ANOTHER BOWL OF KAPUSTA

The True Life Story Of A World War II Luftwaffe Fighter Pilot and P.O.W. in Russia

DIANNA M. POPP AND GOTTFRIED P. DULIAS

authorHOUSE®

2009 revised and expanded version

AuthorHouse™
1663 Liberty Drive
Bloomington, IN 47403
www.authorhouse.com
Phone: 1-800-839-8640

First published by AuthorHouse 8/25/2009

ISBN: 978-1-4184-8836-9 (sc)
ISBN: 978-1-4184-8837-6 (hc)

Library of Congress Control Number: 2004096143

Printed in the United States of America
Bloomington, Indiana

This book is printed on acid-free paper.

Special Note: Because the Author, Gottfried, was born and educated in Germany, he is not completely familiar with the Russian language. Therefore, whenever Russian words appear, they will be spelled phonetically, as he remembers hearing them being spoken.

To Rich: "Horrido!"

06/03/11

Me 109G-14/AS of Lt. Gottfried Paul Johannes Dulias 3./JG 53 ,
Budapest , March 1945

"Ace of Spade Squadron"
("Pik As Geschwader")

JG 53

Gottfried P. Dulias as a Cadet,
Berlin-Gatow, June 1944

Lt. Gottfried P. Dulias

CONTENTS

FOREWORD

For many years I have pondered the thought about writing my autobiography. The fact remains that I doubted my capability of being able to portray my story in a comprehensible presentation. So now I had to develop a format and style of writing that would bring forth the many aspects of my personal life in an acceptable and proper way.

These would also be testimonies of my inner feelings as well as many pertinent facts of encounters in my own family life.

I also doubted the interest by the general public for yet another "Prisoner of War" story due to the fact that so many war stories already exist. I wanted this to be unlike the presentations of sensationalized news reporting and Hollywood productions. This was to be a unique contribution to the general public, who are craving for knowledge of the "Real Happenings" of World War II. This can only be told to them by one of the soldiers who actually lived through those times.

So here is my autobiographical presentation I now dedicate to all my many friends, acquaintances, fellow re-enactors and even strangers who for many years encouraged and persuaded me to accomplish this once in a lifetime special mission.

This also serves as a dedication to my family. Particularly to my sisters who were always part of my life and are still here for me. Also, this is an enlightening story to share with my daughters and granddaughters about the actual facts of my life and ultimately will be their heritage.

Still Alive!
Gottfried Paul Johannes Dulias

A Few Words From
Gottfried P. Dulias

**Here are a few words with my sincere thanks to my
dearest friend and Co-Author, Dianna M. Popp**

Dianna, you accomplished what all my other friends, relatives and acquaintances could not achieve. That was, to finally persuade me to write my story. You started to write it for me based on what I had told you about my life's experiences and then handed me the beginning of Chapter One, as a surprise on the early morning of November 13th, 2003. You even came up with the well-suited and brilliant title of:

"Another Bowl of Kapusta"

The almost commanding words of yours: "Here, now you can continue what I started," made me realize that you really meant it in earnest. I somewhat reluctantly read your starting paragraphs and found that I immediately had to make several corrections and additions.

As I really got into it, I found myself liking the idea and began writing from memory about my childhood. The more I delved into writing, more and more memories surfaced from those long forgotten episodes of my life. By your questioning me about further details of the elaborations that I had written, more vivid remembrances of particular events re-entered my mind. The more I thought about it, the more I liked it.

You have awoken the writer in me. Since then we were able to work together by my dictations, your taking notes and then your talent of writing and typing with ten fast fingers. My editing and re-editing and your final printouts proved to be a fine co-operation that gave our project the necessary speed to achieve better progress.

I consider myself so blessed and fortunate to have found you, my best and dearest friend, and I want to thank you from the bottom of my heart for the great help you have bestowed upon me.

Your steady and meticulous research into the prevailing history during my lifetime created a valuable asset to my story. That makes this book not only of historical value, but also as a learning tool.

Without your steady inspiration I would never have started to write. You encouraged and furthered my self-confidence and made me believe, that indeed, I had it in me to tackle this tremendous task of creating a book, of course, with your competent help!

It features a "Never Before Told, True Story." May it bring a better understanding to all of us, that War only brings misery and sorrow. "Let Peace prevail in this World, because common sense tells us, that this is the only way to happiness and prosperity."

In Thankful Recognition,
Your Friend,

Gottfried

A Few Words From
Dianna M. Popp

It was in October of 2001 that I had the pleasure of making my acquaintance with Gottfried. Actually, meeting him for the first time turned out to be a most pleasant surprise. Initially I was given a bouquet of yellow roses, for friendship. He made a most impressive appearance, as a distinguished, mature, polite and wise gentleman. He had originally found me at a personals site on the Internet and contacted me by email. I was "geographically desirable," as he had put it. I always had the belief, "nothing ventured, nothing gained." So, I put my best foot forward.

The more that I learned about him, the more we 'bonded.' The reason was that as a coincidence, we both shared the same heritage and in many ways, despite the difference in age, we thought alike. It was a comfortable feeling of familiarity. The only difference for me was that I had no idea what he was talking about from World War II. He even had a screen name of ME-109, and I didn't have any clue as to what that meant.

As time went on, I learned more and more about him, his life, and the world he lived in. It became more and more fascinating to me. It was as if he was "storytelling." But that was just his persona. I came to realize that he had shared with me his feelings and innermost thoughts that he never dared to admit to or tell anyone else in his entire lifetime.

On the morning of November 13th, 2003, I woke up at three o'clock with a brainstorm. That was when I began to start writing his story. It was after I listened to a news report the day before about children who were starving, nearly to death, here in America. I immediately made the analogy between Gottfried's own true-life story of his quest for survival and the one I heard about. That is how I became inspired to start writing:

"ANOTHER BOWL OF KAPUSTA."

Dianna

Poprika1@worldnet.att.net

Inspiration From The Philosopher Immanuel Kant (1724-1804)

"What can we know?"

"If I am thinking, I exist!"

"Every event must have a cause."

"Experience teaches us everything."

"Human knowledge originates in our senses."

"Objects and subjects persist identically over time."

"How can we escape from the confines of the human mind?"

These are just a few of the concepts from the studies, writings and teachings of the German, Western Philosopher Immanuel Kant (1724-1804). He is considered to be a most influential thinker of modern times. Although he is not well known in the United States, he is highly recognized throughout most of Europe, and particularly by the Russian people. His Philosophy is of a rather deep nature to be fully understood, yet I can cling to his basic concepts which to me, appear simple. Two major Historical movements in earlier modern philosophy (Empiricism and Rationalism) had a significant impact on Kant.

Mr. Kant was born, raised and worked in the very town that I was born in, Königsberg, (East Prussia), Germany (now Kaliningrad, Russia). Immanuel became a Professor and taught Philosophy at the University of Königsberg. His tomb is attached to the North East corner wall of the Cathedral (Dom) of the very church that I was baptized as a Lutheran. After World War II his tomb was one of the first priorities to be repaired and rebuilt and is maintained in the honor of his memory.

Even the University was rebuilt, though not in its former style. In front of it the Russian people erected a tall statue of Kant in his honor and memory.

I was able to see all of this when I returned to my hometown with my wife Hedwig in 1995, for the first time after the war. Seeing a fresh red rose, placed daily at the pedestal of the statue, particularly impressed us. Our "Hotel Kaliningrad" adjoined the front plaza of the University and we were able to see it looking down from our hotel window situated on the fourth floor.

Originally there was a monumental bronze panel attached to the base of a statue of Kaiser Wilhelm I. that was located at the front corner of the Imperial Castle. The castle was destroyed by the war and the ruins were flattened. A modern office building was erected in its place. It was never occupied because it was condemned as being structurally unstable due to poor workmanship. At the same location where the original bronze monument stood there is now a smaller replica of it for everyone to see. Russian words are now inscribed into the plaque. But in between those lines appears the German text of Kant's statement:

Zwei Dinge Erfüllen Das Gemüt Mit Immer
Neuer Und Zunehmender Bewunderung Und
Eh rfurcht ‚Je Öfter Und Anhaltender Sich
Das Nachdenken Damit Beschäftight:

Der Bestirnte Himmel Über Mir Und
Das Moralische Gesetz In Mir.

Translated:

Two Things Fulfill The Disposition With Ever Newer And Increasing Admiration And Awe, So More Often And Steadfast The Mind Is Occupied With It:

The Star-Spangled Heaven Above Me And The Law Of Morale Within Me.

And

Der Friede Ist Das Meisterstück Der Vernunft.

Translated:

Peace Is The Masterpiece Of Reason

My admiration for this man comes from those two statements that he once made, and they often occupy my mind.

INTRODUCTION

This is the true story of my own life. It is based only upon my own experiences as well as my feelings and innermost thoughts.

Because I experienced some' brainwashing' and had other physical setbacks both as a soldier and then as a prisoner of war between the years of 1944 to 1948; I was able to recall only some of the many events presented here as flashbacks.

Perhaps this presentation of my life story to you is like a time capsule. It tells you about what I have encountered and lived through in my entire lifetime.

I would like to stress the fact that what I have written here is in no way any form of propaganda. It is also not written with the intention of offending anyone.

In the USA according to the First Amendment of the Constitution of the United States we are privileged to have and are protected by the freedom of speech and of the press. So this is just my own story, told in my own way and memory.

I managed to live through and survive a most incredible period of time in the History of the World.

During World War II millions of lives were lost and people did what they were compelled to do, or what they were forced to do. I have since learned to forgive and forget. It is best to move on, for the best is yet to come. That has been and continues to be my positive outlook.

Yours truly,
Gottfried P. Dulias, in God's Peace…

Former Luftwaffe Fighter Pilot and Prisoner of War in Russia, WW II

ONE

(From Before My Birth: 1918/Born: 1925/ Until 1934)

THE EARLY BOYHOOD YEARS

As a young boy I lived in Königsberg, the Capital of the former German Province of East Prussia. I later became the only surviving son in our family. When I was born, I had a brother who was two years older than I, who died young. His brief life ended after he became mentally impaired due to complications from an outbreak of measles with high fever that caused him to develop encephalitis. Inoculations for that particular illness did not exist at that time. Preventive medicine was in its infancy. Perhaps if he had been born in later years, he would have survived, and lived a long and healthy life.

When I was born on June 25, 1925, I had an older sister who was four years old. Two more sisters would arrive in the next four years. Like clockwork, my siblings and I were all born two years apart, and in odd numbered years: 1921, 1923, 1925, 1927 and 1929.

I was born at our home with the assistance of a midwife. That's just the way it was done in those days. Our home in Königsberg was located in the center of town, on the bank of the Pregel River. **Weidendamm** No. 3 was the street and house number. It was a busy commercial as well as residential area. My maternal grandfather, a merchant, Friederich Franz Reschke, owned the house we lived in. He maintained his business office on the first floor of that 2-story building, and our family occupied the upstairs apartment.

After my two younger sisters were born I became the middle child. At my birth things did not go well, and I almost did not make it into this world. My older sister ran excitedly to all our neighbors, clapping

her hands shouting: " I got a new baby brother and he is a Negro."
Well, the fact is, that I was born a "blue baby."

My color was the result of a most difficult birth, during which I did
not receive proper oxygen and was nearly strangled by the umbilical
cord. When delivered, I weighed in at 11.480 German pounds (13.20
American pounds). You cannot imagine any woman having to go
through that today. Today a hospital birth by caesarean section would
be the preferred option.

I was named Gottfried Paul Johannes Dulias. My first name when
translated from German to English means God's Peace. **Gott** means
God, and **Friede** means Peace. My second name was after my father,
Paul. My third name was appropriate to my birth date as it was in
honor of **St. Johannes Nacht**, (St John's night) the customary time of
Midsummer celebration. Then finally, I received the family name of
Dulias.

Well, I came into this world with a fight and a struggle and it was
a matter of life or death. That set the precedent for what was to follow.
I was fated to fight long odds in my life, both as a fighter pilot and as a
human being, but my destiny was to survive.

A LITTLE BIT OF HISTORY

*I would like to begin telling you my story by briefly outlining the
historical events that occurred just before I came into this world.
Historically, during the time I was born Hitler's power was once
again on the rise.*

By 1918 World War I officially ended with Germany defeated.
The new German Government of Prince Max von Baden asked the
President of the U.S.A., Woodrow Wilson for armistice. Wilson was in
office from 1913 to 1921. Unfortunately, at the same time, in Russia
there was the Bolshevik Revolution. Bolshevism signaled the beginning
of a new revolutionary challenge and change to Europe's social order.

By 1919 The League of Nations was founded and the Treaty of
Versailles was signed. But no one saw or anticipated the future ahead.
By 1919 in the United States the eighteenth amendment to the
Constitution was ratified prohibiting the sale and transport of alcohol

(Prohibition). At the same time a quota system for immigration to the United States of America was put into action.

My parents got married in September 1919 when my father was thirty-two and my mother was only eighteen years old. The difference in age of fourteen years between them, caused no problems in their lives, and their union lasted for forty-four years, until my father passed away in 1963. He died as a result of complications from cancer of his kidney. It was discovered too late and an operation to remove one kidney was unfortunately unsuccessful. May he rest in peace, forgiven by us children, for his misunderstood love that he was unable or too proud to show to us.

My mother, Lucie Reschke Dulias, was the only child of my grandparents, a well-to-do merchant family. My father was a Machine Engineer who worked for the **Eisenbahn,** the German railroad, as a senior civil servant.

By 1920 Hitler's group was known as the National Socialist German Worker's party **(Nationalsozialistische Deutsche Arbeiter Partei,** or NSDAP). That party slowly grew and was based mainly in the region of Southern Germany called Bavaria.

Also in the 1920's, Stalin, literally "man of steel", began interpreting Lenin's precepts to a new generation coming of age. In the United States the nineteenth amendment to the constitution was ratified and for the first time women could vote. Having had women voters also helped the Republican nominee Harding win a victory. Warren Harding insisted that the country needed "normalcy."

For America, the 1920's were a time of accelerated economic growth. Hollywood started the Motion Picture Industry. The number of cars produced in the Automobile Industry increased as the amount of cars in use tripled.

From 1921 to 1923 Warren G. Harding was the President of the United States. When Harding died Calvin Coolidge succeeded him.

By 1921 the new Nazi party in Germany adopted, as it's official emblem a new flag. It consisted of a red background with a centered large white circle containing a black swastika standing on its edge.

By 1922 Stalin was named Secretary General of the Communist party.

In 1923 Hitler established the newspaper *Völkischer Beobachter* (National Observer) as the official daily tabloid. Then propaganda began to spread. The propaganda was about Bolshevism, conspiracies, democracy, dictatorship and so on. Also in the same year Hitler and over six hundred storm troopers *(Sturmabeilungen, or SA)* marched on the *Bürgerbräukeller* (a large beer hall) in Munich where the head of the Bavarian government was addressing a public meeting.

Hitler took the leader Gustav von Kahr and his associates as prisoners. As a result of this failed "Beer Hall Putsch" Hitler was tried and imprisoned for five years and the NSDAP was outlawed. In the Landsberg prison, Hitler told his story to his aide Rudolph Hess creating the book *Mein Kampf.* After one year he was released from prison.

Lenin died in 1924. So, by 1925, at the time of my birth: Hitler was back in action, Stalin was in control in Russia and Calvin Coolidge was the President of the United States.

I am the only member of my family who carries on the Dulias name. This name can be traced back into the history of both France and Germany. My ancestors were Huguenots, persecuted in predominantly Catholic France, who were forced to leave their homeland during the 16th and 17th centuries because of their Protestant beliefs.

They were invited by the King of Prussia to repopulate East Prussia, which was ravaged by the bubonic plague in earlier times. Given free land by the King, my French ancestors toiled and cultivated, built farms and villages and contributed to the culture by bringing along much of their own customs from France. They even introduced their skills and trades, many of them un-known there in earlier times. They were hard working and welcomed new citizens, who helped shape their new country.

Paul Dulias, my father, was a man of medium stature. He was always dressed in his neatly tailored double-breasted suits and had a military-style short haircut, with his white hair neatly parted in the middle. I never saw him in any state other than clean-shaven.

In his younger days he sported a small mustache, as it was fashionable for men of distinction to do. He stood very straight and had both a refined and stern appearance, which stemmed from his Prussian military training.

When going out, he always wore a hat and coat. He never failed to lift his hat in greeting those he knew on the street. He was always the gentleman in every way, opening doors for the ladies and offering his seat to them on crowded streetcars. Gentility was his mark of distinction. As children, these habits were relentlessly taught to us, always enforced with demands of obedience. "You must do it this way, I will not accept it any other way!" Those were the commanding words that were the "law" to us.

As the patriarch of our family and being so much older than my mother, as well as his being a pedantic perfectionist, he was of course, always right. Once again, his word was law in our family. He called my mother ***"Lu-chen,"*** meaning little Lucie; and ***"Puppchen,"*** his little doll. I often heard him nickname and address my mother in this endearing way. But when something wasn't to his liking, what she did, or didn't do, it was just ---Lu!

My mother, Lucie, was a natural beauty. She had an angelic face that radiated love and compassion. Though a little on the heavy *(saftig)* side, this did not deter my father. He preferred a Rubenesque type of woman. Rubens was a famous Dutch painter who portrayed full figured women depicted in classical poses. Today, Rubens is still recognized throughout the world as a famous painter from the Renaissance. That is how I remember my mother. She had bright blue glistening eyes and blonde curled neatly styled hair. Her wardrobe was always of the latest style, befitting the lady of a fashionable upscale house, as was customary at that period. That is how I like to remember my mother.

As children we were fortunate to have household help. A Governess **(Kindermädchen)** and a Housekeeper **(Dienstmädchen)** were both hired by my grandfather to make his only daughter's life easier. Therefore, with her tasks and duties lightened, she could devote more time to being the lady of the house. This allowed her the freedom to accompany my father to social gatherings. She also had the responsibility of being an employer, and found herself exercising skills that she never knew she had before her marriage. The same two servants were employed in our household in Königsberg for all the years that we lived there.

Looking back, I can clearly remember when I was no more than two years old, and living in the house where I was born. I am now amazed as to how vividly I recollect many things about that time and place.

Our house had a large courtyard divided in half by a fence separating one half as a garden and the other half as our backyard play area. Sometimes I was locked into the fenced garden part as punishment for some misbehavior. I clearly recall that on one of those occasions, out of anger, I tossed some of my toys over the fence, into the Pregel River. When my Uncle Gustav came for a visit he fished them out with a rake from the sandy shallow shore.

Each day, when my father returned home from work, he expected a full report from my mother detailing the daily activities. As children, we cringed as he opened the door and greeted our mother. Although we hugged and kissed him as was customary, we knew my mother would have to report truthfully of our good and bad behaviors. He was not easy on us in any way.

Often we received our punishment at the instant he found out the truth. That was usually before dinner, so not only were we hungry but we also hurt. Yet my mother had compassion and defended us by trying to diminish the severity of our punishment.

But I can still remember many times when I was severely punished by my father. I could never understand why it was always me—perhaps because I was his only son and had to set an example to my sisters?

I can't imagine what terrible things that I might have done, but often times I was locked in the basement after being whipped. That basement was used mainly as a cold storage especially for fruits and vegetables. It was cold and dark, without any windows. With the lights turned off it was frightening! I think there were even rats or mice down there. I remember that I felt something running across my feet....

SUMMER VACATIONS AT THE BALTIC SEA

Summer vacations during my early years of life (1926-1928) were spent with my family at the resort town of Neuhäuser, located on the Baltic Sea, and situated to the north of my hometown. That northern area that bordered the **Ostsee** (Baltic Sea) was called **Samland**. Neuhäuser was a half hour train ride from Königsberg. The rail net of **Samland** was not connected to the inland part of Germany and it had it's own railroad station, the **Nordbahnhof.**

Neuhäuser was a town of elaborate villas that could be rented by well to do families for the entire summer. We spent all day on the STRAND (sandy beach). My mother, Aunt Anna, and my Governess all took turns caring for my older sister and me. A large blanket covered the sandy ground and we had our daily picnics there.

The Baltic coastline at the **Samland** was known for its steep cliffs of eroded land formations. During those summer months we were able to search for and collect pieces of Amber known as **Bernstein** in German. The Amber --East Prussian Gold, as it was called, was plentiful. Every day more and more pieces washed ashore. We each had our amber collections to take home with us.

The Amber was formed over twenty million years ago from the sap of pine trees. Often small particles and insects got caught and trapped into it. Both then and now, those particular pieces of Amber are the most valuable.

As land eroded in that area, and ancient forests were submerged below today's sea level, the sap became fossilized, thus creating Amber. Even today Amber can be found washed ashore on the beaches of that region, and it is also mined in controlled areas.

My paternal Aunt Anna and Uncle Gustav always stayed at the resort with us for the entire summer. My uncle received a pension from his job with the railroad after he retired early due to a disability. With the two of them around, my mother could enjoy more freedom to join our father back in Königsberg. Occasionally my father joined us on the weekends.

My first steps as an infant were taken at the resort. My Governess would lead me as she held my hands for guidance. Then she would let go, and I would walk until I fell down. Getting up I was eager to walk some more. It is just incredible how today I can remember these little details.

Playthings were model sailboats; small toy cars made of metal, wind up and pull toys, balls, and my pail and shovel. My Governess often read Fairy Tales to me at bedtime. One favorite storybook of mine was ***Max und Moritz*** by Wilhelm Busch. They were funny little characters that were always doing naughty pranks. I thought the boys in the story were clever, and they gave me ideas to do similar things later in my youth.

When I was a little older, after my younger sisters were born, my family and I continued vacationing in the ***Samland*** coastal region. We also found other more suitable areas to stay for the entire summers.

The place we frequently returned to was Großkuhren where we would stay as guests of Rudolf Lück and his family. It was a fishing village and was located about five to ten kilometers west of Neuhäuser. What made the area quite unique was that on the beach there was

To Rich: "Horrido" June 3, 2011
Lt. Georgfried D. Hughes
JG 53 "Pik As"
1944/45 —

a huge mound-like mountain structure called ***Zipfelberg***. Created by erosion, the inner core was of a sandstone composition surrounded by loose sand. Amazingly this structure stood about three hundred and thirty feet high with a small flat platform of sandstone at its peak. People were discouraged from climbing it so that it would be environmentally protected in that shape and condition.

To reach the beach from the upper coastal level, you had to descend a long winding wooden stairway with over three hundred steps, which was called ***"Himmelsleiter,"*** or Heaven's Ladder. This area resembled in many respects the north shore of Long Island, N.Y., at Rocky Point.

The parked sailboats were rolled resting on their keels from the higher rear of the beach to the shoreline by the fishermen as they shouted a "heave, ho" while they struggled to bring their boats to shore. They went out to sea daily pulling their nets, attempting to make their catch of the day. By the early afternoon they returned with their catch. They caught herring, sprats, flounder, fluke and a larger variety called ***Steinbutt.***

Upon their return they pulled the boats back onto shore by using a hand-operated winch. The boats were usually held steady by a total of eight to ten men while they were winched up onto the shore, their keels glided over rollers imbedded in the sand. Once the boat reached its higher resting place it was braced with wooden supports to keep it from tipping over.

I spent many hours each day observing, and was later invited to help them with these tasks. I gladly accepted their offer and was rewarded by being invited to go along on one of their trips. Since they went out each morning at the crack of dawn, Mr. Rudolf Lück and his two sons woke me up so I could get ready.

As we left the shore one clear morning in June, we could see a beautiful sunrise. The sails were set and we gained a fairly smooth speed as the wind started to increase. We went so far out to sea that we could no longer see the coastline. Then the nets were cast overboard and dragged behind the boat. Next the boat turned around and made a zig zag back to shore. While traveling the net scooped up the fish, it was like filling a sack.

Only Rudolf and his sons knew exactly where the different schools of fish could be found. The boat steadily slowed down, as the load of fish being dragged got heavier. Then it was time to return home. At the shore the fishermen's wives and other fishermen came and helped to drag up the full nets, after they were disconnected from the back of the boat with a "ho-ruck," until the entire catch was ashore.

That was some sight -- the heaps of live wiggling and squirming fish. Then they were quickly sorted out and selections were made. The nets were then hung up to dry, and some skilled fishermen went about carefully repairing the damaged parts that always showed up after each use. I watched them with fascination, how quickly they could weave those little knotted squares, so that after the repair was done, one never could distinguish any difference from the undamaged sections of the net.

On another occasion I had the opportunity to go out to sea with a group of divers. The boat they used was smaller than those used by the fishermen. These divers went out searching for rocks that were not far from the shore. So I would estimate they dove into about twenty feet of water. The water was so clear that we could see down to the rocks lying at the sandy bottom of the sea. These rocks were later used for building purposes. Most houses in that region were built from those natural stones. Fishing them out of the water was cheaper than buying bricks for home building.

The divers wore a heavy gauge rubber body suit. The helmet was made of copper and had glass windows protected by brass bars. Rivets fastened those safety bars to the helmet. Two long air hoses came out of the back of the helmet. Those hoses were connected to a two man operated hand pump. One hose supplied fresh air to the diver while the other hose retrieved the depleted air.

The diver was harnessed at his back to a long rope that was attached to a winch on board the boat. This same winch also heaved up the huge pouch filled with the harvested stones from below. After a few hours of hard work there were enough stones harvested for the capacity of the hold on board and we returned to shore.

For me it was an interesting experience, and I felt proud. Not just as an observer, but also as a participant because I was allowed to man the air pump that supplied the divers with air. I also had to watch the air hoses and keep them from being kinked as they moved alongside the boat's top edge. The wind and waves swung the boat around its anchorage, and the divers below moved with it too, collecting the rocks. I felt so grown up in helping the men in their hard work and was proud to be treated as a crewman.

The Lück family offered a section of their home to my family because they had a place large enough to accommodate summer guests. This practice afforded them an additional income in case their fishing expeditions were not too successful and helped to supplement their income during the winter months.

We returned to stay with the Lück family for many years. My sisters and I considered them as sort of additional grandparents and we called them **Oma** and **Opa** Lück. Their sons were like uncles to us.

We always dined together in the evenings sitting in the **Gute Stube**, a huge dining-living room. The ocean breezes from the Baltic Sea constantly permeated the air around us. Fresh and smoked fish were served at most suppers

They smoked some of their catch down at the beach on a clothes line-like cooking device, made from two large low standing poles with cross bars on top connected by several horizontal wires. From the wires the fish were hung neatly spaced in rows by hooks. Below those rows was a wood burning fire in a shallow trench dug out under those lines of wires.

When the fire had simmered down, freshly cut green branches from a bush called **Kaddik** were laid over the glowing ashes and that produced an aromatic spicy smoke. What also contributed to the good taste was the fact that after a few hours of smoking, the fish-oil dripped from the heated fish into the fire below and created more distinct aromatic smoke while keeping the fire going.

This way of smoking and cooking the fish took most of the day, but when done, the fish looked very appetizing with a golden sheen and tasted delicious. They were then packed there at the beach into wooden boxes lined with oilpaper, ready to be shipped to the markets. My favorite fish was smoked and or fresh fried flounder. Followed by lox, smoked eel, smoked sprats and herring. Freshly smoked fish, still warm from the fire was a really fine delicacy and one never gets tired of the joy of eating it.

Another thing that was of great interest to me was the fully equipped carpenter shop at the Lück house. I was fascinated with what I saw at that backyard building. There his master carpenter made and repaired parts for their fishing boats. Rudders, replacement planks and anything that was worn out, broken or damaged from either the home or the boats, was brought there to be worked on. When repairs were done and more time was at hand and also during the winter, **Opa** Lück and his sons manufactured furniture to be sold as a supplement to their income.

I tried out the hand tools and made some small model sailboats on the **Hobelbank** (carpenters work bench), and that was fun. The machinery was off limits to me, but I watched how the men used them for the various carpentry and cabinet making projects. Being in the workshop and seeing the endless possibilities of what could be done there planted a seed in me. It also gave me the training I needed and I imagined that some day I would also like to have one of those shops so I could make some wonderful things.

There in Grosskuhren, in 1933 my father helped me to build a huge sand castle. At the upper part of the village there was a Beach Club for summer guests, which was something, like a Community Center. As recreation it sponsored a sand castle building competition, which my father and I entered.

Our creation looked like a real palace. Together we had built it with just our own hands, a pail and a shovel. It was a wonderful piece of architecture. My pail served as a mold creating towers. When we were done we topped it off with a flag. It was our fortress, and castle, surrounded by a moat. I was most proud of our accomplishment To our surprise, we won second place, got a prize and received a ribbon.

Besides building the sand castle, my younger sisters and I had so much fun in the sand. We even filled up each other's swimsuits with sand. One day my swim trunks became so full of sand that when I stood up, it fell down. That was rather embarrassing in front of my sisters at the public beach where everybody could see me. There I was, standing before them completely naked. But I quickly pulled my bathing trunks up to be covered again. Many small children did run around the beach in the buff anyway. That was just natural! We were all free spirits.

We were always digging in the sand, even down to the water level. We would build various structures and holes and buried ourselves in them up to the shoulders. Sometimes, walking along with the tide we became so deeply imbedded in the sand that we had to help each other to get pulled out. The waves would come up and gush around and through our little legs and as the water retreated, the sand became packed down around us. That was some experience of feeling trapped and we depended on each other to get free from the tightly clinging sand.

The water was crystal clear. We could swim under water and keep our eyes open to look below. We always continued searching for pieces of Amber. The sea mostly had mild rolling waves that broke just before touching the shoreline. So sometimes we jumped and splashed into them. When we were out of the water we often sunbathed or ran about testing to see who was the fastest. We molded the sand to the contour of our small bodies, and we positioned ourselves lying down in the best possible direction to the sun.

We played at the beach from early morning to late afternoon. It was a joy we never got tired of. Then it was time to return to the house to have dinner.

In the morning it was fun when we walked or ran down the steps of "Heaven's Staircase" but it was really a chore to climb back up later in the afternoon. We dragged our tired and hungry little bodies all the way up to the top.

Often we would carry our "catch of the day" of amber, seashells, and **Donnerkeile** (Thunder Wedges) up the steps with us. The **Donnerkeile**, I believe, were formed by lightening striking the sandy beach and melting the sand into a round pipe-like stony wedge, sometimes with a hollow core. They were about 3/8 of an inch thick and mostly of various lengths from one to 3 or 4 inches and of amber color with smooth outer surfaces.

And so, our days at the beach were always really so much fun that we never got bored or tired of it.

It was late in 1927, when my family moved to Ponarth, a southern part of our town, Königsberg. We moved because my father received a promotion which included new living quarters provided by the railroad for the "Upper Echelon".

Our new home was one of the lower apartments on the west wing of an apartment building at **Werkstättenstrasse** No.12. The East and West wings were of a two story type, while the bigger center part had three stories, each with spacious attics and a flat roof. Both outer wings had their entrances at the end sides, while the center apartments had a front-and-rear-door.

When we first moved there each room was heated by a tall ceramic tiled heating stove. It reached almost to the top of the nine to ten foot high ceiling. The heating material was wood, coal and or brown briquettes and tending to it was the duty of our maid.

Once fired up, after approximately one hour's time, those stoves maintained a comfortable room temperature for twenty-four hours. Later on, we moved to the upstairs apartment of the same wing and then we were privileged to have central steam heating with radiators and the furnace was in the huge kitchen. The maid had to carry firewood and buckets full of coal and or briquettes up from the basement, for all ovens and the steam furnace. That was quite a task to keep the entire floor warm and comfortable. Even the water heater for our bath was coal fired.

While we were living in this building, my two younger sisters were born. I cannot recall the birth of my sister who was born two years after me. I do, on the other hand, clearly remember the birth of my youngest sister. Unlike me, she came into this world in a hospital. Perhaps my parents decided to use the convenience of the town hospital because of the earlier difficulty with my birth.

After she was born, my older sister and I accompanied our father to the Hospital to visit my mother and see our new baby sister. We stood in the huge room that was the Maternity Ward to view the newborn babies. I saw rows and rows of curtained baby bassinettes. We looked and looked around until we found our new baby and as she was sleeping we went to see my mother in her private room.

I remember later on, early in my youth, when I was angry with my youngest sister, for some forgotten reason, I complained to my mother and told her that we picked out and brought home the wrong baby from the hospital. She explained to me that we did not select our baby, but that my sister was indeed her own baby because it had her name clearly marked on her beaded wrist bracelet which she received right at birth.

We had a big beautiful Garden surrounded by a fence at the south side of the courtyard, which I was able to overlook from the window of my second floor room. At the rear of the garden (my father's pride and joy), we had a swing that he had constructed for us children. It was made of steel-pipes for safety. A chain swing would have been too flexible and prone to collisions with the main side pipe posts. We often had lots of fun using it and also shared it with other children from our building and friends from the neighboring houses.

In the center of the garden stood a painted white **Laube** (garden cottage). The front of the cottage had an open latticework face, with an entry arch at the south side. The solid sidewalls had large stationary windows. There was no need to have windows that opened, since the entire south wall was constructed of wooden latticework. At each side of the arched entry stood huge black cherry trees and each summer they were loaded with delicious fruit. They were of a special sweet type called **Schattenmorellen,** and we ate them to our hearts content in season, right from the branches.

Inside we had a large table and some chairs. When it was not in use for garden parties, my friends and I would go inside and it would be our playhouse.

Adjoining and attached to the back wall, there was a former chicken coop and my father kept his garden tools and supplies there. Attached to it further back was a **Werk-kammer,** (work room) with a carpenter's workbench, and wall cabinets containing lots of tools. This workshop also had an anvil, another workbench and other necessary tools and equipment to do almost every type of work needed for the upkeep of house and garden. It had no machinery though, like the shop of **Opa** Lück in Großkuhren.

My Great Uncle Hermann, my father's uncle who was, in fact, younger than him, was an expert carpenter and cabinetmaker. He did much of the work there and kept everything for the house and garden in top shape. He built step-up platforms so that we could reach the sinks that were present in one corner of each of our bedrooms, and he lowered the height of all the mirrors accordingly. He also built some of our kitchen cabinets and shelves with his great craftsman's ability.

Uncle Gustav would also come over often and help us with our garden chores of weeding, raking, and watering the many varieties of flowers. Some of them were dahlias, tulips, asters, poppies, honeysuckles and lilies of the valley, etc. The many fruit trees that yielded harvests of great abundance each year needed a lot of attention as well. Trimming off the "water-branches" that would never bear fruit and fitting each tree stem with glue-rings to prevent insects from climbing up and ruining the fruit were just some of the many tasks that were my responsibility. The loose bark had to be scraped off, so that no bugs could nest under it and that was also my job.

I also had to further maintain the rings by applying fresh glue from time to time with a brush. The very rich and steadily fertilized soil made everything grow to utmost beauty and size. My father was especially proud of his huge dahlias that grew to over six feet in height and had unusually large blossoms. Vegetable beds had to be tended to and be kept free of weeds. Walkways between them had to be raked and kept clean. Everything had to be watered periodically if there was not enough rain.

My father proudly gave tours of our garden to guests who would often visit. Very seldom did we receive any praise for our work in 'his' garden. It was mostly criticism, that we did not do our tasks properly. He was such a perfectionist in everything. For example, when we were writing, every letter "i" had to have its dot exactly on top of it. The slightest deviation from his idea of perfection was pointed out to us and we had to make the corrections, but even when we did so, praise came sparingly from him.

To some extent, I often caught myself becoming just like him later in my life, but it was to my advantage. I was often admired and praised for my quality of work, and I never had to advertise for jobs because I established an excellent reputation for quality work.

Uncle Gustav also taught me how to ride my first two-wheel bicycle that was a present from my Opa Reschke. Training wheels were not known during that time. So, my Uncle kept me upright on the bicycle by holding onto the back of the saddle and walking alongside of me while I slowly pedaled to get the feeling of riding the bike. I steered it in large circles and straight lines in the courtyard behind our building.

I quickly gained confidence in riding, and without me realizing it, he let go. On my own I kept riding up to the East end of the long courtyard and to my surprise, saw him still standing at the other end as I turned to make the return trip. At first, I felt a little uneasy being on my own. But since I made it so far by myself without my uncle holding my bike steady, I kept going proudly making several more rounds all by myself. Once the ice was broken, I rode with increasing confidence and later became an expert at riding my bike "free hand"-- the proverbial "Look Ma, no hands!"

I later taught my friend Dieter Pfaff to ride my bicycle the same way that Uncle Gustav taught me. Dieter caught on quickly, as I did, and for his next birthday he got his own bike. From then on we made the neighborhood "unsafe" doing all kinds of tricks. We raced each other and did daredevil runs to see who chickened out first. Needless to say, we had our fair share of crashes and falls, scraped bloody knees and elbows, but that didn't deter our fun. The "battle scars" of our escapades are to some extent still visible today.

Each morning the housekeeper would see to it that my sisters and I had fresh milk, bread and rolls on our breakfast table, but more importantly, I anxiously awaited the arrival of the Baker. Since the age of about four or five my dream was to become a Baker or Pastry Chef. I so loved the heavenly smell of the warm, freshly baked goods. I could never forget that wonderful aroma coming from the Baker's delivery buggy.

That's what really had me dreaming of becoming a Pastry Chef. I imagined having that "Heavenly" Life on Earth. I thought that if I could make these creations every day that it would be fantastic! I would derive great satisfaction not only eating them, but by being able to make them not just for me, but also for everyone else. I had illusions of grandeur.

As far as I can remember, I always had a sweet tooth. I surely could make a little extra room in my stomach for cookies, cakes, candies and ice cream. I also loved eggs in any form, raw or cooked. My mother also did some elaborate fine baking. She made the best *"Torte."* That was a round cake having filled layers and was decorated and topped with various fruits, nuts, chocolates, *marzipan* (molded almond paste) and other confections. I also thought that if she could make such wonderful creations, so could I!

Another delight was when we went to see my Uncle, Julius Lappe who owned a well known established Confectionery Store. The shop was located near the Imperial Castle and the main feature in his store was the genuine *Königsberger Marzipan* that my hometown was famous for.

Marzipan is made from ground almonds, which are then mixed with almond oil, sugar and other ingredients to form a paste. The paste can be molded like dough into various shapes and decorative confections. When baked in a special oven, a lightly browned top crust is created making it most appealing.

Uncle Julius' shop featured fine pastries as well as assorted chocolate. What I distinctly remember was that during Lent, just before Easter, on Maundy Thursday it was the tradition for him to bake and sell a huge Pretzel pastry known as a *Kringel.* It was filled with marzipan and candied fruits and covered with a sugary glaze. My *Opa* Reschke always visited us on that day bringing along one of those huge *Kringels* and other sweets. He too was always anxious to go to Uncle Julius' Store.

I clearly remember the numerous parties given by my parents at our home. As young children our **Kindermädchen** made sure that we were in bed by seven o'clock, so that we would not be deprived of sleep during those noisy gatherings. We had to relocate to the attic room for the night. It was a semi-finished room with skylights and was spacious enough for our four featherbeds.

Nevertheless, we still heard the subdued noises from the party, especially when my father played the piano. It was an upright console type made by the well-known manufacturer, Theden of Königsberg. I could never forget seeing the golden print above the keyboard with its name. So my father supplied the music and the guests danced.

Before retiring to the attic for the night, my sisters and I participated in the dinner celebration with the invited guests. We were the only children present and the guests praised our exceptional good behavior.

The formal dining room table setting taught us the way of society, and we knew no other way. The scrumptious meals that were served were plentiful and prepared by our **Dienstmädchen** under the guidance of my mother. Coming from the **Höhere Töchter Schule** (upper class Daughters School) my mother had been trained in various household skills and Culinary Arts. Also, this schooling enabled her to know how to prepare and serve meals worthy of a Master Chef. Any of today's four or five star restaurant's Chefs would be proud to present those meals as one of their own creations.

Whether or not we participated at a dinner with the guests, we still had to keep a certain formality and discipline at the dinner table. I surely remember that we said prayers before and after our meals. Before the meal: *"Komm Herr Jesus, sei unser Gast und segne, was Du uns bescheret hast. Amen,"* In English translation: "Come, Lord Jesus, be our guest and bless what you have given to us. Amen." After the meal: *"Wir danken dem Herrn Für seine Gaben, Denn Er ist freundlich und seine Güte währet ewiglich. Amen."* The English translation: "We thank the Lord for his gifts, for he is friendly and his goodness lasts eternally. Amen." I remember it was my youngest sister who was expected to say the prayers at each and every dinner. When the after-dinner prayer had been said we had to respectfully kiss our father's hand and then our mother's before we exited the room.

Often times after dinner, the male guests would join my father in the parlor to enjoy either a cigar or cigarillo of a fine blend of tobacco. My father never liked to inhale the smoke, but a few times I remember seeing the smoke fuming from his nostrils. The aroma from the smoke permeated the air, and even while we were tucked away upstairs, we could sometimes get a whiff of it. It seemed like it was just the thing for the men to do after dinner, perhaps to talk about their jobs or even have a game of chess or play cards.

The Parlor Room was always a most fascinating place. First of all it had my dad's gun and saber collection, which he was always proud to have on display.

My father had a fellow WW I comrade and friend who lead quite a different lifestyle. I remember having heard the many tales of his adventures and his being on safaris in Africa. After the war, Mr. Schebsdat became a Counsel General for Germany and was stationed on the island of Fernando Po, which were located midway along the coast of West Africa. He sent us numerous gifts of African artifacts and those items were also on display, decorating the room.

All of them were most unusual conversation pieces. That collection included a crocodile carved out of ebony, a totem-type Fertility God wooden sculpture, skins from huge lizards hung on the wall as well as colorfully native made woven patterned hangings. There was even a hand carved chess table that had the figure of an elephant as its base. Leopard skins and leather toss pillows of different sizes were on the large leather chairs.

A line of elephants in graduated sizes, resting their trunks upon one another that were hand carved from a whole elephant tusk. That entire piece was with Mr. Schebsdat but when it fell off his mantel it broke into fragments and we received a larger part from that ivory carving. (I still have one of those pieces today, as does my youngest sister). However, it is so unfortunate to kill an endangered species for decorative purposes.

Later in the evening all the furniture was moved to the sides of the main room so the guests had a dance floor. My father was a "Champion of Dancers," particularly of Waltz's. He and my mother danced a most beautiful Viennese Waltz together doing both right and left turns. Sometimes **Opa** Reschke would play his mandolin or guitar. When we were somewhat older we were able to stay up later to join in the festivities.

Those gatherings continued, no matter where we were living, because with our parents and family, it was an established tradition.

TRADITIONAL CHRISTMAS CELEBRATIONS IN OUR FAMILY

Our Christmas Celebrations turned into a "Grand Performance." The setting of the dining room table was always formal, but for this occasion it had a white linen tablecloth that was freshly starched and ironed. My father sat at one end of the table and my place as his only son was directly across from him at the opposite side of the table. To my left were my older sister's, and also my mother's seat, she sat at Father's right hand. To my right were my two younger sisters nicknamed **Die Kleinen** or "The Little Ones."

In the middle of the table was the holiday centerpiece, a Christmas Advent Wreath with four candles on it. Advent was the start of the Holiday Season. In anticipation of Christmas, an additional candle would be lit on each of the four weeks prior to the holiday.

This pre-Christmas tradition was and is also common to many European (particularly Nordic) countries. It was a way of counting down to the day of celebrating the Birth of Jesus. The twenty fourth of December was Heiliger Abend (Christmas Eve), and for us that was our big Christmas celebration.

The Parlor Room became the Christmas Room. Our parents made it "off limits" to my sisters and me for many, many days before the holiday. We did try to sneak a peek through the keyhole making an attempt to see what was going on behind closed doors.

The Swedish artist Carl Larsson brilliantly illustrated this very same scene (1853-1919) by his pen and ink drawing of 1892 titled: **The Day Before Christmas Eve.** Coincidentally, in that picture you will also see four children peeping through the keyhole. As I look at the works of Carl Larsson I am taken back in time to the exact scenes (genre) that I experienced as a child. Carl Larsson could be compared to Norman Rockwell of the twentieth century.

Yes, we were extremely anxious for our Christmas celebration to begin, as we had great expectations. We knew that something was going to happen soon because everyone was busy scurrying around. The tree was hidden until just before Christmas Eve. One evening our father brought the live tree into the house. I don't know where it came from but it must have been from a nearby forest. To us, as little children, the tree looked so huge. It stood tall from floor to ceiling. It was a wonder.

In preparation for Christmas Eve my sisters and I had a special assignment. First of all, we had to do a little research and select traditional Holiday songs and poems. Then we had to write them in a painstaking manner with a fountain pen and ink, in German script and put them in a folder. We then had to memorize and practice whatever we were going to recite. Each of us had to make our own folder and then hand decorate it with something significant or appropriate to our celebration. We often made paper cutouts of pine branches with candles attached and pasted them onto the folder. Other times we drew a picture on it or pasted appropriate Christmas pictures on the front.

Besides making a Christmas folder for our evening presentation, we also had to memorize Bible verses, the Christmas Story from the Second Chapter of Luke, verses one through twenty: "In those days Caesar Augustus published a decree ordering a census" …

Our Christmas Eve dinner was at noon **Mittagessen**. Actually, the largest meal of any day was always at that time. It was traditional to serve **Weihnachts Gans** (an oven-baked goose for Christmas). It was freshly killed and sold to us by farmer merchants that came to our street with their wares. First the bird was weighed and then sold. We had an icebox in our kitchen to keep it cool, but for those who did not, it would be hung outside the window in the cold fresh air awaiting preparation and roasting. In those days the iceman came and delivered blocks of ice twice a week to keep the icebox supplied.

The Goose Dinner began with a blessing said by my youngest sister, followed by a toast. It appeared to me that it was most often a fine white German wine that was served with the meal. Each child was permitted to have a small sample of the wine and it was served in a little cordial glass. Together we all toasted: "**Fröhliche Weihnachten**;" Merry Christmas to each other.

The first course was Goose Soup that was made with fresh vegetables and giblets as well as the feet and neck from the goose. The feet were wrapped with the cleaned intestines of the goose. For my mother this was a special delicacy and I couldn't understand why it was considered a delicacy.

Salted potatoes, peas and carrots, stuffing and delicious gravy were all served with the goose portions. The meal concluded with a salad of greens that was topped off with smoked and fried bacon cubes. That was a delicacy for my father. I abhorred it. It made me feel nauseous but I had to eat it anyway. My father insisted that I had to eat everything that was put onto my plate before I was allowed to leave the table; and he meant it!

After dinner, my little sister said the prayer concluding our dinner session. Afterwards we took a short break and then spent the afternoon with coffee, cakes and cookies. My sisters and I did not get the **Bohnenkaffee** (made from freshly ground coffee beans). Instead we got **"Kathereiner's Malz Kaffee."** It was a brew made of roasted barley grains having a slight semblance of taste like the "real thing" but without caffeine, as found in the bean coffee (as kids would become too 'hyper').

There were an array of cookies, cakes, **Torten** (a type of layer cake decorated with marzipan, fruits, butter creams) and my mother's famous gingerbread holiday cake, the **Pfefferkuchen.** The maid, under the direction of my mother, had decorated all sweets and confections. Among the cookies were some of my favorites: **Lebkuchen, Pfeffernüsse,** butter cookies and **Speculatius** (windmill spice cookies). After this our family went to a four o'clock church service at the **Evangelische** (Lutheran) Church. We children couldn't wait for the service to end. We had great expectations of things to come.

Upon returning home, the time had finally come when the doors to the Christmas Parlor would open and we would start celebrating Christmas. Our mother and father had decorated the tree. They kept the tradition of using real burning candles. The candles were attached to the branches with metal clamps and a weighted small wire device that kept the attached candle in an upright position.

The doors opened, we being the little children, stood in awe of the wonder of the Christmas tree all aglow. There was the tree in its splendor and we exuded happiness as the smell of the lit tree permeated the room. The festivities began as we entered the room and had to form a line. That was the beginning of our "Grand Performance."

My older sister was the first one to recite her Christmas poem selection. First she had to hand her folder to our father. The folder resembled a large greeting card. As she began her recital she did a curtsy, followed by her presentation, then a hug and a kiss first for our father and then the same for our mother. They in turn wished each of us a Merry Christmas.

My presentation followed after my older sister's. I started with a bow and recited my selected poem. Then it was my two younger sisters turn. It was a rather somber yet festive occasion that we always eagerly anticipated. There, before our family standing tall was our **Tannenbaum** (Christmas tree) in all its glory looking down on us.

This was then followed by our memorized presentation about the Birth of Jesus, the Christmas Story, as taken from the Bible scriptures starting with the second chapter of Luke from the New Testament. "And it came to pass in those days, that Caesar Augustus sent out a decree"… Each of us recited five verses, while our father held the Bible and coached us, in case we got stuck during our recital.

Then it was our mother's turn to entertain us. She played the piano and we all sang traditional German Christmas songs: **Stille Nacht, O' Tannenbaum, Ihr Kindelein Kommet, Leise Rieselt Der Schnee** and others. When the sing along started we knew that the time was coming nearer for us to receive our gifts.

After the piano recital and sing along the candles on the Christmas tree were extinguished. The same device that lit the candles also extinguished them. It was a long five-foot sectioned pipe- like pole that was blown through. A lit candle stuck onto one end of the pipe when it was used to light each candle on the tree

Once that was done, we were then able to "dig" into our sweets and goodies that were on the special gift table. Each of us got a **Bunten Teller** (colorful plate) that was heap-loaded with all kinds of candies, nuts, cookies, fruits, marzipan and a chocolate **Weihnachtsmann** (St. Nicholas).

Our decorated Christmas plates were lined up on a large long table covered with a white tablecloth. It was set up just for the purpose of displaying and distributing our goodies and gifts. Sections of table were divided and assigned to each child and sometimes to the servants if they remained with us over the Holiday. There were rows and rows neatly arranged presents. Our mother then individually led us along as she pointed to each of the assigned section of the table. There, just behind our plates were the unwrapped presents. Depending on what the gifts were, they were stacked about two to three feet high.

The one thing I remember about Christmas was, that it was always something to look forward to, a time when the family was together and my parents were generous to us. I remember that on the next day, Christmas Day, we repeated a similar celebration at the home of my maternal grandparents, **Opa** and **Oma** Reschke.

A similar performance with self made folders containing poems were also recited for the traditional Birthday Celebrations of our parents. Early morning on their **Wiegenfest** (Cradle Fest) as the **Geburtstag** (Birthday) was also called; we entered into their master bedroom. We stood in lined formation, bowed and curtsied and then recited our congratulatory poems while our parents sat up in their bed to receive our presentations. That was followed by hugs and kisses wishing them a "Happy Birthday."

At Christmas we did miss our older brother Ullie (Ulrich). When I was about two years old, he was then four. Due to his mental impediment he had to go to live at the children's hospital in Rastenburg, East Prussia. It was evident that Ullie was not functioning in a normal way and he needed twenty-four hour care.

I remember him standing up in his crib and all that he could say was "eee,eee,eeee." That was the last time I saw him and I felt so sorry, that my only brother was unable to be my playmate. It became more and more difficult for my parents and the servants to care for him.

Not to mention his bed-wetting. My parents did not want us to be saddened by his presence and decided, that it was best for him as well as for us, his siblings, to have him live in an institution for handicapped children.

In Germany both for the Christmas and New Year's Eve Celebrations you could hear the ringing and clanging of the many church bells all around town and countryside. The echoes of the ringing bells were even heard from very far away. They made a beautiful festive concert all by themselves.

FURTHER MEMORIES FROM LIFE IN KÖNIGSBERG

When I was about five years old my *Opa* gave me a large kite as my Birthday present. I guess I was his "pet." He nicknamed me *Jungchen*, the youngster, and would often spend his free time with me. Well, that kite was really too big for me, taller than I. The strength of the wind, with it's pulling force, lifted the kite up and me with it. So my father had to help me hold onto it when my *Opa* was not around.

Flying that kite was so much fun. It was then that I realized how I could make things fly in the air. So I developed an interest in making my own kites. I also made paper planes out of folded newspapers and even had a toy sailplane. That little plane was made out of wire, covered with starched cloth, had a catapult (sling shot release) and a rubber nose, so it would do no damage hitting something delicate or breakable.

Besides flying my kites and planes I also admired aircraft in flight. Quite often, while I was playing I would look up into the sky and see the huge five engines Junkers Lufthansa Airliner Hindenburg on its daily route to Berlin. Actually, I could distinguish its sound from all other planes. It sounded like hammers hitting large steel plates. The sound could be heard from far away.

Every day I could clearly see high above me those passenger planes and wished I could be up there with them going to wherever they were going. The planes always flew the same pattern. The Devau Airport of Königsberg was to the North East and as the planes took off they flew southwest, directly over Ponarth on their way to the *'Reich'* (the mainland of Germany).

Wow, I really loved flying my playthings and watching any type of aircraft in flight. It was then that I realized that my first choice for the future was definitely to be a pilot, not a Pastry/Confectionery Chef. My real love and passion now, was to become a pilot. So I thought, that if I could somehow be both, that would be fantastic!

It was about 1928 when my Grandfather, Friederich Franz Reschke had an apartment building built. It ended up being a three storied, thirty-six apartment complexes. More importantly, I remember that there was a large backyard behind it and it was there that he was also a Beekeeper having about twenty wooden hive boxes.

That fascinated me whenever I visited him, observing his routine of being a keeper of bees. When I was old enough, I helped him to remove the honeycombs from their hives and put them into the honey centrifuge where the honey was collected on the bottom of the drum. Opening a valve at the bottom, the honey would be dispensed into individual jars and sealed by screwed on lids. Because of the abundance of Linden trees nearby in full bloom at Springtime, the bees flocked to those blossoms. I observed, that when they returned to their hives, they had "saddlebags" full of pollen.

In the German language there is a distinction between the words for dying, a human life is of the highest caste-level. The animal kingdom is a lower secondary one, but the bee is the only member of the insect world which in dying , was of that higher caste. Its death was described with the same word equivalent to a human death. In German a human death is described as: **sterben**, an animal death as: **krepiert**. The bee's death was the same as the human and called **Die Biene stirbt** or is **gestorben.** That was out of respect to the hierarchy of the diligent bees.

I graduated from the **SpielSchule** (Kindergarten) and by the age of six I started Public School. My Elementary School was built of red bricks and was named after a famous person, "**Pestalozzi Schule.**" Johann Heinrich Pestalozzi (1746-1827) developed what became known as the

"Pestalozzi Method Of Teaching." He believed that children should learn through appropriate activity and by example.

In Germany it was a tradition that on the first day of school you would receive a **Schultüte**. I did receive several from my extended family. A **Schultüte** looked like an upside down dunce cap or straight horn of plenty. It was a huge cone shape made of decorated cardboard, had a shiny paper cover and was filled with all kinds of candy, sweets, and chocolates. My grandparents gave me the biggest one. My **Tante** (Aunt) Anna, **Onke**l (Uncle) Gustav as well as my other Aunt Elisabeth and Uncle Bruno, also gave me a large one. I was so proud going to school carrying my huge candy filled cone.

My **Tante** Anna, my father's sister, always made a wonderful impression on me. She had such a kind and caring manner towards my sisters and me, being her nieces and nephew. She never had any children of her own so she was very protective of us. She intervened and always showed kindness when our father was harsh with us. She made him aware, that we were just small children and that he should be easier on us.

Our home was located on the outskirts of Königsberg , Ponarth near the repair works of the Railroad where my father worked. It was also famous for its **Ponarther März Bier** (Beer), made in its huge brewery. I had to pass it every day on my way to school nearby. I remember enjoying the steamy fresh smell of the malt mash.

Local farmers loaded it onto their horse drawn wagons. They took the malt mash home to feed it to their pigs. Dieter Pfaff (my school buddy and neighbor in our apartment building) and I, often dug deep with our hands into the heap of warm mash and ate some of it. It was a very delicious treat. In retrospect today, I can't imagine why, but we boys had to try everything once to satisfy our curiosity. and liked it.

I also fondly remember, walking to school and passing a Blacksmith shop. The men were shoeing the large horses. the Hanovarians (**Hannoveraner Pferde**) of the Ponarth Brewery. I don't know horses that well, but maybe they were like the "Clydesdales" here in the U.S.A.?

Sometimes I arrived late at school because I got lost in time watching them nail the new horseshoes to the horses' hooves. The blacksmith also often forged some fascinating wrought iron artwork, forming them from red-hot bars. I watched with amazement how, with a large pair of long tongs in one hand and a hammer in the other, he beat and forged some useful things on that huge block of iron, the anvil.

Needless to say, my tardiness to class earned me some "light" punishment in the form of one to three whips on the outstretched inner hand with the teacher's bamboo twig. It was called ***das Spanische Rohr*** or ***Rohrstock.*** The "heavy" punishment, on the other hand, was a double whammy. For that you had to bend down, place your head under the teacher's desk and " whoosh", the ***Rute*** came down on your behind. In agonizing pain you hit your head on the underside of the desk. Hence, the "double whammy."

The number of strikes for your punishment depended on the severity of your misbehavior. Hitting from one to even five or six strikes really hurt and made your behind hurt for hours. After the severity of the punishment, any rubbing with your hands to alleviate or diminish the pain did not help. Not to mention the "pain in the neck" caused by the un-intended second "whammies," and the painful pressure of your body weight, when sitting down at your desk after this punishment.

Yes, corporeal punishment was not only allowed in German schools, but was also encouraged by the parents, and often you got a second punishment by them when you returned home. That was after reading the letter the teacher gave to us to take home informing our parents of the "crimes" we 'committed.' They had to sign the letter to acknowledge having received it and their child had to return it next day to the teacher.

The teacher was entirely in charge in the school and you would not dare dispute that issue. The parents respected the teacher and vice versa. That was the rule and you did not dare question the system. It was the common discipline.

At that time, in the early thirties, up to the end of WW II, the German school system was segregated by gender. There were public schools for boys, and public schools for the girls. Later, the ***Gymnasiums*** were for boys, and **Lyzeums** for the girls. This combination became the equivalent to High Schools in the United States. Later, Universities were attended by both genders.

Girls very seldom made it to the Universities; instead they were trained in household skills in the **Höhere Töchter Schulen** (upscale Daughter's Schools). That was of course if one had affluent parents who could afford to pay for their expensive training.

According to the evaluation by my teacher, Mr. Zabel, I was a bright yet somewhat lazy student. I can't say that I was Mr. Zabel's proverbial pet, but whatever I did, I did almost to perfection. My father, a veteran Prussian Artillery Officer of WW I, made sure of that, raising us children rather strict. Nothing we ever did was good enough, he insisted on utter perfection. In our fear of him, and to avoid the sometimes-cruel punishments we could expect for our misbehavior, we tried to do our dire best, mostly in vain, to please him.

He once told me during one of his lessons: "When I say, that wall is green, then for YOU it IS green, even if it is a hundred times white--- because I SAY SO!--- Period!" Needless to say, as children we lived in fear of him. We had the feeling, that he did not love us, no matter how hard we tried to please him with our given tasks. After having done our homework for school, we had to work in our huge garden, weeding, watering and tending to his prized fruit trees, etc. The Garden was his beloved passion and he took great pride in it.

Only later in our lives, we came to realize, that indeed he loved us and was proud of us, but he was inept to show his feelings of love, a result of his own stern upbringing and especially of his training as a Prussian Officer.

From 1929 to 1933 Herbert Hoover was the President of the United States and the entire world was in a period of economic depression. At the same time the stock market crashed in New York City.

It was a terrible time for everyone, especially to the people of Germany. The flow of foreign capital into Germany ceased and the country's foreign trade declined. Industry slowed, unemployment increased. Germany went deeper and deeper into depression. The party movement of the ***Reichstag*** came into being and rapidly grew. The Nazi party took advantage of the situation from 1929 to 1932.

In 1932 Hitler lost in the Presidential Elections to Paul von Hindenberg. Shortly after, Hitler refused to join in a coalition and demanded sole power. Therefore, the ***Reichstag*** was dissolved. Despite further set backs the Nazis were still the strongest party in the ***Reichstag.***

Following further turmoil between opposing parties, the attempts to create a new party became a crime. The National Socialist party became the only legal one at that time. A law acted upon in December of 1933 joined the Nazi party to the state. Thus totalitarian control of the state and of German society was established. Party members of at least eighteen years of age or older swore allegiance to the ***Führer***. Millions joined and those not willing to join were compelled to do so.

In a family photo, dated from 1932, my sisters and I looked like we were of the Von Trapp Family. Nicely posed in our crisp, neatly tailored sailor outfits. I still have that black and white photo today. It is now framed and hangs on the wall above my computer. It is a proud reminder of an age of innocence, my childhood and the fine upbringing I had in an upscale German Home and family.

By 1933 Franklin Delano Roosevelt was the President of the United States. I believe it was about the same time that I enjoyed sleighing during those cold snowy winters in Königsberg. We had a few sleighs. One was a large four seater, another, a two seater, that was not as good, and a third that was nicknamed by us, the *"Ziegenbock"* (male goat). It was designed with a high rounded neck and sharply bent front skids and it often got stuck. Even though it was a pretty sleigh to look at, painted in dark purple shiny lacquer with gold stripes on the edges, it was simply not practical for our use. So we fought amongst ourselves to get one of the two good sleighs.

Our sleighing escapades took us past part of the brewery to a fork in the road at a pasture to the right. Because the brewery was built on a fairly steep hilly platform we could slide down the incline passing over the creek of waste water from the beer bottle washing facility, the **Biergraben** (Beer creek).

A large open sewer pipe protruded from the incline half way up between the outside wall of the brewery and the bottom of the hill. It was covered with soil and grass in the summer. During the snowy winter it served as a great hump, over which we became airborne on our way down by skis or sleigh. It was our ski jump from which we could fly into the air. We called that hump *"Hoppsassa."* Not everyone was brave enough to go over it with a sleigh or on skis. If you were lucky, your landing would keep you all together to continue with the ride unscathed.

Often times we connected a few small sleighs together so we could steer better and our heels would become our brakes, but only down the hilly road. The **Hoppsassa** was too dangerous for the coupled steering sleighs. For this, of course, the *"Ziegenbock"* was utterly useless. You never could make it over the hump; it was too slow because of the sharply bent front of the skids. It never gained the speed needed to "get over the hump."

I guess altogether we were often a group of twenty to thirty children with almost everyone bringing his or her own sleigh or **Tonnebretter** (barrel boards). We were in our "Winter Wonderland." There were occasional snowball fights and many days after a fresh snow fall we made snow Angels. We created this by lying on our backs, and spreading our legs wide apart. Then we moved back and forth to form an Angel gown while we swung our arms in a flapping motion to create the wings. We competed with each other as to who could make the best Angel.

Some boys had home made skis made from barrel boards of discarded beer barrels. A strap from an old bicycle tire formed a loop to slip the feet into, and that was securely nailed down on top of the boards. In case of a downfall, your feet easily slipped out from it. These poor mans type of skis were used by kids with parents who were less affluent, and could not afford the real thing.

I had a pair of the "real McCoy" to the envy of the other kids, but often let them borrow mine so they could see the difference between their primitive contraptions and a good set of "boards." In turn, I tried out their barrel boards and found them to be not so primitive after all. They had the advantage of being shorter and were easier to steer.

My playmates and I often took turns having our **Mittagessen** (lunch) in each other's homes. After playing in the snow for many hours we welcomed a hot bowl of homemade soup to warm our chilled bones. Sometimes it was a seasonal vegetable, other times chicken and noodles, and occasionally a soup made from the white leaves of the cabbage.

One day, when I was maybe eight years old I saw an odd shaped item buried in the snow, by the **Biergraben** hidden in a small bush. I was sleighing when I was tossed into the bushes and made the discovery. It was then that I saw an odd shaped box. It turned out to be something heavy, with a zigzag angle. I asked myself: "What could it be?" Curiously I opened the box and discovered a real gun. I took it out of the box and aimed it into the air. My friend Dieter said: "Oh boy, we can shoot it." So we pretended that we were soldiers. I had some knowledge of guns from my father. I thought what we saw had been a Luger (50 caliber pistol) fully loaded with three extra full magazine clips tucked into a separate compartment of the box. I felt so grown up and important, but at the same time I knew that this was extremely wrong and dangerous. I told my friend that we had to bring our find to the **Polizei** (Police).

I packed the gun back into its case and we went to the nearby Police Station to report our find. The Policeman wrote a report and then came with us to see the exact location of where we found it. It was then for the first time after holding a gun in my hand that I felt like a soldier and a man, because I held a real gun and not a toy.

Another time I made a similar find in the snow. But this find was something most strange and unusual. It was a bag filled with black and white photos. I studied each one very carefully. I could not imagine why people were naked and in such strange poses. I found out a little later in my life that what I looked at were pornographic pictures.

So, that was just an added attraction to what I could find in the snow and more knowledge that I had gained relating to my own sexuality. I sold the whole package of pictures to some older boys for the then 'enormous' price of one ***Reichsmark***, a good-sized silver coin. That was immediately turned into candies and licorice at a nearby Kiosk. That silver coin would have "burned a hole in my pocket" and I certainly could not let that happen. Candies were of more importance to Dieter and me, than those useless pictures.

One very negative memory I have of my life in Königsberg came during wintertime. We children were dressed in woolen ***Bleyle*** sweaters with long sleeves. On our legs were long woolen socks reaching up over our thighs held there with a broad rubber band. Allergies were never heard of in those times. I later learned that I was allergic to wool touching my bare skin. ***"Es kribbelt"*** I complained to our ***Kindermädchen.*** With a disbelieving smile I was rebuffed and told, it was just my imagination. The constant itching was a real agony and that grew intensely stronger as I worked up a sweat while hard at play wearing my heavy coat and ski pants. I was always glad to shed the dreadful woolen garments at night after returning home. I had a rash each evening and even after being relieved of the wool clothing, I was still itching for hours. Just this fact alone, made me wish, never to have to return to my old boyhood times and go through this misunderstood agony again, especially when wearing long sleeved woolen sweaters

Now, in today's modern and more informed times, it appears that my youngest daughter inherited that allergy from me. When she was a toddler and my wife dressed her in woolen clothing that touched her skin, she always complained, that it "hurts." When my wife told me about it, I told her of my early experiences with wool and then realized that our daughter had an allergy to wool, just as I continue having today.

But a fond memory I have is of the time when I learned how to swim. The ***Hubertusteich*** (Hubertus pond), just East of the Ponarth Brewery had a ***Badeanstalt*** (Public Bath). For an entry fee, one could go swimming and bathing. ***Badmeister*** (Bath Master), Mr. Falk was in charge of the entire facility and was also the swimming instructor. For a fee, I took swimming lessons and I was one of his most eager pupils.

It really was fun to learn to swim and make it to the ***Freischwimmerzeugnis*** (Free Swimmer Certification), in a short time. As closure of the course and to receive my certificate I had to make a head first dive from the one-meter board, which I reluctantly did and received my certificate. When I hit the water, my head got a fairly strong welt that was mildly painful for hours. The Free Swimmer Certificate required a non-stop swimming time of fifteen minutes in deep water. It was not hard and not a problem for me either.

The ***Fahrtenschwimmerzeugnis*** (Travel Swimmer Certificate) required a swimming time of one full hour, which also was not a problem for me. But I dreaded the required dive from the three-meter board. I feared the strong jolt I would surely get on my head when I hit the water. I climbed up to the three-meter board and stood there for what seemed like an hour refusing to jump. I had often jumped feet first from there, but was deathly afraid to do it head first.

Everyone who was watching me urged me to dive. They said, "It won't hurt!" But I steadfastly refused and finally climbed down. Mr. Falk then told me of a little trick: By placing my stretched arms high above my head and clasp my stretched hands together like in prayer, it forms a penetrating point and I would pierce the surface of the water. Diving from that height, creates a cushioning whirlpool between my arms, which then protects my head from hitting the hard water surface upon impact.

Finally convinced, that this would be the solution to my fear of hitting my head, I gathered all of my courage, climbed up again to the three-meter level and forced myself to do that dive, no matter how it turned out. To my surprise, it really worked just as Mr. Falk had predicted. Nothing hurt after that and from then on I enjoyed diving from even higher boards without fear. I got my certificate and proudly showed it at home to my parents.

A few years later, when we had moved to Bavaria I made it to the ***Rettungsschwimmer-zeugnis*** (Rescue Swimmer Certificate), the equivalent to becoming a Lifeguard. That was a lot harder to achieve and required much practice.

My Mother with her parents, Reschke

My Father, Paul Dulias

My Mother, Lucie (18yrs.)

My Oldest Sister, Me at One, Brother Ullie at Two.

Me at 2½

Me, a "Terrible Two?"

Family Vacation at The Baltic Sea
(in center - Grandparents Dulias),
Along with Aunts, Uncles

Grosskuhren, Opa Lück (left) Boats and Nets

Tante Anna, Onkel Gustav

The Sandcastle My Father and I Built

First Days of School

Holding My Schultüte

Didn't We Look Cute?

A School Boy   Proud of My First Bicycle

Our Class 1933 At Pestalozzi School
I was in second row, second right from Mr. Zabel

Our Play Group. I'm hiding,
but my hand is on
Irmgard's shoulder

Fun On The Swing

1932 We looked like the Von Trapp Family

Zeugnis

von der

Pestalozzi -Volksſchule zu Königsberg Pr.

Schuljahr 193⁴/₃₅ 1. Halbjahr,

für .... *Gottfried Dulias* .... , aus Klaſſe 5a

Zeugnisgrade: I ſehr gut; II gut; III genügend; IV mangelhaft; V ungenügend

Führung:	gut
Aufmerkſamkeit:	
Fleiß:	genügend
Ordnung:	

Leiſtungen:

Religion:	genügend	Rechnen:	genügend
Leſen:	gut	Heimatkunde:	noch genügend
Rechtſchreibung:		Zeichnen:	faſt gut
Sprachlehre:		Muſik:	
mündl. ⎫ Ausdruck:	genügend	Turnen:	genügend
ſchriftl. ⎭		Handarbeit:	fehlt naſſe immer!
Schreiben:	faſt gut		

Verſäumt: 7 Tage. — Verſpätet: — mal.

Bemerkungen: .

Königsberg Pr., den 28. September 193⁴

Rektor.   Klaſſenlehrer.

Dulias

Report Card - Pestalozzi School

Two

From Königsberg to Osterode (1934-1938)

By 1933 Germany was a totalitarian state led by the dictator Adolf Hitler. That was the beginning of the Third Reich. By that time the majority of German voters supported one or the other of the two major totalitarian parties, the Communist or the National Socialist.

In 1934, when I was nine years old, my father got promoted to a new position as: **Reichsbahn Amtmann** and our family had to move to Osterode, East Prussia, my father's birth place. There he became second in command of the railroad repair works. We had just about settled there, when we had to make a return visit back to Königsberg. We went back to attend the funeral of my Uncle Julius Lappe, the owner of the confectionery store.

After seeing the lifeless body of my deceased Uncle at the funeral parlor, it left me with a frightening remembrance. Awaking in the middle of the night, from some undetermined noise, I opened my eyes and imagined that I saw his lifeless face as an image formed by my pillow. It was almost as if I had seen a ghost, really weird. Uncle Gustav and Aunt Anna had to comfort me and stayed with me until I could fall asleep again.

In Osterode our three- story house was located at **Wilhelmstrasse** No. 39 alongside the railroad tracks that separated the train station from our street by a high fence. The station stood diagonally across from the right street front of our house, and to the left there was the railroad repair and maintenance plant. The railroad owned the building in which our family lived. Housing was provided for their upper echelon employees. We occupied the entire first floor, which was an enormous living space. It was a modern building with two entrances, and was built around 1930.

Upon entering our apartment by the second entrance stairway hall in the courtyard, there was a seventy five feet long L-shaped hallway. All rooms were accessed from there to each side. My room was located at the far left end on the right side of it, near the front of the house. In the hallway next to my room there was a trapeze swing mounted on the ceiling. My sisters shared a huge bedroom right next to my smaller one.

We all enjoyed the swing, especially on rainy days. It gave us an activity in exercise and fun. For us it was about the best plaything we had there. Swinging on the trapeze we often jumped onto a couch, right at the end of the hallway. It actually was an extra sleeper that I had to use when overnight guests were given my room to sleep in.

In the wintertime it was still dark in the early morning when the railroad workmen bicycled past our house on their way to work. The headlights from their bicycles reflected through my window onto the wall at the foot end of my bed and the ceiling, producing a moving light show as they passed by. Awakening, I loved watching the constant motion of dancing lights and shadows from my bed. The rapid succession of shadowy figures that passed along my wall was like a shadow puppet show. By seven o'clock in the morning my show was over because all the men had begun working at the plant. That was also my signal to get up and ready for school, which started at 8:30 AM.

Each and every school day, in all kinds of weather, I had half an hour walk to school. It took me the same amount of time to return back home in the afternoon. School buses did not exist in those times, as they do for today's youngsters here in the U.S.A., who enjoy that ride and take it for granted.

One day on my way to school while passing by a nearby apartment building I found a cigar box on the front steps. As I opened it up I discovered inside of it a number of bundles of paper money. I immediately entered the building and began knocking on doors asking if anyone had lost anything.

It so happened to be that a group of students visiting our town were staying in that building and they claimed my find. They told me that it was their traveling money. The teacher of the group told me that the box contained over three thousand marks. I returned the box to them and they in turn gave me a "Thank You" reward of five marks. To me at that time it was a lot of money, and I was able to buy many things with it. I kept my reward "treasure" a secret from my family and slowly spent it over a period of time.

After the fourth grade in public school, I started in the "Sexta," the beginner's class in the **Kaiser Wilhelm Gymnasium** of Osterode. It was there that we started learning the dreadful foreign language of Latin.

Then in following classes, the Quinta, Quarta and Unterterzia, came English, Greek and French on the agenda, none of which were to my liking. Thinking to myself: What do I need those for? Well, I had to reluctantly learn the Latin: "flamma flagrat" (the flame flickers), "agricola laborat" (the farmer works), "puella vocat," (the girl calls), etc. and later full sentences and chapters depicting Roman history.

Latin and **Mathematik** (mathematics) were my weak and sorely disliked subjects to learn, but I managed to get a "G*enügend.*" The **Genügend** in my report cards (**Schulzeuginisse**) would be the equivalent of a "C" according to the American Educational System. The other subjects were more interesting to me.

I liked: Geology, Biology, Art (mostly drawing and painting), Science, German orthography, also Music and Gymnastics too, with and without the use of gym equipment. Swimming and nature studies were taught out in the open at Lake Drewenz.

I achieved *"Sehr Gut und Gut"* (very good and good) markings for my efforts in those subjects. That was the equivalent of "A's" and "B's" in American schools. However, sometimes I got an *"Ungenügend"* in one or the other categories, a "D" for missing homework, or a *"Mangelhaft",* which equaled an "F" on my **Zeugnis.** That surely meant punishment by my father in the form of curtailed privileges and of whippings with a dog whip, or both.

The dog whip originally was more than two feet long. The last time I saw it when we were living in Fürstenfeldbruck, near Munich, in the nineteen forties, I remember that it couldn't have been more than eighteen inches long. Worn out from too much---- "use!" Sometimes, when I was due for punishment for one reason or another, I hid that **Hunde-Peitsche**, so my father couldn't find it. But soon I produced it again, after being "worked over" with the **Sieben-Penter,** (seven tailed carpet whip) with a wooden handle, that had seven leather strips attached. Knowing, that the leather strips did not inflict the intended painful "results," my father used the wood end on my behind, and that really smarted, as anyone can imagine!

Today all those beatings are classified as corporal punishment, amounting to child abuse, especially here in the States. But back then in Germany in most families it was a common practice and was never debated or challenged.

Towards the rear corner of our hallway was the combined dining/ living room on the left with a connection to the Parlor. A wall with an eight-foot wide pair of pocket doors separated the two rooms. Our long dining room table could comfortably seat about sixteen people when it extended to full length. Normally it was set for six, just for our family.

At the corner of the L-shaped hallway was the master bedroom of my parents. Their room had a most magnificent large custom made oak vanity. It was an outstanding piece of furniture that had a natural black marble top, white veined, in its natural design.

In the middle of the top was a sunken basin. A large porcelain floral decorated water pitcher was filled daily and placed onto the counter top. When in use, it was emptied into the huge basin for washing. The water drained into a reservoir below in the cabinet. It had to be emptied each day by the maid; there was no plumbing connection. At the rear wall above the marble backsplash was a glass-shelf for cosmetics, toothbrushes and glasses. A huge mirror with beveled edges and matching oak frame hung above the shelf and at its top were four crystal globed light fixtures.

At the right end of the shorter part of the 'L' angled hallway was the hotel style kitchen that was equipped with more than ample work and pantry space. It had a large butcher-block table and additional counter tops for food preparation. The stove was of a commercial type and was fueled by natural gas. Liesbeth Traufetter was our new live- in maid and cook, she took excellent care of the whole family. Her room was also off the long hallway on the left side, its window facing the courtyard.

An equally large apartment was above ours and was occupied by another upscale railroad family. The **Werkdirector,** who was the first in command of the plant and his family lived there. The entrance to their upstairs apartment was the one at the street side and front of the house.

On the third floor, up from our courtyard entrance there were two smaller apartments. One occupied by maintenance foreman of the plant and his family. The other apartment was for the Kallweit family. The husband, the Main Foreman and Supervisor of the Railroad Work Plant and his wife had only one child, a son named Erich.

When I met Erich he was about thirty years old. Unfortunately he was disabled since childhood due to Polio. A vaccine had not been developed then and Erich was left handicapped with limited use of his legs. He alternately used a wheelchair and/or walked with crutches.

I often spent a lot of quality time with Erich. He was a most brilliant and fascinating person. All of his education and expertise had been acquired by taking correspondence courses. As an exceptionally talented artist he drew and painted intricately detailed pictures that amazed me. Some of his subjects were of a great variety of floral arrangements, still life, portraits and landscapes.

I was in awe over his ability at calligraphy. He wrote beautifully in skilled penmanship. In fact, his writings were so perfect that the correspondence school returned the work to him. A note was enclosed stating that he should re-submit his work in a "handwritten format" not a "machine printed" one! He showed me that correspondence as I too, thought that it was mechanically printed. He had to actually prove to them that yes, indeed it was hand-written by him. This could be done by holding the written page up to a strong light so as to detect a variation of strokes, thickness and flow of the black ink.

His works were unlike anything I had ever seen before. His knowledge of just about anything was fascinating to me. I absorbed a great deal of it and furthered my own education through his instructional teachings. We often played board- and card games as well as doing puzzles that needed clever skills to solve. I was taught how to play chess, checkers, and another, called *"Mühle"* (mill), as well as other games of strategy.

Mr. Erich Kallweit was my mentor and his teachings and friendship were priceless to me. I remember one day in 1938, just before we moved to Fürstenfeldbruck we were listening to a speech by Hitler on the radio. He attacked the integrity of President Roosevelt by calling him a *"Lümmel"* (punk, rebel rouser, delinquent, and troublemaker). Erich then made a comment: "*That means War, sooner or later!*" How right he was, because just one year later in 1939, his prediction came true.

Fondly I think back to the wonderful times I spent with Erich. I learned so much from this great teacher. The knowledge and skills I gained from my acquaintance with him were always a great advantage for me, priceless!

Thank you, Erich Kallweit, wherever you are now, I will never forget you. I owe a tremendous debt to you for this gift that has influenced my life, even to this day.

Attached to our apartment building, on the ground floor in the courtyard, was an addition containing a laundry for the use by all tenants as well as storage rooms for each apartment. The Kallweits used theirs as a stable for Erich's pet rabbits.

Every day he laboriously came down the three flights of stairs on crutches to feed and tend to approximately twenty pets. Together we fed the rabbits fresh vegetables, grain,

clover, and hay. I can even remember peeling a few leaves from a head of cabbage and letting the rabbits eat from my hands. He taught me to respect and care for animals, as creatures created by God, as living beings that needed tender care. No wonder, this genius of a man gave me more education than I ever received in school or at home.

It was somewhat around this time that we made a visit to Danzig (now Gdansk) to visit another one of my father's old World War I buddies. Hugo Behrend owned a huge Ranch Estate. Well actually, he was a landlord and practically owned an entire village whose inhabitants were working for him. His thousands of acres of land were agriculturally cultivated. On his property he had many horse stables and from what I saw, there had to be about one hundred horses and many cows, pigs and flocks of chickens. While we stayed there I learned an awful lot about agriculture and farming.

For the first time I learned to ride a horse bare back. I remember falling off one horse, right in front of him. Luckily, and to my surprise, the horse immediately stood still, and I was not trampled upon. I got back on, and held on tightly to the horse's mane.

Eggs were always one of my favorite things to eat and there they were plentiful. Sometimes I ate them swirled with a spoon and stirred in some sugar because they were so tasty to me, sweetened. Other times I had fun punching two holes in them, sucking them out. On command, I ran a competition with their big hunting dog. He lapped his up from a dish and I sucked mine empty. Time and time again I won the competition.

Back at home I also frequently punched holes in top and bottom before 'drinking' them. Then the intact preserved hollow shells were saved for a later time to hand-paint them, especially for Easter. Occasionally, our maid would punch a single slightly larger hole at the side center and empty the egg white and yolk, then use it's shell as a mold. With a pastry bag that had a narrow metal point she filled the hollow eggshell with molten chocolate, sealing the hole with a small foil-label and so created a delicious Easter egg after cooling it in the 'icebox'. These were all nice things that I experienced, and still have fond memories of from my childhood.

I was a Little Rascal

Above the storage rooms and Kallweit's rabbit stable there were two storage attics, accessible only by a ladder, and in one of them my father stored his garden equipment and fertilizers. My close friend was Gerhard Buick, who was a year younger than I and lived in the apartment building next door. He was my steady companion at play and in doing pranks, that we often loved doing, for kicks.

I recall that many times we climbed up the ladder to the loft attic and threw handfuls of *"Thomasmehl,"* (a black powdery fertilizer) down to the courtyard. This produced a cloud of dust, like an exploding bomb. It really was fun to create these fake explosions, as we imagined we were flying a plane and "bombing" the landscape below us.

Needless to say, that "stunt" earned me a severe punishment with the dog whip by my father. That expensive fertilizer was a derivative of the "Thomas ovens" that were found in steel producing plants. It was of a very potent type that made everything that grew, develop to it's utmost potential. So, when my father wanted to 'feed' his plants and flowers he found most of the *Thomasmehl* missing. He knew right away who the culprit was who had "squandered" the plant food and made the grass in the courtyard grow with surprising speed.

A further punishment was, having to "mow" the fast growing grass with a sickle, while on my hands and knees. We did not have a mower then, since previously we had no lawn to speak of. The garden was completely cultivated with vegetables, berries, bushes and trees, as well as a great variety of my father's prized flowers. There weren't any wasted areas, such as a lawn. Only the courtyard had a somewhat poor grass growth that now, with the rich fertilizer, came to life in a most amazing way.

The house next door from ours was one of a long line of apartment buildings occupied exclusively by railroad workers who were employed at the plant across the street. My friend Gerhard Buick had a sister one year older than him named Ilse. She was a tomboy like my youngest sister but was the same age as me. Ilse always joined us at play and often my youngest sister as well. Ilse and I spent many times alone together when Gerhard was otherwise occupied with tasks he had to do for his father.

She was a pretty girl with blue eyes and blonde braided hair interwoven with colorful ribbons. For her age she was an early bloomer and was well developed but in pleasant proportion. The way I like to remember her was as a free spirit, with a happy-go-lucky attitude. We also knew exactly what was on each other's minds, and almost always fully agreed with one another.

One early winter's evening Gerhard and I took a walk around our neighborhood, in search of the colorful glass globes that adorned many a front yard and garden. The idea came over us to quietly swipe some of them while it was dark, and we could not be seen. Each of us hid two small spheres of about 4" in diameter inside our winter coats and also carried an additional larger 6" to 8" one on our way back. There we hid them in our garden under some debris in the compost bin. I had a plan for next day and that was to climb over the low fence at the rear of our garden and walk to the creek that flowed through the pasture adjoining the rear of our garden. The creek was partially lined with some bushes along the shore, and flowed towards and into lake Drewnz at the lower part of Osterode.

I planned to take the swiped hollow (blown glass) globes and insert a cork plug into their necks at the bottom of each. Then to toss them into the creek and watch them float downstream. ---- I supplied the corks because we had plenty in my house, saved from the many bottles of wine, champagnes and liquors, which were left from mt parent's many parties.

That plan was my own idea and it turned out just the way I had imagined it would as Gerhard assisted me. The larger champagne corks were an exact fit to the neck openings of the larger globes, some of the wine corks fit also into the smaller globes, some we had to cut thinner with our pocketknives to fit the necks

The next day as we got home after school, we had to do our homework first. Around 3 PM we were free to continue our shenanigans. So, that afternoon we retrieved the globes from our hiding place, went to the creek and let them float one after the other downstream and they became a floating parade along the length of the creek until they emptied into the Lake Drewenz.

Gerhard and I imagined what the town's people would think and say when they saw the parade of floating and bobbing colored balls. We ran down along part of the creek to follow our parade, to watch that none of them got broken, but since we spaced them far enough, it did not occur. We were also careful not to be caught doing that. People were standing on the street bridge over the creek looking and pointing down to the creek wondering, what was going on? Gerhard and I were hiding behind some bushes. Observing from afar, we saw mothers on the bridge with their children looking at those strange glass bulbs bobbing towards them and disappearing under the bridge. The kids shouted happily and ran to the other side of the bridge and watched those shiny balls float further down disappearing in the distance and then winding up in the lake. I wondered what people thought of that strange flotsam appearing from nowhere and maybe tried to "fish" them out from their boats? This was another shenanigan done without being caught.

Each apartment in our section of the four family house had it's own storage room in the attic. My father kept his World War I memorabilia there as well as other forgotten treasures. One day I took the key from the hallway keyboard that was marked "attic." Gerhard and I went secretly up there exploring.

This really took courage because it had been "forbidden" territory, "off limits" for my sisters and me. So we saw a long, tall package tied and wrapped in newspaper. We lifted this heavy parcel up and started to unwrap it. To our surprise it was a military Karabiner (rifle). Then I knew right away what the ammunition was for that I discovered earlier in my father's Parlor desk. That gave me the idea that we could try to use the rifle at a remote site far away where we would not be heard or seen.

I slid the gun into my pants leg to hide it. We went downstairs out to the courtyard and temporarily hid it in the huge garbage bin.

Gerhard stood watch while I went back inside to our apartment and to the Parlor room. I grabbed two packages of ammunition, put them into my pocket and snuck back outside. We took our sleighs pretending that we were going sleigh riding. Gerhard and I retrieved the gun and wrapped it in a burlap sack and pulled it along on the sleigh. We traveled out of town towards a small lake, way past the West end of Osterode.

About three miles down the road we came to a forested area by a small lake and looked for a place suitable for our target practice. The steep slope at the shoreline was a perfect launching spot for our sleighing. Sliding down from the top of the plateau, we landed onto the frozen lake. What fun that was and we almost forgot about the gun. At the base of the lake's shore, we saw rowboats stored upside down for the winter.

That gave me the idea to use those for target practice from a position half way up a slope. I had inserted a clip of five shots into the breach of the gun and closed the lock. Knowing that it would produce a sharp kick to the shoulder upon firing it, I braced it into the slope behind me and aimed it from my hip towards the boats and pulled the trigger.

Lo and behold I hit the boat right in the center. We saw the impact as the snow covering the boat burst into the air. That reaction was an amazing sight we certainly did not expect, but now we felt proud of our achievement.

After I completed my first try at shooting I let Gerhard take his turn. I gave him some instructions on how to repeat what I had done. He was eager for his first handling of a real gun. I had already had some experience while in the summer camp of the HJ (Hitler Youth). I think that was when I had been instructed at a rifle range with smaller 22 caliber guns.

The result of his try turned out to be completely different from mine. He missed the boat entirely. Instead he ended up shooting a hole through the ice of the lake. That created a huge burst and shower of snow and ice particles, like the impact from a grenade. It was really fun watching the results of the thirty shots of ammunition we had taken with us.

Upon inspecting the damage we had done to the boats, I found to my amazement, that the bullets went right through the one side and had exited the other, leaving a large hole there, unlike the small holes on the impact side.

After taking a few more sleigh rides down the slope we decided to return home, as it was beginning to get dark. We put the gun back into the burlap sack and placed it on the sleigh, pulling it back home. I then returned the gun to the attic the same way that I had brought it down. We both re-wrapped and strung it so it would look as close as it originally did when we found it. No one ever had even the slightest clue about what Gerhard and I had done. That time again we both got away with another prank unpunished. We were young and did not fully realize that our antics would cost the boat owners dearly for repairs.

During the Spring and Summer my sisters, Gerhard, Ilse and I went to the same forested lake area. We carried baskets and empty milk canisters with us to be filled with collections of wild berries and or mushrooms to bring home.

At school, in Biology class, we were taught how to find and select edible berries and mushrooms. We were shown pictures in books to identify the edible ones and our biology teacher pointed out the differences between the poisonous and edible berries and mushrooms. One of the keys to look for, when uncertain about our find, was to cut a mushroom in half and see if the cut surface turned purple in a short while. If it did, then it was poisonous. Another key, which was obvious, was never to pick the red-capped ones that had white dots on them, called the *"Fliegenpilz"* (fly agaric). They were not only the most beautiful and decorative but also the most poisonous mushrooms.

According to the season, or the month, we would find different varieties of berries and mushrooms. The springtime and snowmelt created a lot of moisture on the ground of the forest, and the mushrooms usually sprouted up first.

Week's later blueberries and wild strawberries were harvested. After we brought our finds home, we gave the baskets and canisters to Liesbeth (short for Elisabeth), our maid. We ate some of the raw berries with milk and sugar for dessert. Marmalades and compotes were made from the remaining berries. The mushrooms were washed, and prepared for meals. One particular mushroom type called *"Pfifferlinge"* was my favorite. When prepared the right way, with a cream sauce and served with salt potatoes it was a scrumptious meal.

The purpose of our basement was to store dry goods as well as jars with assorted homemade marmalades, jellies, jams, whole fruits, berries, vegetables, and my favorite dessert of pickled pumpkins and sweet rhubarb compote. Most of those were harvested from our garden. There were also large wooden barrels full of varieties of herrings. Among them were the **Bismarcks, Essigs, and Schmants. (Soaked in cream)**

Also in the basement there was a workroom containing our old carpenter's workbench, wall hung cabinets, and shelves stacked with tools. I often spent many hours there creating things like sailboats, Go-carts, and airplane models as well as other hand crafted items and toys. This brought memories back from my first attempts to craft some useful things in the workshop of **Opa** Lück in Grosskuren, where for the first time I was introduced to such carpentry and cabinet making. When I was older and wiser, this knowledge came in handy for the task of building bigger and more useful items.

I WAS A PIMPF

National Socialism in Germany was in many ways similar to Italian fascism. The difference was, that the roots of National Socialism were German. One example was the Prussian tradition of military authoritarianism and expansionism. All German youngsters under the age of seventeen were required to join the Hitler Youth organization,

(Hitler Jugend) which was under the direction of the SA (Nazi party). The supreme leader of the HJ was Baldur von Schirach

In 1935, when I was ten years old it was mandatory that I join the Hitler Youth organization (HJ) as a *"Pimpf."* That was the equivalent of being a young Boy Scout here in the United States. My uniform consisted of wearing a brown pocketed shirt accented by an insignia pin, and a black kerchief around my neck held in place with a woven leather knot.

I also wore a black boat shaped cap *(Schiffchen mütze)* and black short corduroy pants with a chrome buckle along with a shoulder belt. As an accessory we wore a travel knife *(Fahrten messer),* which was attached to the belt at the left hip in a sheath and holster. Oh yes, I remember the inscription on my 'mini sword/dagger', *"Blut und Ehre."* That meant Blood and Honor.

Girls were required to join the B.D.M. *(Bund Deutscher Mädel)* that was the equivalent to today's Girl Scouts here. They were taught skills that would be important for later woman / motherhood and the care and keeping of a home. As the old expression goes: *"Küche, Kinder, Kirche." (kitchen, children, Church)*

The girls wore a uniform similar to the boys. Theirs consisted of a black skirt and a white blouse with an insignia pin on it, accessorized with a black neck scarf slipped into a knotted ring. I remember that my sisters were also members of the B.D.M., as ordered.

About once a month our group assembled and bicycled ten to fifteen kilometers out of town to various campsites for a weekend sleepover. I clearly remember that it was on one of those trips that we had a tremendous thunderstorm.

When we got there we went swimming in the lake. Our camp and tents were set up at the shore of a beautiful lake, I can't remember its name and our camp counselor called us to rush out of the water quickly, and run to our tent as the storm approached and it started to rain. Each tent was large enough to accommodate about a dozen boys.

While inside it safely, there was an un-familiar very strange sound, the pitter-patter of the rain, but then the sound changed.

What we experienced was a tremendous hailstorm, and that was a very different if not frightening type of experience for us. Once it was over we came out and had fun making ice balls and started throwing them at each other. Only they did hurt, being of solid ice, as opposed to a wintry snowball

Our mornings began by doing various exercises and warm-ups as well as a sprint in the woods. On those same weekends we learned different warfare strategies between groups with different color armbands and acted them out. During the evenings for entertainment, we had Campfires with sing-a-longs, accompanied by the Counselor playing his **Ziehharmonika** (concertina) which was similar to an accordion, but had buttons to push instead of piano keys for playing songs. Some were specific songs composed for the Hitler Youth Groups. Along with those we told our usual "Ghost Stories." In the darkness with kerosene lamps as well as small flat battery operated flashlights illuminating the area surrounding us.

We were responsible for preparing and cooking our own meals. Those who were somewhat knowledgeable, or thought that they were, attempted to do just that. I remember one morning one boy tried to make us a hot cereal. The milk was brought to a boil in a huge pot on a gas-fired camp stove. Then he dumped an entire bag of Farina into it and started to stir the mixture. It turned out lumpy, became scalded and burnt, got stuck to the pot and turned into a big mess. All had to be thrown away because it tasted awful and no one could eat it. But what a tiresome job it was to clean that pot! It had to be scraped and washed out again and again by using a rag with some sand at the lakeshore.

Then I volunteered for the job of making the breakfast cereal, because I had some previous experience having done it before. Back at home I not only watched our maid making cereals daily, but also helped her. I started from scratch. First, using that cleaned pot I brought the milk to a boil, and turned the flame to a simmer. Then, slowly, I added the cereal mix while I kept steadily stirring. After it thickened I then removed the pot from the fire. Adding some sugar into it, it was ready to eat. All complimented me on my success, and within a short time the pot was scraped clean empty. There was an ample amount so many of us took second and third helpings. From then on I was the appointed cook.

On the day of the six hundred year Anniversary Celebration of Osterode, we marched proudly in the parade behind the " SA", the *"Sturmateilungen"* of the National Social German Worker's Party, NSDAP (as the Nazi party was officially called). The parade commemorated the founding of Osterode by the Order of the Knights of the cross, who started out by building the *Burg* (fortified castle) around which a market place later developed.

My two younger sisters, dressed in 19th Century ladies garbs and gowns with pompous hats, posed as passengers on a float supplied by the Railroad plant. A miniature replica train was displayed on it, modeled after the ones from the 1880's.

The whole town was festively decorated with garlands and a multitude of swastika flags. Every house had to display the new national flag. It had replaced the black/white and red banner of the old Kaiser Reich since 1933, when Hitler came into power as *Reichs Kanzler* (Chancellor) and Führer (leader). The enthused German people, who were looking for the better times that this charismatic man promised us, elected him. What ensued, after this new Government took over, is a sad memory of history, most Germans are certainly not proud of. Germany would never be the same. Although, in the first few years of his rule before WW II, there were many significant accomplishments that made most German citizens embrace Nazism.

Under Hitler there was no more unemployment. Super highways were introduced, the Autobahn, as it is known today became the "Super Highway." You could drive at more than one hundred kilometers or more per hour, or as fast as your car could go.

Affordable housing for every working family was available. The Volkswagen automobile was available and sold for the price of only eight hundred *Reichs Marks* and was well within reach of the working class, thus the "Peoples Car" (Beetle Bug) came into being. That is the meaning of "**Volkswagen**." The idea came from Hitler and he specified the criteria for it. Professor Ferdinand Porsche created the design upon his request. But in 1939 the war started and further production of it ceased. The factory was handed over to the German Air Force **(Luftwaffe),** who then built a military version of it, the so called Geländewagen, (all terrain wagon) often wrongly referred to as Kübelwagen (bucket car). In reality that was a later design of the wagon which was amphibious and had a fold-down small boat-screw driven by the transmission.

Pensions and welfare for disabled workers were established. Wages and salaries rose as the economy improved. "Made in Germany" markings on exported goods were known throughout the world as a guarantee for the best quality possible, and at the same time, the least expensive. The two major manufacturing markets in the export business were, at that time, Germany first and also Japan.

No wonder most countries preferred German wares, machinery and other heavy equipment from the well known **Krupp Werks**, chemicals from **IG Farben Werks**, and many more goods from other Companies, such as those manufacturing optic equipment like Zeiss,etc. which made the German Economy grow and prosper phenomenally.

Though I am not a politician, never was, or will be, this is the way I saw it and my young mind was fed with plenty of propaganda which made me believe, that indeed, Germany, my fatherland, was a well respected country and nation. At that time I was proud to be a German and honored to be a member of the Hitler Youth group.

Besides, that was just the way it was when I was a young boy growing up, I didn't know it as being any other way. There was no choice in the matter.

Now looking back, I think it was in 1936 when I saw a Zeppelin for the first time. We were in our Public School Classroom when the teacher told us that the Graf Zeppelin was scheduled to fly over Osterode that day. Our class was led outside to a large nearby pasture. We were told to form a line, standing side by side at arms length, from end to end that was to represent the entire length of the Zeppelin to give us a perception of it.

It would give us some idea of the huge dimensions that it had. Then suddenly, off in the distance we heard a deep humming sound coming from it's engines. Shortly as the noise grew louder, the Zeppelin appeared and was flying towards us. At first in full frontal view it appeared like a huge round balloon. Once closer, it was more clearly defined and we could see it in its entirety as it came directly above us.

We were in awe looking up at this huge "flying machine." We raised our hands high above our heads and waved upwards as we looked to the pilot, crew and passengers. They acknowledged our waves, and also waved back to us. They were flying low, so what we saw was a clear close-up view. You could also clearly distinguish the motor gondolas and propellers at both sides outside the cigar-shaped entity.

When we returned to the Classroom we continued with a discussion about what we had seen and experienced. Our teacher shared with us more information about the History of the Zeppelin, dating back to Pre World War I. For us, it was a brand new, and "once in a lifetime experience" being able to clearly see that clever invention above us passing by.

In June of 1937, there was a competition that I decided to enter. It was to build a dollhouse, of free style without any particular specifications. The purpose of the competition was to sell the doll houses. The event was held as a fundraiser before Christmas and the money collected would be for the purpose of helping less fortunate people and their children, for the holy days.

My design was of a modern type having a basement garage and a first floor with a living/dining room with double doors leading out to one side. There was also an exterior winding stairway to the second floor platform and from there to the flat roof garden, all guarded by railings. The second floor had two bedrooms and a bath as well as a kitchen. All rooms had a ceiling light fixture, even at the platform roof garden as well as at the upper stair landing and also the exterior wall above the double doors featured exterior lights.

A switchboard in the basement garage controlled all of the lighting for it. The fold-down door of it included a lock and key. The power for the lighting came from a large lantern battery, also stored in the garage.

I had purchased the small bathroom light fixture and the otherlight fixtures, as well as the mirrors from a craft store. These small-scale lights had intricate detailed lampshades. For the living room I picked a larger tri-light hanging fixture for the roof an umbrella shaped one. I crafted all the furniture myself, including an elaborate buffet with glass doors in the upper setback china display cabinet. I made the dining room table with its six chairs and a couch in the living room out of oak wood. The couch was neatly upholstered with velvet material. Even a Grandfather clock decorated the dining room. Each room had windows with glass and dividing frames.

Floors were carpeted. Only the kitchen and bath were tiled with artificial tile boards. I even papered the walls with some leftovers from our apartment. The various wallpapers were of a motif suitable for the small scale of the Doll House rooms.

The exterior walls and railings I painted with white oil paint and the flat roof garden floor with slate gray. My younger sister made the curtains for each of the windows and they were skillfully folded to look like the real ones in our apartment. She also sewed the bedding for the bedroom set and I made the mattresses out of dried peat moss encased with a silky cloth.

I painted all the ceilings flat white after filling in the grooves for the all hidden wiring with wood filler. Inside the lower living room a straight stairway led to a landing halfway up to a bedroom above the garage and from there continued to the upper rooms. A single door from the master bedroom led to the platform of the outer winding stairs.

In full scale, the house I created looked very much like a Florida beach house. It took me several months to complete that project with the largest part of my time spent creating the furniture to scale.⁻

I got it ready just in time for the exhibition in town before Christmas 1937 and lo and behold, I won First Prize, a blue honorary ribbon. A picture of the dollhouse was printed in the local newspaper with a brief story about the twelve and a half year old builder. I declined to be photographed for an accompanying picture, (being too shy for that kind of publicity).

After Christmas, to my surprise, I was notified by letter from the main office of the HJ at Berlin that my dollhouse had been bought by Baldur von Schierach for his children. He was the ***Führer*** of the entire Hitler Youth, the top leader of that organization. I felt really honored, that my work had made it to the 'top'. Our troop leader awarded me with a Gold Merit Medal in front of the whole troop. I proudly wore that medal from then on at all our uniformed functions and events. My fellow members and the entire troop were just as proud to have one of their own in their midst as a winner of that honorable badge.

I was proud to be a PIMPF

My younger sisters
Dressed for the Parade

Float 1890's - 600 Anniversary Osterode

Staatl. Kaiser Wilhelm-Gymnasium
Osterode Ostpr.

ZEUGNIS

für den _[handwritten]_

von _[handwritten]_ bis _[handwritten]_ 193_[?]_

Allgemeine Beurteilung: _[handwritten]_

LEISTUNGEN
Urteile: I sehr gut; II gut; III genügend; IV nicht genügend.

Religion:	_[handwritten]_ genügend
Deutsch:	
Latein:	
Griechisch:	
Französisch:	
Englisch:	gut
Geschichte:	genügend
Erdkunde:	gut
Mathematik/Rechnen:	genügend
Biologie:	gut
Physik/Chemie:	
Wahlfreies Fach:	
Zeichnen:	
Musik:	genügend
Leibesübungen:	gut
Handschrift:	genügend

Schulbesuch: Versäumt: 28 Stunden   **Verspätet:** — mal

Besondere Bemerkungen: _[handwritten]_

Report Card - Kaiser Wilhelm

66

Camping with Hitler Youth Group

In our Garden with Guests.
Table set built by Uncle Hermann

Views of the Doll House that I built

Graf Zeppelin
over Catholic Church in Osterode

View of Lake Drewenz (Osterode)

THREE

Osterode to Fürstenfeldbruck
The Teenage Years
(1938-1943)

Early in 1938 my father was promoted to a higher position as *"Reichsbahnrat"* (Railroad Advisor). That title was one of the highest ranks in the career of the Railroad echelon. His re-location would be to Munich, which was and still is the Capital of Bavaria, in the Southern Region of Germany. My father relocated first in preparation for our forthcoming move.

My mother and our maid as well as Great Uncle Herrmann made preparations and arrangements for the move in Osterode. He came down from Königsberg to help us out. The name of the moving company was **Korn & Spudich** and both families were friends of my parents. They were often guests at our house during those lavish dinner parties.

In those days eighteen-wheeler moving trucks did not exist. Instead, boxcar wagons that were horse drawn were the only way to make a move. The wagons resembled those of a traveling circus of the early fifties here in the United States. The horses pulled the loaded wagon to the local train station. Then the entire wagon was loaded and secured onto a flat bed railroad freight car. For our move, we needed at least two such wagons *(Möbelwagen)*.

When the wagons reached the town of Fürstenfeldbruck, near Munich, they had to be unloaded from the rail car and then connected and pulled by another team of horses supplied by a local moving company. The entire moving process took about three or four weeks.

During that time, my younger sisters stayed with Aunt Anna and Uncle Gustav in Königsberg. My older sister preferred being with **Oma** and **Opa** Reschke who also still lived there. I was a little more privileged and had the opportunity to stay at a farm that belonged to the sister of Miechen Bolzio, our previous **Kindermädche (nanny)**. That farm was near Nikolaiken, in Lubjewen in the lower Eastern "1000 Lakes" region of East Prussia. This area became part of Poland after World War II. I recall that I stayed at their farm for about one month.

I had my own small room and enjoyed playing with their young son. I was thirteen and he was just a few years younger than I. The most vivid thing I remember is, that for the first time I was allowed to sit on a horse and plow the field. The horse was very gentle and accommodating to my inexperience, and it knew the routine, so I didn't have to command it very much.

There was a frog pond on the farm and my new little friend and I tried to catch polliwogs while watching insect-like creatures called **(Wasserläufer)** water runners, running along the surface of the water without sinking in. That reminded me of Jesus, who could walk on water as told in a Bible story.

While at the pond, a small flock of honking geese flew overhead and the boy shouted: "Look, Look, there are wild airplanes!", as the frogs scattered about.

The two cows on the farm grazed daily at the lowland pasture. My job was to herd them home for milking each evening. Peat moss was harvested in that swampy lowland pasture area creating small deep ponds with shallow shores around them.

One day I led a cow on a rein past one of those deep water holes and she stopped to take a drink. She knelt down at the edge and promptly plunged into the deep water as the soft edge gave way under her weight. While I held her head above water by the rope, she tried desperately to get up out of the water, but all her efforts were futile. The soft edge gave way under her front hooves and the cow sunk back into the bottomless edge of the pond.

I told the boy to get help, and he ran back to the house and got the farmer who brought some more rope along to lasso the cow behind her rear end and pull her up. It was successful but the farmer was mad at me because I allowed a thing like that to happen. I felt unrightfully scolded because all I was doing was goodheartedly allowing the cow to drink the water. I had no idea that she could plunge in! I simply did not expect this accident to happen.

For the first time I witnessed what it was like to participate in a funeral. A neighbor had died. Funeral parlors and the process of embalming did not exist at that time in such a rural farmland area. Therefore, the man was laid out at his home upstairs in his bedroom To keep the body at a cool temperature, to be viewed, wet cool sand from the local lake shore had to be collected and was placed under and around him which then was covered with white linen.

The next day the man was carried down the steep staircase and was placed into a coffin. The flower-draped coffin was loaded onto a horse drawn flat farm wagon and a funeral procession formed and walked behind it. At the nearby cemetery the gravediggers had prepared a sizable hole six feet deep in the ground awaiting the dearly departed. The coffin was placed on two logs bridging the grave and the Preacher held a short devotional speech with prayers.

He blessed the departed soul with the sign of the cross. After this, the coffin was lowered with ropes to the bottom. Each one of the mourners then stepped up to the grave's edge and tossed three handfuls of earth and a flower down to the coffin. When this was done, the gravediggers quickly shoveled the dirt to fill the hole and form a mound. Then it was decorated with numerous wreaths and flowers that were brought along by the mourners.

Following this, they walked back in groups to the house of the dearly departed, exchanging stories about his life. Back at the house a *"Totenschmaus"* took place. It was a feast celebrating eternal life with lots of delicious foods, wine and beer as well as *"Schnapps."* (Liquor) The men enjoyed that potent drink made from rye grains. Everybody had a great time celebrating and then walked home happy, some in a "zigzag" pattern.

It was a totally different type of experience for me. Being part of a funeral and procession left a lasting impression with me. It was a somber, as well as a happy occasion, never to be forgotten.

At the farm there was also a workshop. It reminded me of the one I worked in by *Opa* Lück at the Baltic Sea coast. It was also a Carpenters Shop with machinery. I was able to spend a little time making some toys there. I also loved to watch the geese and duck hatchlings with their peep, peep, peep sounds. Once hatched, they ran and peep peeped all over the place. I saw them hatch, breaking through the eggshell, coming out all wet and fuzzy. We had to feed them chopped nettle. Their feed looked like a small salad. An older hen who stopped laying eggs served as a surrogate mother for the ducklings and goslings and she gluck-gluck and glucked as she led the little ones all around. It was an interesting little parade. These little creatures were so cute and I enjoyed playing with them and letting them run all over me; they were my favorite animals, so delicately cuddly and loveable.

Often we traveled over a bridge by horse and buggy to do some grocery shopping in the town of Nikolaiken. The bridge spanned a narrow arm of the big lake there. A large colorful wood sculptured fish, about six to eight feet long, floated there wearing a golden crown on it's head. It was chained and moored from the bridge's center support column.

This chained fish, called "***Stinthengst***" was named in an old legend the "Stint Fish-king." Supposedly he would bring good luck to the fishermen as long as he was there, held in captivity. Even today, one can see him floating attached to the chain with the golden crown on his head, just as I remembered seeing him as a boy. To this day the Polish people continue to pass on this legend.

On other days I watched and helped the farmer's wife make homemade bread. She kneaded and mixed the new dough with saved sourdough from the previous batch in a large wooden trough, also adding some caraway seeds. Rounded shapes were formed and were left on the countertop to rise.

While waiting for this, they were covered with moistened white sheets. Then, they were knocked flat and re-formed into loaves and placed onto wooden boards to start rising again. Shortly after that they were shoved with flat long-handled wooden paddles, and placed into the brick oven that was built next to the main farmhouse.

About four hours after baking in this outdoor brick oven, the bread was done. It smelled so delicious and reminded me of when I was a child back in Königsberg and the Baker delivered freshly baked goods to our front door with his buggy.

There was a nice batch of ten to fifteen loaves of bread, each about ten to twelve pounds. I couldn't wait to take the first bite of that nice fresh crispy golden bread. It was a delicious treat for me, spread with either sweet butter or marmalade. However, I didn't like the two together on the same sandwich, individually they tasted much better to me.

Soon it was time to leave Lubjewen because our family's move to Bavaria was eminent. During my stay there I learned first-hand what farm like was like. It surely furthered my experience and education.

I felt so sad and sorry to be moving again after having lived in Osterode for just four years. I feared not only missing my best friends, Gerhard and Ilse but also starting over in a new and different life, school and un-known surroundings

When the move was complete, my sisters and I rejoined our mother in Königsberg. We took the train and traveled to Fürstenfeldbruck, Bavaria by crossing the Polish corridor, a strip of Polish land between East Prussia and the main Reich. The treaty of Versailles created that strip of Polish land after WW I, leaving East Prussia separated from the main part of Germany. While traveling through the corridor, we had to pull the window shades down, since we were not allowed to see the Polish land stretch, that in pre-WWI was German. Border patrols came through the RR cars and we had to show them our passes. Sometimes, some individuals were taken off the train, never to be heard from again. Not only did that begin to happen more often, but Polish troops often opened fire across the border and killed German farmers who were out plowing their fields.

Hitler did not tolerate this. Enough was enough and that turned out to be one of the reasons among many others, that Hitler ordered the German army to march into Poland. World history today accuses Hitler of having 'invaded' Poland for no reason at all; nobody ever talks about the reckless atrocities the Poles committed that actually caused WW II to start. Poland, England and France were Allies by a treaty, so naturally, Poland's two Allies declared war on Germany. WW II started in 1939 after our family had been living in Bavaria for one year.

All this was blown out of proportion by the Propaganda Minister Göbbels to rile-up the support of the German people to stay with the Führer's leadership. Since I personally encountered some of it first hand, I believed what we were told.

When we arrived in Fürstenfeldbruck, we found out that the furniture had not gotten there yet. There would be a one-week delay for the arrival of our belongings. The decision was made to stay at the "Hotel Post," the best and largest Hotel in town until the move was completed and the loads of furniture were placed into the villa my father had rented at Pucherstraße # 56.

The Hotel Post was a well known first class establishment. When retiring for the evening, we placed our shoes in the hallway outside the entrance door of our upstairs rooms. The next morning we found them polished and shined. We had never stayed at a hotel before and that impressed me as an exciting and novel experience. Excellent meals were served in the lower dining rooms and it was a pleasure for us kids to have so many choices to pick from.

A week later we moved into our nice and roomy three story villa. Naturally, it included a large garden to my father's delight. Once again we children had to resume our dreaded garden tasks. Our new residence was located in the upper part of that idyllic town. Fürstenfeldbruck was located a half hour train ride west of Munich, towards the **Bodensee** (Lake Constance).

Our villa actually had four stories, counting the lower basement. We occupied the entire building. There were a total of eleven rooms and two additional walk-in attics. The basement was semi-finished, had a section for the central heating room, an adjoining coal storage area, a laundry, large storage room and a workroom which contained the same carpentry bench and tools from Osterode and before that, Königsberg.

My bedroom was on the second floor next to the huge living room. It had a half-moon shaped bay area with large windows and that's where we kept all our houseplants. I particularly remember a magnificent large cactus that bloomed once a year for only twenty-four hours. Its bloom was an enormous white lily-type flower with a strong pleasant aromatic scent we smelled throughout the room and farther. Another outstanding plant was the multi-stemmed room palm-tree that occupied about half of that bay area.

To our surprise my father had purchased an unusual piece of clay pottery that stood on a pedestal and was sculptured of raw baked clay in the form of a full-scale man's head. It was hollow and had a small opening at the top from where the entire head could be filled with water.

Every day we had to add water to it because of evaporation. The surface of the head had grooves in it representing slick hair growth. By sprinkling grass seed into the grooves, they sprouted and green grassy hair grew. It was amusing to look at that man growing green hair. Something quite similar, called Chia pets are sold here in the United States, but they are much smaller.

From the bay windows we could look to the East on the left, and to the West on the right along Pucherstrasse. Straight ahead, to the South we could see the entire length of the ***Adolf Wagnerstrasse***, so named in honor of the Governor of that region.

Once a week our maid prepared rye dough and it was my job to bring it to the local Baker, ***Lukas Drexler***. I pulled my wooden ladder-wagon to the Bakery about two blocks from our house down our street in the morning on my way to the Bahnhof (RRstation). I commuted on the train each week day to high school in Munich. I dropped the dough off at the bakery to be baked in their huge ovens and left the wagon there. In the afternoon on my way home I picked it up, bringing the warm and crispy bread back with me in happy expectation to have a bite of it.

Once I got home it was a real treat for me to be able to get the first crispy end-cut from that fresh delicious rye bread. I put a heap of our homemade marmalade onto it and enjoyed eating it to my heart's content along with a glass of milk. That was my reward for doing my job well. My sisters did not have that same privilege, but I let them have a bite.

My little wagon was a very useful item. Often I had to go to the forest area to collect the thick bark from the long needled pine trees. Lumberjacks, who felled the trees, had peeled the bark off and left it on the ground for anyone to pick. There was plenty of it and I filled my wagon to capacity to bring the load home as firewood along with some cut off branches from the forest floor.

In our basement laundry there was a huge hearth with an enormous cast iron glazed kettle built into it, which served as a laundry cooker. By burning the bark in the fire chamber underneath the soap-water filled kettle, the laundry cooked to a boil. I still remember the name of the detergent that was used, *"Persil."* It was a well-known product name and widely in use. In addition, there was another frequently used soap, which was of a gel-like consistency called *"Grüne Seife,"* green soap. After boiling the laundry, our maid removed it from the kettle with a long wooden paddle and placed it in a washtub filled with cold water, to rinse it out. Then it was rinsed again and wrung out by a hand-turned mangle attached to a manually operated washer and carried by basket upstairs. It was then hung to dry in the garden. There were long laundry-lines strung between pipe poles anchored in the ground. This took place once a week and in our neighborhood one could see which day of the week was chosen as the family's "wash day". This is how laundry was done at the time

I often shared my wagon with my buddies. We steered it while kneeling in it, then rolling down the incline of the *Wagnerstrasse*. That was very thrilling and we rode it in competition, taking turns to see who could steer and roll it for the longest run. So, in essence our idea was comparable to the go-carting, that became popular in the United States during the 1950's or even earlier.

A gigantic garden surrounded our Villa, but somewhat more confined than the one in Osterode. It had many fruit trees and berry bushes as: gooseberries, raspberries, strawberries and three varieties of currant-berry. The currants were the common red ones, and the rare white and black ones. It was most enjoyable to pick and eat them right off the vine. The white currants were the sweetest, the red were somewhat tart as were the black ones. A huge cherry tree grew in the middle of our yard and below it stood the wooden garden set with its round table and benches that Uncle Herrmann had built for us in Osterode.

There were several types of pear and apple trees also one Quince tree. To the rear left corner of our garden was a high multi-stemmed hazelnut bush, beneath it was our compost pile where our food wastes of vegetable peels and shavings were turned into fertile soil. It was often sprinkled with lime to neutralize acids.

To our delight a cute little Hedgehog *(Igel),* took residence in that compost pile and in the adjoining pile of twigs, which were cuttings from the numerous fruit trees. Every day we fed him a bowl of milk, and that was his reward for controlling the snail population. The snails took a great liking to the strawberries and other vegetable growth that was planted in our garden, so our little *Igel* did a good job in keeping the yard free of those pesky creatures.

To the other far corner of the garden we kept four ducks in a fenced in area. I had built a shallow cement basin for them, sunken into the ground. They were such wonderful pets as well as a good supplement to our food supply during the following war years.

My youngest sister had a flop-eared pet rabbit she named *'Schlusele,'* and another one, which were kept in a cage along the rear shaded veranda wall which was part of our house. I decided to build a wooden cage, elevated on stilts with a pitched tarpaper roof featuring a chicken-wire door for these bunnies.

Rows upon rows of vegetable beds took up a large area of the backyard. There were beans, peas, cabbage (both green and blue), radishes, carrots, onions, tomatoes, lettuce, endives, and a variety of salad greens. Dill, parsley, peppermint, rosemary and other herbs were also grown. A field of potatoes took up another large parcel of the backyard.

My "not so nice job" was to empty and distribute the liquid waste from the *"Odelgrube"* (in-ground septic holding tank) throughout the yard. That stinky job of removing the lid from the concrete holding basin and then spreading bucket after bucket of that stuff around the garden as fertilizer, was almost sickening, but I got used to it! With a long- handled scoop, I dunked into that swampy mess and scooped it up to fill the buckets to carry them once a week to 'nourish' each of the trees, bushes, flower- and vegetable-beds.

Another task I was assigned to do during the fall, was to spread lime all over the now harvested vegetable beds. By using a small hand shovel I sprinkled the raw lime powder over the beds. But, it made such a cloud of dust as the force of the wind blew it into my face. The calamity of it was that my eyes started tearing and I began sneezing uncontrollably. Since the lime powder was uncured raw limestone, I knew its capability of getting hot when mixed with water.

So, I devised a very efficient method for getting the job done without getting 'blasted'. I mixed one third sand to two thirds lime powder, added water and kept stirring the mixture until it thickened. Then I placed the bucket in the middle of a vegetable bed and from a distance of about twenty-five feet waited for the expected results.

Within a minute I saw steam coming up from the bucket, and suddenly the whole mix exploded upwards, like a shot out of a canon, making a "w-h-o-o-s-h" sound up into the air. Then the now cured lime rained down onto an area of approximately twenty-five feet diameter.

I repeated the same 'procedure' at the other vegetable beds until my job was completed. So my knowledge of chemistry certainly came in handy, and no one ever knew the secret of how I got the job done without the effects of lime powder all over me. Wow! I don't know what would have happened if my father had ever found that out. Would I have been congratulated for the new method I invented? Or would I have received punishment (with the dog whip) for doing such a dangerous thing?

From a Little Rascal to a Big One

I continued to live dangerously, and once again I had a "brilliant idea." I knew from an earlier time, that I had seen a big box of ammunition for an elephant gun in my father's desk. So I opened the desk and took the box and brought it to the workroom in the basement. Those bullet shells were lead slugs of about 5/8" in diameter and 1" length with rounded tops. I pulled one of the bullets from it's casing and took a look to see what type of powder it contained. It turned out to be the granular pre World War I type, which was highly potent, (more so than the black-powders from World War II).

I tried out a half teaspoon of it and lit it with a match on a tin surface. To my surprise it went up with an explosive force, unlike the black powder used in the shells of modern military ammunitions. That gave me the idea to make a homemade experimental bomb that my friend Helmut and I could explode in some secret place.

I began by emptying all the shells that were in the box, and pressed the lead slugs back onto them so nobody could ever tell that they were empty. With a pound or more of black powder, I tried to think of the best way to make a bomb. How could I make it more powerful? Then this brilliant idea came to me:

By putting the black-powder into a very small metal pillbox I started building the bomb. I punched a hole into its cover with a nail before closing it. I then placed this box into a slightly bigger one, surrounded with more gunpowder. I also punched a hole into the opposite side cover before filling the rest of the tin box and covering it, and then placing that into the next larger one.

This process I continued with a gradual increase in size of all metal containers. The final size was a large cookie tin can of about ten inches in height and diameter that had all succeeding interior chambers filled with gunpowder. The cover of the cookie tin already had a small hole in it for it's secondary use as an aid for knitting purposes to pull yarn through so the ball of yarn in it would not roll onto the floor. Now I had to come up with a way to ignite the bomb.

Since I did not have a fuse, I had to devise another way. At the same time it appeared to be too small. So I had a better idea to make it bigger. I took a five-gallon marmalade metal bucket that had a tight press-on lid similar to a paint can.

Using sawdust I filled it up half way and placed the cookie tin bomb into it. I then completed filling the bucket to the top with sawdust and pressed down on it to pack it as tight as possible. Before placing the lid on it, I soaked the sawdust thoroughly with benzene. Then I took chicken wire and wound it around the entire bucket to tightly secure the lid. Now we had an odd shaped ball bomb of approximately two and a half feet in diameter. It looked like a wad of chicken wire (but it had a 'powerful load' hidden inside).

Helmut and I loaded it onto the rear parcel carrier of my bicycle. We then headed down to the lush overgrown and forested area of the Amper River, near the Fürstenfeld Monastery. We found a tree alongside the raised pathway by the River bank, which was leaning over towards the water. That gave me the idea to blast the tree off its roots and let it fall into the River.

At least, that was what I hoped to achieve. We built a small campfire of twigs and dry branches at the base of the tree. When the fire was big enough it developed glowing ashes. Then we quickly placed the chicken wire bomb on top of it. We speedily leaped back behind the embankment of the raised path by our bicycles and waited excited for something to happen.

So we waited and waited and thought we had created a "dud." We didn't dare come out of hiding, we just continued waiting. Suddenly there was a t-r-e-m-e-n-d-o-u-s fireball and blast that deafened our ears.

A huge black mushroom cloud rose up to the sky. Today I would compare its appearance to that of a miniature atomic bomb explosion. The tree fell over in one piece into the rushing water of the River and floated away bobbing up and down. The stump of the tree was cut level with the ground, (as if by a huge razor blade). The campfire was completely blown away and not a trace of the bomb's components or chicken wire could be found.

We quickly grabbed our bicycles and sped away, fearing that someone would appear to look around for the origin of that enormous mushrooming black cloud-ring that formed and lingered for quite a while above the location of the explosion. Along our escape route we passed a Policeman on his bicycle and were glad that we were far away from the location of our successful prank. He asked us: "Did you see that big mushroom cloud?" We replied "yes," and that we were also looking to see where it came from. So, we kept on going, and were relieved that we did indeed pull off a remarkable and most dangerous experiment without getting hurt or being caught.

A LITTLE BIT ABOUT FÜRSTENFELDBRUCK

The monastery *Fürstenfeld* is like a jewel, built in the Bavarian Baroque style. It was erected during the years 1099 to 1109 under the guidance of the Englishman, Stefan Harding, who was the third Abbot of the Zisterzienzers .

He established the Law of the "Charta Caritatis," which established how all monasteries were to be built in the future. The Fürstenfeld Monastery was the prototype, and at that time it was called "Citeaux." All new Monasteries were then built under the Benedictus Rule. The Monks who wore gray robes were of the ruling order, the Benedictines.

This all took place at the time when Pope Pachalis II was the Shepherd of the Catholic Church. By his >>*Privilegium Romanum*<< he guaranteed Abbot Stefan Harding and his order of Monks the freedom of absolute exemption from being ruled by the Dioceses of the local Bishops. They only had to answer to the Holy Chair in Rome.

On August 14, 1263 Citeaux was renamed *Fürstenfeld* (Prince's Field) at the Feast of the Ascension of Mary, Mother of God. A beautiful gilded statue of her, holding baby Jesus is just one of the many statues displayed there. Numerous nameless artesian masters from the Baroque period created all of it. The beautiful, elaborately decorated Monastery/Church was the place where my wife Hedwig and I took our wedding vows, in 1951.

The near-by marketplace, *Bruck*, was located on the banks of the Amper River. It was located along one of the biggest and most heavily used trade routes that dominated the flow of merchandising. The town collected tolls at the *Brücke* (Bridge) over the Amper River. *Brücke*, also called *Bruck* in old German, gave it its name.

As the market place grew bigger and later became a town, it's boundaries encroached on the territory of the Monastery *Fürstenfeld*. The town fathers and Monks agreed to merge the two entities and so, Fürstenfeldbruck was created. That is how it's name came into being.

My new school was located in Munich and I had to commute there by the local train each school day. Because my father also commuted daily to Munich, we traveled together. This made me feel more at ease because it was an entirely brand new experience.

The first day my father accompanied me to school and introduced me to the **Rector** (Principal). There was a big difference between the **Gymnasium** I left in Osterode, and the new **"Oberschule."** The Gymnasium taught Latin as the first foreign language to be learned. The **Oberschule** started with English as the first foreign language. That meant that I had to "catch up" with the help of a tutor and learn two years of English to be on par with the new class. But to my advantage, I was two years ahead in Latin.

Mathematics posed a slightly different problem. The bearded teacher in our class spoke mostly in Bavarian slang, which was extremely difficult for me to understand, in addition he mumbled into his beard. It was not until later that I became more familiar understanding the spoken dialect. So, because I failed Mathematics, my father transferred me to a different **Oberschule**, which was located in the borough of Munich called Pasing. It was just a couple of train stops before reaching the **Haupbahnhof** in Munich.

In Pasing I could clearly understand our Teacher for Mathematics. So, I passed the test and remained at that school until I met their requirements. We had a magnificent Professor named **Herr** Süssengut (Mr. Süssengut) who was a very well liked Biology Teacher. He formulated his lesson plans in such an appealing way that made studying with him an interesting and captivating experience.

We were a class of about thirty to thirty-five boys. Two of my classmates commuted with me and we became friends. One was Helmut Link and the other was Hans Korn. While commuting back and forth to school we often played cards on the train, and were joined by other boys like Gert Nolde and Werner Barthel.

However, the cards that were used in Bavaria were of a completely different type than what I was used to. Therefore I usually lost in the games we played, because I was an inexperienced player with those strange looking cards. I never could quite get used to them and preferred the traditional ones I was familiar with.

After school I met with Helmut and Hans who were enrolled in different classrooms of our school and together we took bicycle rides to the surrounding areas including forests. Just like in Osterode, we collected berries and mushrooms to bring home. Sometimes Helmut's sister, Sieglinde as well as my younger sister would join us. We all got along very well and were "pals," and the best of friends. Helmut's father held a high position in Law, perhaps something equivalent to a District Attorney here in the USA. He was an ***"Oberstaatsanwalt"*** of German Law. One time Sieglinde and I biked together up a forested hill called ***Engelsberg*** (Angels Mountain), which was located behind the ***Klosterkirche Fürstenfeld.*** Up there, I found a huge old Beech tree in which I carved a heart, our initials and date for posterity.

By early 1939 Hitler decided to honor mothers who gave birth to more than three children with an honorary cross, called: the 'Mother cross" Actually, there were several stages of it to honor those mothers who bore even more children: For four: (Bronze), six: (Silver), eight: (Gold)). Our mother was the proud recipient of that Mother's Cross.

It was an honorary ribbon necklace with a large bronze semi-Maltese cross and was accompanied by a certificate. My sisters and I proudly posed with our mother for a photo to celebrate the occasion. A system was also devised whereby parents would receive extra stipends called ***"Kindergeld."*** The more children you had, the more money you could receive from the government.

It was about that same time, around 1940 that my parents received a telegram. They were informed that their son Ulrich had died. The notice of his death stated that he was one of many children along with several Doctors and Nurses who had passed away due to an undetermined "mysterious" illness.

My sisters and I were told the sad news that our brother "Ullie" had died. The next day I cried while in school with tears for the loss of my only brother. We knew it was a fact that under Hitler's dictatorship a plan for Euthanasia was put into action. The Program called "Aktion T4" started in 1939 and officially continued into 1941. By that year over one hundred thousand men, women and children were systematically killed. We strongly suspected, that our Ulli was one of them.

All those who lived a life "unworthy" of living were usually drugged before being put to the gas chamber. It was also a fact that if a patient lived for at least five years in such an institution they were condemned to that 'Action' Program. Today we know that Ullie was one of them because of the tireless research by my co-author and best friend Dianna Popp. She also found out, that known high officials in command of executing those "special purposes" had ordered those deaths. Later on, deaths continued unofficially by the use of drugs and or starvation. The "Aktion T4" Program became the precursor to the Concentration Camps.

By September 1, 1939 Germany went to war when it marched into Poland. Most eighteen year old boys that my older sister knew from the neighborhood and Dancing School were immediately recruited into the Military. Within a very short period of time about two thirds of them lost their lives. Some had married before they were drafted, and unfortunately, the young brides became widows.

On December 7, 1941 Imperial Japan attacked the United States Naval Base at Pearl Harbor in Hawaii and that action brought the U.S.A. into World War II.

During that time I was sixteen years old and in my last year as a member in the Hitler Youth group. By age seventeen it was mandatory to join the **Arbeitsdienst** (Labor Force). My predecessor was too old to remain in the HJ, so I then was inline to fill the position of leader for our group. I was required to arrange get-togethers and send out notices telling the members that it was mandatory to attend all our meetings.

I definitely relished the opportunity of having that power and being able to dictate requirements to my group. It was almost like I was acting the part of a Luftwaffe officer.

I distinctly remember my strongly demanding letters. We were a group of between ten to fifteen boys and this was my first leadership experience.

In Fürstenfeldbruck we met at the **Hitler Jugend Heim** (Hitler Youth Home). It was especially built for the youth group and was a meeting place only for the boys. It had a gym and meeting room, which was used to give instructions to the group.

During that time, both the girls and boys groups as well as their parents were involved in collecting scrap metals of aluminum, brass, copper, and iron to contribute to the defense industry. Actually, all German people were asked to contribute any useful scrap metals for the program.

These recycles were put to good use for the manufacturing of new weaponry and ammunitions. Brass and copper were preferred for the making of ammunition shells. When those were not available the shells had to be produced with other metals, I believe steel was used, which was covered with a lacquer to prevent rusting. The color of them was olive green. Copper was still needed for bullet jackets containing lead. Inserted steel bolts were used for penetrating bullets and special gunpowder was used for tracers.

It was my job to remove the solid brass bars that held the carpet runner on our staircase leading to the second and third floors in our villa. It was a tedious job to remove the aged screws and eye hooks. They were attached in pairs, to each step of the staircase and held the bars in place, where the risers of each step met the top of the step below it.

The collection of scrap metals took place mostly in local schools, where larger rooms and halls were available. Huge containers or bins, specially labeled for depositing diverse types of metals, were there to be filled with the donated material by the population.

There was absolutely no exchange of monies involved in the recycle program because it was entirely developed and executed by the Nazi party system. It was mandatory that everyone should participate and follow their guidelines.

There was also a clothing drive. The purpose was to supply the fast advancing German army in Russia with warm clothing. They were caught unprepared for the early cold winter of 1941, which stopped them from reaching Moscow.

There was a special decorative medal created for those soldiers who made it through alive that particular winter. It was nick-named: "The

Frozen Meat Medal." Many of them lost limbs as a result of frostbite. Their limbs turned black and had to be amputated. Those poor souls became unlucky invalids. They were awarded that medal and sent home. The band of the medal had two white and black lines woven into it. It was sewn in triangular form onto the upper left side of the uniform jacket near the front edge by the buttonholes. The medal itself was kept at home and only worn on special occasions.

In August of 1942 I went to visit my oldest sister in the area of Alsace Lorraine, (Lothringen) near Luxembourg. She lived there for three years and worked in a defense plant. The management provided a plush elaborate room in a feudal Castle. We had a very nice time together doing some sightseeing and also took many photographs as well. I just recently looked at them in my older sister's photo album as we reminisced about our life during the War. One of the pictures we took of each other; showed us standing under the huge arch of the Luxembourg stone bridge spanning the river valley. It was a marvel of architectural accomplishment I had never seen before or ever after.

Our Villa at Pucherstrasse No. 56

View of our Villa from Adolf Wagnerstrasse

Interior of Klosterkirche of Fürstenfeld

Our Mother proudly wore her
Bronze "Mothers Cross" 1939

1941 Clothes Drive

Confirmation Day

The Dulias Family About 1941

FOUR

Challenges Ahead,
Being Introduced To The Luftwaffe

While I was the leader of the HJ (Hitler Youth) group, I found out about a sub-division that was specifically for those interested in aviation. I decided to switch over to the Flieger HJ.

We always had our meetings and workshops in the Air Academy No. 4 located on the northern outskirts of Fürstenfeldbruck, called **Luft Kriegs Schule** (air war school). There we learned to build our own aircraft school gliders, and upon completion we were then taught how to fly them. We started young with actual specific training. The materials and flight instruction of pre-military training were supplied and controlled by the **Luftwaffe** (German Air Force). Luft is air, and **waffe:** meaning weapon. The entire command of the Luftwaffe was non-political as were the other branches of the Armed Forces, except the **Sturmstaffel** (SS). The SS was originally an elite political military troop controlled by the Nazi movement.

The Luftwaffe was very interested in teaching and training future recruits how to fly and then teach others all aspects of the Luftwaffe. That was required and a mandatory pre-requisite before being accepted, and sworn in as a member of the Luftwaffe.

The Specific Requirements Were:
1. Build (as a group, your own individual) gliders.
2. Learn how to fly the gliders.
3. SG38 school glider training: That particular design was developed in 1938. The plane was a basic first glider used to teach us how to fly.

4. You would be seated on a plywood seat, and harnessed to it. In front of you was the steering stick (**Steuerknüppel**) and your legs were stretched out to the foot pedals. (**Seitenruder**)Those pedals operated the rudder of the plane, while the steering stick operated the elevator in the tail by a pull-push motion. (**Höhenruder**)

5. The pulling movement caused the lowering of the tail of the craft while bringing the front up. Pushing it caused the opposite motion. It brought the nose down. This actually produced the rising or lowering of the aircraft in flight. It gave the pilot the impression of the nose rising or falling. In other words, this procedure was the elevator control of the plane.

6. Pushing the stick left, banked (leaned) the left side down; to the right, the right side down. Holding it in center position kept the wings level or holding the desired banking angle after reaching it. Those flaps on the back edges of the wings were called ailerons. (**Quer-ruder**)

7. The rudder pedals activate the right and left movement of the vertical tail part and that changes the forward direction of the aircraft, to the left by pushing the left pedal, to the right by pushing the right pedal. Unintended outward shifting sideways while changing the direction of the craft making a curve to left or right is prevented by simultaneous banking the plane in the direction you are aiming it.

8. Being able to then teach others what you have learned.

This particular glider model that I first learned to fly on, is now permanently on display at the Deutsche Museum in Munich, Germany, and other Aviation Museums, including the United States.

LEARNING HOW TO FLY.

The *Flieger HJ* boys were a group of fifteen to seventeen members being taught by Luftwaffe Instructors. We had completed building our first SG 38 glider and waited with great expectation for our first day of flight instruction.

The glider had to be test-flown by our flight teacher before it was certified as trainer aircraft. Our work passed the instructor's test flight, and the next suitable day without too much wind movement was a Saturday in the summer of 1942.

The disassembled SG38 was loaded onto a specially designed transport trailer and was then pulled by a Luftwaffe troop-transport truck, similar to the ones in the US Army, to our destination, the training field.

We climbed onboard and off we went towards the Fore-Alps, a region that was ideal for our training. The village of Peiting had an open level wide pasture that gradually inclined into a fairly steep grassy hill facing towards the South. It was located about twenty to thirty kilometers South of Fürstenfeldbruck, about a half hour's drive.

After arriving there, we re-assembled our brand new glider to be ready for us to make the first "Rutscher" (shallow ground slide) on flat pastureland. This was done in the following way: The first in line of our group got harnessed onto the plywood seat, which had a backrest, with shoulder straps.

There were thigh belts to hold him securely to the seat and backrest and he wore a *"Sturzhelm"* (crash helmet). He sat there with his heart pounding from excitement, and received last minute instructions by our friendly *"Fluglehrer"* (flight Instructor), on what to do. We were to keep the wings level by using the ailerons, and had to aim a straight line into the gentle wind by using the rudder for correction if the plane should deviate from the intended direction of flight. The elevator was to be held in a neutral (level) position. To keep the aircraft from becoming airborne, you had to push it slightly down, in a forward motion. The skid-equipped SG 38 had no landing wheel, as was the case in the bigger more sophisticated soaring planes that we flew later.

A forked long twin and strong bungee rope was hooked to the front end of the glider. A running crew of five members towards each side of the forward facing open 'V' fork of about sixty degrees spread, positioned themselves way ahead of the plane, holding the front ends of the bungee ropes.

They were ready to run forward in their directions to stretch the bungee to get sufficient tension so that the aircraft would have enough velocity to slide along the ground for about fifty meters. The two or three men "holding crew" held the craft by a short-knotted rope attached to the tail end of the fuselage frame until they got the command to let go. Meanwhile, the ten men launching crew ran in the two forward directions, thus forming a slingshot to give the SG 38 its forward motion.

Strict orders for keeping the plane down and skipping along on the ground had to be obeyed, because we had to get the feeling step by step of operating an aircraft. Each of us had our turn with this procedure. Only one of the novices panicked and pushed the elevator stick too far forward and wound up making a ***"Ringelpiez."*** That is known in aviation terms as a "ground loop." Fortunately, our glider was not damaged and we could continue taking turns to perform our first ***"Rutschers"*** (ground slides) one by one.

When my turn came to sit alone at the controls of an airplane for the first time, my heart began to beat faster. I got a funny feeling in my stomach, that later, during my training flights and especially later at each combat mission became all too familiar. It can't be described as fear, rather as a heightened sense of alertness, with a flow of adrenaline, as the saying goes: "to steel yourself"

The running crew at the bungee rope and the holding crew at the tail were ready waiting for the command "Los" (let go), by the Instructor. He looked at me quizzically to see if I was ready. I nodded my head, while looking straight ahead and then he gave the crew the command.

The bungee crew ran forward in their angled directions and I felt the tension of the rope building up in that giant slingshot. Then the second "Los" was given and away I went, straight forward, no deviation from the intended distanced sight target point. I immediately, with a careful short forward push of the stick, corrected a slight attempt of the aircraft to lift from the ground, slid gently along the ground holding the plane level by aileron movements until I came to a stop about seventy meters from the starting point. Then the left wing came down slowly touching the ground, a perfect accomplishment. What a feeling of relief! I was proud of myself for doing all that was expected of me.

The crew came running to retrieve the glider, bringing along the two-wheeled pulley. We lifted the craft up onto it and pulled it back to the starting point for the next candidate in line, to test his courage.

It was late afternoon by the time everyone had completed his turn. We packed up for our trip back to the base. We stored the craft in our designated hangar and proudly went home, with a feeling of accomplishment. We were eagerly anticipating the next event of our training, where we would lift off the ground to an approximate height of three, four, five or more feet, if the initial speed and lift allowed it without stalling the plane.

Later on, when the weather permitted good flying days, we went back to Peiting for more training. The next phase was still on flat ground, but the bungee crew had to run farther, stretching the rubber rope almost to its capacity. We were lifted off the ground and leveled the aircraft at about two meters (more than six feet) altitude. Leveling the craft, we descended downwards in a straight line preparing for a gentle landing. By getting the right feel for it, you had to watch your rate of speed for the descent. Those short and later longer and higher hops made us more familiar with the operation of the controls. By repeating this procedure over and over again we gained more confidence.

Then it was time to test for the "A" certificate. The starting point was half way up the hill, about ten to twelve meters above the ground level of the flat pasture. Our task was to maintain a straight flight pattern. After being launched and staying up in the air for at least twenty or more seconds we were to gently come down for a smooth landing. Running downhill, the crew had it easier and the bungee rope was stretched almost to its capacity as the holding crew at the tail was increased to three or four. With the increased tension-load, they had to hold the plane until the "los!" command was given.

After passing the test, I received my "A" certificate. I later flew from the top of the hill and received my "B" certificate. That required each of us to fly a forward

"S" figure while gliding down and ending up in a straight line with the flight direction. One had to time it just right in making the turns to wind up in the prescribed straightforward line upon landing. It was not too easy, and several of the ***Flugschüler*** (flight pupils) had to do it over and over again to pass the test. I am proud to say, that I did it at the first try. I did not have time to achieve my "C" status because I received my orders to report to the mandatory ***Arbeitsdienst*** (Labor Force).

ARBEITSDIENST, DECISIONS AND TRAINING

I made my decision for my chosen trade just before entering the Military Service. I had taken a correspondence course while still in the **Oberschule,** and was convinced that I was on my way to becoming an Architect. Three years of apprenticeship to become a carpenter was required to get a certificate as a journeyman and pass the test.

I learned how to make three-dimensional Architectural drawings according to scale and do the needed drafting. That prepared me for a future trade of carpentry and cabinet making which was one of the main requirements to be admitted to the Polytechnic institute in Munich. I had all of the positive "vibes" to study to become an Architect.

An additional two years apprenticeship was required before entering the Polytechnik Institute to study Architecture. The combined studies of various building trades included learning of masonry for a few months, followed by plumbing, roofing, heating systems, locksmith as well as bridge-building and so on. Only after accumulating five years of apprenticeship in major building trades were you then allowed to continue to become an Architect.

Before I could complete the two years of extra training, I was called to serve in the Arbeitsdienst (Labor Force) Camp. There I was selected to be part of a separate group of eight or nine men. We all had creative talents and previous training in woodworks. Having already been an apprentice in carpentry and cabinet making, I was qualified to be a member of the newly formed "Fiddle Builders Group." Our camp was located in **Tennsee,** near **Mittenwald** in the lower Alp Mountains of Bavaria.

Herr (Mr.) Harlan headed the group and was a **Geigenbauer** (violin builder) hired by the Labor Force to teach us the building of string instruments. Originally he came from the town of Mittenwald, which was well known for its violin builders. He was a member of the Tennsee Fiddle Group and as the "Fiddle man" he was a jovial, somewhat heavyset yet friendly soul. Not only was he excellent in his craft but was also a great teacher who had a very patient nature.

The fiddle that we were to make was a blend of a violin (which had four strings) and a guitar (having six strings). The unique difference between the two was when combined, it created the Tennsee Fiddle.

This fiddle was strung and tuned like the guitar. The bowed bridge allowed it to be played like a violin or a knee fiddle with a bow.

The Fiddle man, Herr Harlan, supplied all the materials necessary for the making of the instruments. Each and every one of us had to make a fiddle of our own. We were taught how to select the proper pieces of aged and dried wood. Making the proper selection by clapping the wooden parts together to test for their certain sound was what would later give the fiddle the right resonance (tone). Mr. Harlan showed us how to do that and listen carefully to the different variations of the fine tones and then decide on some carefully made selections to go ahead with building our fiddles. We also went to neighboring farms and collected long strings of horsehair to create our own bows. There was a small woodworking shop at the barracks where each student had his own workbench. It took us about two weeks to complete our fiddles and then two more weeks of practicing to play them before holding a group concert as a crowning achievement of our diligent efforts. The entire workshop and training lasted for about one month.

Then we had to wait for further orders for our deployment to do defense work

On our free weekends we took up some light mountain climbing at the surrounding lower mountains that were walkable instead of steep rock climbing. While we, the selected group, were training in fiddle building, the rest of our unit had to undergo pre-military drilling and naturally, they were envious of our 'easy' treatment.

After the Fiddle making ended, our entire group of about one hundred young men received our orders from the Labor Force command to report to the North West Coast of France known as Bretagne (Brittany). We were transported there by freight train.

We were stationed directly at the coastline near the town of Brest. The landscape there was an interesting contrast to the coastal farm villages in Germany. The noticeable difference was that three-foot high fieldstone walls separated the farmer's fields, as if sectioned off into territories. Fieldstones lined the roads and also paths. They were used in the building of most homes and churches too. Those building stones were of various grayish tones and appeared perhaps to be of granite.

We were billeted in an empty school, living dormitory style. I was assigned the position of Medic in a small infirmary and when needed to administer first aid, I had acquired some previous training in that field while in the HJ.

My job was to keep medical records, take temperatures, and to administer medications. I remember being nicknamed "Aspirin Stud" because for the most part I handed out lots of aspirin to whoever had a fever or dysentery.

The main purpose for being sent there was to wait for orders to build fortifications at the coast. Orders telling us what we were supposed to build never arrived. Because of that there was a lot of free time. However, we still had to participate in the daily routines of military training. That included infantry, digging trenches, acting out and playing war games. We were each given a French rifle and ammo, captured by German forces.

Also, we were taught how to throw real hand grenades, German ones with the wooden handles. You had to know how to throw and toss them standing up as well as lying down.

While on the ground, I tossed one but it didn't fly far enough away from me. As a result of that, when it exploded, a small piece of shrapnel hit my left sleeve and made a hole in it. Fortunately, my skin was not touched. I made sure that the following tosses landed at the intended target far enough from causing any harm to myself.

The food we were given there was satisfying. It came from a German field kitchen. But one very annoying thing, at least for me, was that we always got salted butter. I could never get used to that so I traded the butter for another man's marmalade as I always did have a sweet tooth.

Besides that, the most annoying thing was the "toilet." It was by far nothing like what I was used to and I could not easily become accustomed to that new 'contraption'. It seemed very strange to have a hole in the cement floor with two-foot indentations to place your feet on while you squatted down. There was also no privacy and the flushing system ran out from a wall in front of you for all the units in the row so they could be flushed at the same time. You really had to be careful to aim right!

During our free time we enjoyed swimming by the coastline when it was high tide. At that time the high boulders in the water were almost completely submerged. When the tide went out at ebb time you could walk out onto the shallow sandy shoreline and find starfish, exotic shells and other sea life.

Attached to the boulders was a type of shellfish, which must have been mollusks. The French fishermen pried the mollusks off with their knives, carved them out from the shell and ate them raw. I couldn't understand how they could do that and I was not interested in trying it either! For them it must have been a raw fish delicacy, like sushi, but to me it did not look appetizing at all.

One day a British twin-engine short-range bomber was shot down in our area by the German 88 Flak *(Flug Abwehrkanone)* air defense cannon. The plane crashed to the ground on a nearby open field, which had a three-foot high fieldstone wall surrounding it. As a matter of fact we saw that all farm-fields were 'framed' with those fieldstone walls. It was probably the custom in that region of France to mark the boundaries of their different farm properties.

We were assigned guard duty that day in pairs on two-hour rotational shifts to guard the wreckage against pilfering.

The plane had crashed down in the afternoon and my turn to guard it with a partner was from ten to twelve at night. The pilot and co-pilot did not survive. A German infantry detail of soldiers came to pick up the bodies so they could be buried in a local "heroes cemetery" with military honors. They were probably then listed as missing in action by their home unit in England.

While on guard duty, just before midnight I heard some rustling and thought that someone was approaching the wreckage. I shouted: "Halt or I'll shoot!" There was no reply so I just shot a few rounds at random in the direction I heard the noise from. The next morning, after searching the area I didn't find anything indicating trespass, maybe it was a dog?

Then I started to examine the wreckage more closely because it was extremely fascinating to me. I looked at the heap of twisted metal that was once a plane and now no longer recognizable as having been such. It was remarkable to me that it crashed but did not explode or catch on fire. In its condition, it could not be determined what type of aircraft it once was. Only the two engines had some identification. That was also the first time that I actually used a rifle having followed orders to do so. I also had to file a report as to what action had been taken in the matter.

My otherwise uneventful stay in France lasted for two months. When it ended we were transported back to the Tennsee camp by train. As we rolled through Paris in cattle cars, we saw for the first time, the famous "Eiffel Tower."

Before leaving that lovely alpine area of Germany, I took advantage of the opportunity to do some more mountain climbing while wearing my military boots. It was not a cliff but more like a steep grassy incline. The reward for reaching the top was a spectacular view looking down on our camp.

I captured that view by taking a photo from atop that small mountain adjoining it and that is still in my possession today. I was searching for the alpine flowers of **Edelweiss, Enzian, und Alpenrosen** (alpine roses). I was only successful in finding Enzian, which is a small blue bell-shaped flower and is most common in mountainous areas, particularly in the lower Alps. That same flower is also used for brewing a cordial drink appropriately named *"Enzian."* I placed a few of the little flowers in a book so they would become pressed and dried for posterity.

After being dismissed from the Labor Force I returned home to Fürstenfeldbruck. I was waiting for my notice to be called to join the Luftwaffe because I had already submitted my application before serving in the **Arbeitsdienst.**

The Luftwaffe, Testing and Interviews.

One day I received official notification in the mail from the Headquarters of the Luftwaffe (German Air Force) that I should come to Munich for testing. The letter also outlined what items I was to pack, including specific articles of clothing, swim suit, sweat pants, shirts, and so on.

When I received the notice I was happy as well as anxious as I had been patiently waiting to hear from them. I packed my overnight bag and took the train to Munich to stay for the three days of testing.

Day one began with an early morning arrival followed by getting acquainted at meetings. We were a group of about twenty-five to thirty aspiring young brutes. Initially our gathering was informal. Instructions were given as to what attire we should wear and what sort of behavior was expected for the rest of our stay. We also received a detailed outline of the upcoming events for the next three days of testing.

The first command to the entire group was "Strip Naked!" Then we had to line up and one of the Air Force physicians paraded up and down the lines, looking us over for any visible defects. Then we went before other desks, each having a special type of doctor who would be taking notes as we answered questions about our medical history. There were dentists, internists, ear, nose and throat specialists and orthopedic Luftwaffe doctors. After completing this physical examination we continued with the testing process.

Next we were detailed into groups of five, and were escorted by an Air Force sergeant to the first test site. Test one was for writing skills. I recall writing several compositions. Some were creative and also imaginative. Others tested my knowledge of academics, including mathematics, geography, science (physics, geology) and I was questioned if I had any knowledge of foreign languages. I wouldn't doubt that there might have been some handwriting analysis involved. But I had to write in the old *Sütterlin* type as well as Latin and Germanic penmanship in print style.

We had breaks between test sessions. Meals were served in the mess hall for breakfast, lunch and dinner. Sleeping arrangements were dormitory style, three men per room. We were also critiqued and scored as to neatness and housekeeping skills, after a strict inspection; we had to conform to their high military standards. But I was prepared for it after having been trained thoroughly in the ***Arbeitsdienst.***

Day two started with a morning run of about one half hour, followed by breakfast. Testing in all areas of physical fitness took place. Some of them were: Gymnastics, climbing ropes, vertical bars, parallel bars, chin-ups, sit-ups, push-ups and swimming as well as diving.

We were also tested on how long you could hold your breath and for how long you could remain underwater. For each specific test a different instructor made checkups, took notes and ran a stopwatch timing our progress. They looked mean, did not crack a smile and upheld their authoritative demeanor.

To be accepted as a trainee fighter pilot of the Luftwaffe you had to go through a most unusual interview process. Not every aspiring pilot in training could meet the requirements and challenges they presented. Today, I still remember some of the odd and strange questions I was asked. In one's entire lifetime, a person would never have to go through what I had to do for this 'job' interview.

The third and last day was the most challenging. First the questions started with very basic information about who I was and what my education consisted of. Then it continued as bizarre psychological testing and a challenge of my stamina and my decision making.

I stood alone before a committee of eight Luftwaffe psychologists. Their tables were arranged in a semi circle. All eyes were focused on me. The psychologists were in full dress uniform with complete regalia. Their hats were neatly placed directly in front of them on the table. Each member of the group had a writing pad with a fountain pen and took notes. Pitchers of water with glasses for them were also part of the set up.

The psychologists shot impromptu questions at me, one after the other, in rapid succession and I was not allowed to hesitate for a moment because they wanted a quick response. I had to have an answer for every one of them within a second, proving to them that I was capable of thinking fast and making split-second decisions.

I believe it was about a two hour long interview process, or at least it seemed that way to me. As a pilot it was vital to have those capabilities in situations that could be a matter of life or death, especially in air combat.

Some of the questions that I still remember were:

1) Suppose you are an officer and you are dancing with a Lady; so what would you do if your monocle fell into her cleavage? I replied: "I would grab her by the legs and turn her upside down and shake her 'til the monocle fell out."

2) What would you do if you had a woodenhead? I replied: "I would become a Luftwaffe psychologist." With that response I made them turn beet red! But it was a quick answer and that's what counted.

3) Ok, very well! Now, tell us about the love life of the cobblestones under the influence of the rays of the sun. I replied: "There was a cobblestone Hans and another one Gretchen and they loved each other and wanted to be together, and their love heated up under the blazing sun, and they got married and lived happily ever after."… Or something to that effect.

4) Ok, next question! If you were teaching in front of an imaginary forum, what would you say about different races and mankind? I replied: "Existing in Europe are the Germanic, the Celtic, the Middle Land People (A grouping of Italians and other Mediterranean's), the Baltic, the Slavic, and the Mongolian races. I continued by describing the individual ethnics. Differences relating to pertinent facial and structural body features, etc.

And so it went on and on shooting more of those types of questions at me for the duration of the session. Never once did they nod, smile or show any emotion. It was strictly a business. When my session was over and I was dismissed, I saluted and immediately exited the room with a sigh of relief. I was sweating profusely, practically soaking wet, and felt like my clothes had become glued to my body. On my way out I passed the next 'guinea pig' in the hall and he asked me how it was. I replied: "Just keep talking, and don't hesitate."

I returned to the briefing room where the rest of the group was assembled to receive further instructions on what was expected of us for actual situations in combat. This briefing was ongoing while each man was called one at a time to be singled out, and 'psychologically tortured.'

When all of this was over and done with, we thought we would receive some kind of indication as to what our status was. To our disappointment we were just dismissed after our three days in Munich, and left in the dark. The only consolation was that we would be notified at a later date as to whether or not we were accepted.

To my pleasant surprise, I received my notification less than a week later. My orders stated that I had to report back to the same testing place in Munich in three days. This time it was for the induction and swearing in to the Luftwaffe.

I was instructed to pack my belongings, according to specifications and be ready to start serving my country immediately. As soon as I received my orders, my parents, sisters, some family and a few friends gathered at my home in Fürstenfeldbruck for a small goodbye party. I had few friends because most of mine were already serving in active duty at the fronts.

I felt so proud to finally be accepted to be a future Air Force pilot. My childhood dream had finally become a reality. I was no longer a little boy longingly looking up to the sky whenever a plane flew by. I was now Gottfried, the young man, becoming a future pilot and officer in a well-respected branch of the Armed Forces, the "Luftwaffe."

The swearing-in was a simple ceremony held at the Headquarters in Munich. We were a group of about fifty men. I held up my right hand and repeated the Oath of Allegiance to the *Führer* and to the Deutsche Reich. This was done while facing the Luftwaffe flag, not the common swastika one.

To my surprise, while this took place, I recognized the same fellow whom I had passed in the hallway after my psychological questioning procedure a week earlier. He was the one who had asked me: How was it? At that time I gave him my advice. So, I guess it worked! So we exchanged winks at each other.

However, after becoming a Pilot I still looked up into the sky whenever I heard a plane above. The "jet age" was just beginning in 1943. The newest German Fighter Plane was the *Messerschmitt 262*. When it flew by we had to look way ahead from where we thought the sound was coming from because of this particular war bird's tremendous speed. Often you heard it, but missed seeing it.

BASIC TRAINING

After the swearing-in ceremony we marched to the main train station in Munich, the ***"Hauptbahnhof,"*** located towards the West end of town. We boarded a specially scheduled train that not only took our Luftwaffe group of new recruits but also recruits of other branches of the military to be dropped off at their targeted destinations.

Our destination was Oschatz, located in the region of Saxony, Southeast of Berlin. On the way there the other military groups were dispatched to their various destinations while our group remained on to the last stop, Oschatz.

Our ***Kaserne*** (Military Base) was on the outskirts of town, and consisted of a huge complex of buildings and facilities. We were assigned to our barracks and were billeted five men per room. Each of us had his own bunk bed, upper or lower.

I had one at the top. The mattresses were of a standard type, filled with horsehair. The bedding set was of a blue and white-checkered pattern. We were supplied with thick woolen blankets and a feather filled pillow, just one per man. After settling into our barracks we had to report to the supply office to get all the necessary apparel and equipment.

Among those items were:

1. A Karabiner (Military Rifle), which was your bride because you were married to it for your entire military career. (But of course, we were not to bring it along at flying combat missions, where I had a Luger side arm.)
2. I was lucky enough to be issued a Pre-War Mauser rifle, vintage 1937 that still had the original walnut shaft. It was so accurately

sighted, with such precision, that I usually hit the bull's eye dead center.

3. A Luftwaffe uniform made of 100% wool in the standard blue-gray color.

4. A pair of black leather boots. The soles had metal cleats and heels rimmed with an iron horse shoe-like reinforcement. Those boots had shafts that ended about four inches below the kneecap, and were nicknamed: ***"Knobelbecher"*** (which was a leather cup that was used for tossing and rolling dice).

5. A few pairs of dark gray woolen mid calf socks.

6. A few pairs of 100% white cotton boxer shorts and t-shirts.

7. A boat-shaped cap to match the uniform.

8. A few long-sleeved light blue cotton shirts.

9. Cooking utensils, containers, and cutlery.

10. A canvas bag called ***"Brotbeutel."*** It had an adjustable shoulder strap and was mostly used to carry pieces of bread and other edibles.

11. A water canteen, which was made of aluminum and was covered with felt. (The felt served as insulation as well as a protective covering preventing dents and avoiding noisy banging).

12. ***Kochgeschirr*** (Cookware / eating device of aluminum painted Luftwaffe blue).

Among my personal belongings were two sets of pajamas. I knew that I was allergic to wool, so I had to devise a way to prevent skin rashes. I decided that a pajama bottom, which was made of cotton, worked fine as a layer between my skin and the woolen pants.

Fortunately, the long-sleeved shirts that were supplied with my uniform were cotton and did not present a problem at all. This was unlike what I later saw the American servicemen wear for their required uniform, which were made of fine wool. It would have been a big problem for me, had our shirts been manufactured with wool material. I get "goose bumps" just thinking about that!

Back in the barracks we had to neatly stack up our issued belongings into our own individual metal cabinet called the ***Spind.*** (Locker) It had a lock and a key. Every two rooms totaling ten men shared one bathroom. Running hot and cold water was in steady supply. They were equipped with five toilets, five urinals and five washbasins accessorized with mirrors and glass shelves. The bathrooms were completely tiled, from floor to ceiling and also featured teak wood benches to sit on, while dressing or un-dressing.

When we toured around the site, we were shown the mess hall. It was so huge; it could accommodate the entire company of one hundred men. We were given three meals a day there. The exception was when we were away on training maneuvers.

On those occasions we were supplied with box lunches, placed into our canvas bag, the ***Brotbeutel.*** Lunch in the mess hall was our main meal. It started with a vegetable soup, sometimes a salad, followed by potatoes, meat, ***Kommissbrot*** (military bread containing special enriched ingredients) and a variety of freshly cooked vegetables. For dessert there was usually a large piece of cake and a mug of coffee.

I had no complaints about the quality of the food. Everything was always fresh and tasty, contrary to what one would expect from institutional or military supplied foods. By tradition, the Luftwaffe always had the best food for their personnel, as did the Navy. That was to the envy of the other branches of the Armed Forces.

There was also a small medical center called: The ***"Revier"*** that had at least two doctors and four nurses on duty at all times. It was fully equipped and functioned as a small hospital. I do recall that on one occasion a few of us, including me, were put into quarantine for one week. The reason was for a suspected epidemic of some kind. While there, we felt quite privileged while the others had to do field duty and training in all kinds of weather.

The daily routine in our base usually followed the same pattern. Wake up call was at 6:00 AM, followed by a shower and a shave, and then breakfast, which was at 7:00 AM. After getting ready for the assigned duties of the day, there was a role call at 8:00 AM.

We marched to the rifle range twice a week, and practiced sharp shooting. Regular rifle targets were placed one hundred meters from the shooting stand. We were not supplied with protective gear for our ears. The sounds were piercing and my ears rang afterwards. If we were out on the field we had our bag lunches at 12:00 noon. At 1:00 PM we practiced marching including goose step, or parade marching in perfect formation and line up.

Sometimes we sang traditional marching songs that we had learned earlier at the ***Arbeitsdienst.*** In the field we practiced advances toward the "enemy", going undercover by camouflage, etc. The Sergeant shouted orders and commands and we had to respond to him immediately.

He often shouted: "You want to be soldiers? You are so timid you could be trampled to death by tiny little duck feet!" "You can shit big piles and hide behind them that you can do, but soldiers you are not! (Yet!!!)" So in response we chuckled, but nevertheless we had to take that shit and hit the dirt!

Other days the program changed and we attended classes indoors in a separate educational hall. There always was a movie screen and a projector set up. We were shown educational and instructional films in regard to military strategies as well as general knowledge required for combat.

Never was there any propaganda involved, it was strictly military topics. A podium made of wood took up the entire width at the front of the room. One instructor sat at a desk to the left of that podium. Tables and chairs were set up facing the podium. Two men were usually assigned per table. Each student in this classroom had a composition book for note taking as well as a hard cover textbook providing us with basic military training information.

AT THE AIR ACADEMY

My basic training lasted for three months in Oschatz. Upon completion I was assigned to the Air Academy No. 2 at Berlin-Gatow on February 1, 1944. I would have preferred to go to the Air Academy No. 4 in Fürstenfeldbruck at my home, where I originally learned to fly the gliders with the Hitler Youth and Air Force instructors.

Upon arrival at Air Academy No. 2 in Berlin, we received our required gear including a brand new dress uniform, visor cap, one piece zippered flight suit, leather flight cap, goggles, underwear, shirts, ties and so on. We had been previously instructed to bring all items with us that we received in Oschatz at basic training.

We started with theoretical training and the continuation of glider and soaring instructions. Since I had already earned my "A" and "B" certificates, I was ahead of most, if not all of the other trainees. They had to start from the beginning to achieve the same goals. Therefore, I had more time to fly the more advanced soaring planes as opposed to the gliders. In doing so, I earned my "C" certificate in a very short time. Flying in the two-seater called: *'Kranich'* (crane)

It was a fairly sophisticated shoulder-wing soaring plane, having great visibility. It was a pleasure to fly because it was very easy to handle and it was 'forgiving' and not too sensitive. A French high wing monoplane called the "Morane" towed us. It had a powerful engine strong enough and very suitable for towing. We were mostly towed to an altitude of fifteen hundred meters, somewhat more than four thousand five hundred feet. We unhitched upon receiving a signal by the tow-plane pilot. We pulled the release knob, and were banking away. Immediately, we searched for thermal bubbles of rising warm air that took us to even higher altitudes; thus achieving a longer duration of flight.

For the first few training flights the instructor accompanied me. Once I had the confidence, I went solo. Then the instructor was replaced with a sand bag that weighed approximately as much as he did. The weight of the bag was needed to keep the balance of the aircraft. I had to practice maneuvers according to the orders of the teaching instructor in order to earn my "C" certificate. By my third or fourth solo, as I remember, I had passed the required tests and received my flight certification.

I was then qualified to fly the most advanced soaring plane that we had, the Mü 13. That plane was so sensitive that the slightest movement on the stick control immediately affected the entire performance of the aircraft. That meant I had to handle the stick delicately like holding a raw egg. The *Mü 13* plane gave me the most pleasure, a real thrill. What a pleasant and free feeling I had flying alone in command of the most sophisticated soaring plane to my heart's content, while my fellow trainees had to contend with lowly gliders learning basic flying maneuvers. It was no wonder that it was also certified for aerobatics. So I put it through some thrilling lazy eights like a curved roller coaster figure eight motion. I didn't fly any loops. Those were a big NO, NO! It was strictly forbidden, even though the aircraft was capable of easily doing that.

When our glider training was completed, we finally started our training in powered crafts. The first one I flew was the *"Fokke Wulf,* FW44D Stieglitz." That was a two-seater open cockpit biplane. It was almost an identical twin to the US Navy trainer "N3N," only smaller. For me, it was a great pleasure to be in complete control over a powered aircraft. The flight instructor flew with me for at least the first ten flights. He often complimented me on my ability to learn to handle the plane with such speed, as if I was born with the ability to fly. After having flown solo for about another ten starts, with assigned orders I graduated to the next level of training.

Once again it was another open cockpit biplane, a two-seater, but this one was capable of highly acrobatic maneuvers. It was the *"Bücker Jungmann"* that had an in-line engine. What made that aircraft unique was that it was one of the most advanced aerobatic training planes in existence at that time in the whole world.

Flying that one was certainly more thrilling than flying the Stieglitz. My instructor saw that I was ready to handle it in solo flights. He told me that I would definitely be a "great" Fighter Pilot! Following this two-seater, I was ready for another Bücker plane, but it was a single-seated one with a radial engine. It was called the *"Bücker Jungmeister."* This was really the "best" aerobatic plane in the world, and it kept that status for a long time after WW II. Its Siemens radial engine gave it more power than the *Jungmann* I believe that even enabled it to "hang on its prop" as the aviation jargon goes.

It had the same characteristics of the *Jungmann,* but was much faster and capable of exceptional aerobatics. Even forward loops could easily be achieved without complications. A forward upside down loop brought the blood rushing into your head. Not every pilot could endure that, but I was fortunate to go through with it.

After being evaluated as a potential future fighter pilot, my training continued in a "Messerschmitt 108"Taifun. (Typhoon) That aircraft was four-seated, with two side-by-side rows of seats. It was a powerful plane and surprisingly easy to handle. Comparison wise, it was like the ME-109 E, a single-seated craft as the fighter plane in which I did my final training. Within a short period of time I was once again ready to go solo. In the108 Taifun I passed with flying colors and was then ready for the next level of expertise.

Emil, a Messerschmitt 109 model, was an already obsolete plane, returned from front duty to become a trainer. At the front, the new 109 "Gustav" was replacing the Emil's. The difference was that the Gustav was faster and better armed and had rounded wing tips instead of the squared off ones that the Emil had.

It included a three-centimeter (30 mm) canon firing through the propeller knob spinner and two 20 mm canons mounted atop the engine covered by the cowling. Synchronized gears enabled them to fire through the spinning propeller blades. Later 109 Gustav models were equipped with a special hood designed and required by one of the top aces, Adolf Gallant. The newly designed hood also called the *"Erla Haube,"* gave you much better visibility and easier egress, at bail out.

I will never forget my first "solo" in the Emil. In taking off, rolling on the grassy runway I felt a slight bump. Lifting off was no problem. The landing gears retracted and I went up, up and away!

I soon became familiar with that new powerful machine and did the prescribed aerobatic maneuvers over the field. It gave me a spirit-filled lifting feeling and the handling was surprisingly easy. It had an immediate and fast response to the slightest movements of the controls. It was sheer pleasure to fly it. Coming in for the landing one day I saw a flagman ahead next to the *Landepiste* (landing strip) frantically waving and at the same time I received a radio message that only my right landing gear was out.

My indicator at the instrument panel showed the green light, meaning the gear was down and locked. Nevertheless, I had to throttle up to gain altitude again and then attempted to raise the landing gear. Nothing moved, the left was stuck in the wing and the right one was down and locked. So I took her up to two thousand meters, about 6000 feet, and did a steep dive starting with a sharp pull-up at 1000 meters…. (to give me enough 'room' for a safe bottoming-out of the dive and not go *" ungespitzt in den Boden "* { un-sharpened into the ground } as the German Luftwaffe jargon goes) ….to shake the stuck gear loose by the gaining G-force. Boy! The way I got pressed down on my behind onto my parachute, which served as our seat cushion in the bucket seats. It was given that nick name because looking at it when empty, it appeared to be a lopsided bucket, hence—the name.

At the bottoming-out I felt as if I weighted several hundred pounds. What a novel but also thrilling experience! Now I had found out what our **Stuka** guys are going through each time they do a dive-bombing mission. I almost got dizzy as I came out of that dive. Nothing moved and then that funny feeling of butterflies in my stomach came up. Now I was really in trouble! I would have preferred doing a belly landing, had the right gear retracted. The ME 109 was known to withstand such a landing easily without breaking up.

By radio communication they gave me a choice of either bailing out or bringing her down on one leg. I chose the latter, because I was not a coward! Besides, my bailing out could have resulted in my pilot-less plane crashing into a populated area, possibly killing someone. I did not want to take that chance and have a life-long regret or a bad conscience.

So I felt compelled to risk bringing her down on one leg to avoid that.

To attempt that type of landing I took a long shallow approach coming in, but was too fast and had to pull up again for another try. On the second one I had the right speed, but was still too high and over-shot the intended safe touch down point. So I pulled up again for the third try.

As the saying goes: "All good things come in threes." My third attempt was just right. I tilted the plane slightly down to the right, so that the strut and wheel were perpendicular to the ground to be able to carry the weight of the entire craft on one wheel alone. I came in perfectly with the correct speed and glide angle to set her gently down.

With full flaps she gently touched down, the right wheel rolled out while I cut the engine. Slower and slower I rolled, and didn't touch the brake as the left wing slowly came down. Finally the left wing tip scraped the ground as the Emil looped to the left, after one and a half turns she came to a stop, completing a perfect **Ringelpiez.** (Ground-loop)

I had unlocked the tail wheel, or more damage could have occurred.

A great feeling of relief came over me when I realized that I really did it, and promptly I slumped down in my seat. I brought her safely home in one piece with only minor damage. The left wing tip showed some paint scrapes and the tips of the propeller blades were bent. There was no other damage to see. I surely was convinced that my guardian Angel was with me!

Bathed in sweat, I got out and saw the flight instructor and a few men running towards me. They "congratulated" me for a job well done! We all looked at the stuck left gear to see what the trouble was.

It seemed that some unknown object had hit the wheel cowling as I took off and bent its edge, forming a curled hook. Once retracted it became locked in its well and couldn't come out. It only took one day to repair that damage and the following day the good ole Emil was once again up in the air with its patched up scars from the old bullet holes and all. After that episode I received a special commendation for bravery and a three-day pass plus the weekend so I could visit my uncle Otto for five days in Berlin.

That was a wonderful visit with my uncle Otto Skopnick and my two cousins Gerda and Irma. They took it upon themselves to "spoil me" with their delicious meals including some rare, hard to find, cookies and cakes. Their house at **Lewetzostrasse** No. 16 was the only house on the block that remained fairly undamaged from the bombs that fell and ruined the neighboring houses on the street. Most of the houses in their neighborhood were completely bombed out, down to ground in heaps of rubble.

The roof garden was a favorite place to spend sunny days playing card games and writing letters home. We even did some dancing to music that came from our modern portable radio. We constantly left it playing to be informed and warned by announcements of any approaching enemy bombers and also by imminent air raid sirens.

After five wonderful days, I left with all sorts of "goodies" and delicacies from my uncle's grocery store-chain; Gruber and Skopnick that normally were impossible to obtain without ration cards. Happy and 'loaded' I returned back to the base after being well fed and royally entertained on this mini-vacation. Of course I shared my goodies with my room buddies who were so surprised and enjoyed things they hadn't eaten in a long time.

After training with the Emil, we also got to know and fly the Gustav mainly to become familiar with the best combat plane at that time. Other academies trained their men piloting the ***Fokke Wulf 190*** fighter plane. Those pilots in turn claimed theirs to be the best fighter plane but that fact remained intensely debatable and that problem never was really solved.

Our entire training process lasted six months, until August 1944. Aerial gunnery practice was also a necessary and important part of it. Instrument training consisted of only very basic concepts, there was not enough time left. We were told that at the front, there would always be a leader who had instrument and navigational training, but in spite of that, could we also get lost?

To some extent, we did receive some limited navigational training whereby we had to fly a triangular pattern from our base to a target town that could be in the range of fifty to one hundred kilometers distance. From that target point we then had to make a ninety-degree turn to reach another target approximately fifty or so kilometers away. From there back to our base, thus flying a triangle. That flight was supposed to last about an hour or so.

While flying VFI you had to use a map to follow the prescribed pattern and compare it with the ground terrain to recognize marked locations. If you got lost, you were instructed to use the "iron compass." That meant that you had to descend from the prescribed thousand-meter altitude down to tree top level.

Searching around you had to locate and fly along railroad tracks in the approximate compass direction of the target point until you came to a station that usually had large marked signs along the tracks with the name of that town in large black lettering on it. Consulting the map you could then find the location and know where you were, climb up to one thousand meters again to continue your ordered course. It could take quite some time finding out where you were.

This however, resulted in a minus point for your training record. Indeed it did happen to me on my very first tri-angle flight; I was considered overdue for my return because after an hour had passed I had not yet arrived. The barometric register that had been placed in the tail section of the plane recorded the proof that I had descended into the wrong altitude. Upon my return that instrument revealed the truth and I got reprimanded by the instructor, but he asked me jokingly: "Where were you, did you stop and have a beer somewhere on your trip?"

Getting lost on those brief training flights was not unusual. More than two thirds of us got lost on the way and one of my fellow trainees had to make an emergency landing on a farmers pasture after running out of gas, miraculously without damaging the plane. Calling our base operations tower on his radio he gave them his position info after asking the nearby farmer where he was. A rescue crew with mechanics from our base went there by truck and a tow trailer to dismantle the plane, load it up and return to base. A fly-out from there could not be risked; the pasture was too short for take-off and was surrounded by tall trees in that forested area. It was sheer luck that the pilot found that pasture in time and landed there, barely stopping in front of the trees. He almost got 'washed out' from the training program but for the fact, that he didn't lose the craft and his skillful landing, and also because of the dire need for fresh pilots at the front.

The same fellow student pilot was later one of the novice pilots also assigned to JG 53.

But he was in another group stationed on the same field base where I was and we met a few times and compared combat experiences with each other. He was ahead of me with air-victories; while I had only two, he already had four when we lost contact with each other as my group got transferred to Hungary.

A sad incident occurred in our training while practicing parachute jumping. We had to make three jumps from a tri-motor Junkers JU 52 transport plane like the paratroopers with their chutes attached to a static line which pulled them out behind them upon jumping off the plane with spread arms and legs.

That was to get used to the sudden jerk when the chute deployed and to get the feel of a descending fall and the proper roll on the ground upon hitting it. Of course before those real jumps we practiced those 'landings' from a twenty-foot high shallow descending angle ending about 50 feet from the tower. Hanging by a harness attached to the cable we practiced gliding down on it, simulating landings by parachute.

Following that training we then had three practice jumps from the JU 52 without any problems or injuries. But the two jumps of a different type, a pilot chute that was worn on your behind and as such became your seat cushion in the bucket seats of the fighter aircraft, was a completely different story. The left vertical main harness strap at the front had a metal pull handle attached which released a small priming-chute, which in turn pulled the main chute out of the packing sack while the jumper is in freefall.

When jumping from high altitudes above two to three thousand meters, you had to freefall to not less than five hundred meters, then pull the release handle to open your chute to come safely down without suffering lack of oxygen at those higher altitudes if exiting too early. Our first such practice jump was done out of a canopied two-seater low wing monoplane, the name and type of it escaped my memory. I believe it was one of the captured French planes. Equipped with two canopies, one for each pilot, it enabled the student pilot to leave the plane and jump down after opening the hinged canopy.

That first jump was done from one thousand two hundred meters. We pilots were wearing an altimeter on our wrist like a wristwatch. So, at our first bailout we had to freefall not more than 200 meters and then pull the handle to open the chute at one thousand meters. One of us fellow student pilots evidently panicked on that first practice jump, perhaps couldn't find the pull handle and in his fright clenched his right fist around the vertical left harness strap and with his adrenalin powered right arm he pulled with superhuman might on that strap and ripped it apart. That pilot harness type withstood-four thousand pounds before failing in stretching tests. Now this poor fellow in his frightful panic was able to rip it apart and fell like a stone to an instant death onto an asphalt road.

His clenched fist couldn't be opened and the belt ends had to be cut off from both sides of his tightly closed fist.

He was buried with military honors at the nearby ***Heldenfriedhof.*** (Heroes' cemetery) So ended a promising career. He had intended to stay with the Luftwaffe to fulfill his goal of becoming a career officer.

By the way, he was one of the smarter pilots, that didn't get lost on the tri-angle flight.

I Met A Goddess

While at Berlin-Gatow we cadets were alternately performing guard duty at the front gate of the base.

We each had twelve-hour shifts. The job required the checking of all incoming and outgoing traffic to our air base. The passengers of all vehicles had to show identifications and explain their purpose for entry. Known Officers and other personnel were automatically acknowledged, saluted and waved on. It was an interesting job and a welcome diversion from our aircraft training.

There were usually two men at the guard booth. One handled incoming traffic and the other, the outgoing traffic.

Air defense duty was another requirement at the perimeter of the base. That duty was performed about twice a month. We manned a twin machine gun, the MG81. That amazing gun had a firing sequence of four thousand shots per minute.

Once you pulled the trigger for a split second, a few hundred shots left the barrels. It made a "swishing' sound unlike the rattling tak, tak, tak from other earlier designed machine guns. Therefore, this one had no gun sight. You aimed it towards the target by tracer bullets. The ammunition was packed in the belts five tracers, five regular bullets, and five armor piercing, in that sequence. I was familiar with this from practice sessions.

I never had to actually use it in earnest. It was meant to fend off fighter attacks, flown at low altitudes, which never happened at our location.

Having guard duty at the front gate was also to my great advantage. Often civilians came to visit their relatives, as well as girls visiting their boyfriends. One day, while I was at the gate, a young woman of about eighteen years of age came up to me and asked for permission to see her boyfriend.

She was wearing her **Arbeitsdienst** uniform and her name was Gerda Meinert-Wunsch. (Un-forgettable to me) She arrived at the nearby train station from Berlin and had walked to our base. Upon checking the list of personnel presently at the base, I found out that the air cadet she was looking for had received orders to report for active duty at the front, just a few days before her arrival.

To me, she was such an appealing, exceptionally beautiful girl. She had strikingly blonde shoulder length hair with a neatly set coiffure, curled inwards at the ends. Being of medium stature she had the most gorgeously shaped body, she was like a "Goddess." As I noticed her hourglass figure, she appealed to me so strongly, in a refreshing way. Her brilliant blue eyes glistened with enthusiasm and radiated warmth that even the bad news that I revealed to her could not diminish.

I took the opportunity to engage her into a long conversation and we shared some of our most recent experiences in our different services for the fatherland. As she was standing by the guard-booth we were frequently interrupted by incoming traffic I was checking. I asked her if she would like to join me for a dinner in a local restaurant, a **Gasthaus.** I knew I could afford that, not only from my military salary but also because I had some additional savings of monetary gifts from my uncle Otto at my disposal; he always asked me, if I had enough spending money and he was always generous.

The following weekend we were able to meet because I had Saturdays and Sundays off. Having our delightful and pleasant date together at that dinner was actually my first experience together with a young lady and it was followed by a visit to a movie. I can't remember what the movie was about because my attention was 'glued' on her. I simply couldn't get enough of her. Also I was strongly drawn to her by the pleasant scent of the perfume she wore. I later realized it was the 4711 cologne, the same one my mother always used which came from the city of Köln (Cologne). No wonder!

She impressed me not only by her exceptional looks and beauty but also by her brilliant intelligence. Writing poetry was her passion and she brought some of her writings along to read to me. They were very inspiring and that gave me the idea, that maybe I should also try to start writing such poems.

(Years later I did when I was courting my future bride and before that, as a POW in Russia being confined for some time in a POW hospital.)

But I can't remember what she read to me, only that her poems were smartly written, I was so mesmerized by her and I just wanted to be with her, nothing else mattered to me. However what I do remember is, that we were about the same age, with no more than just a few months difference. What was it that attracted her to me so strikingly and fascinatingly? Was it by sudden impulse, or was it by her alluring charm? It may certainly have been her amazing warmth and happy spirited demeanor that appealed to me and of course, especially her flawless beauty.

At our next date I met her upon her arrival at the railroad station. Earlier we had planned that we would be going for a swim in lake Wannsee close to our base. It was just the right time at the beginning of the summer, I recall. At one end of the lake there was a public swimming area with facilities and snack shops. At the opposing side of it there was a base owned boathouse that contained rowboats, kayaks and paddleboats. As cadets we had permission as well as the rights to use any of those boats for recreational use during our free time. We headed for the boathouse and selected a neat rowboat and I rowed out from shore so we could enjoy the beautiful scenery while we carried on in a pleasant conversation. I brought some of the goodies from Uncle Otto's store for our enjoyment.

I looked for a suitable place along shore where we could be undisturbed and found a nice open grassy place surrounded by trees.

There Gerda and I had a wonderful romantic picnic together eating sandwiches and cookies accompanied by a bottle of wine.

Our togetherness was so enchanting and I was so mesmerized being in her company. We completely lost track of time. As we were deeply enjoying our time together we forgot about the world around us, putting aside all and any worries or concerns. They didn't matter to us.

In our conversations we shared with each other personal things about our lives, like where we grew up and what our secret dreams were. I learned where she came from; it was a town near Breslau, but I could never remember the name of it, maybe because it was not that important to me.

We also talked further about her enchanting poetry. She appeared to me so immensely brilliant, she was like a God-given heavenly star; I just can't put it into words how deeply I felt about her. Right there and then I reached the conclusion that blondes were not dumb after all, as I used to think so mistakenly, and also according to the widely used and established opinions.

Our get-togethers were repeated from then on for many times to come. We were actually able to see each other over the entire summer during every weekend.

To this day I can still remember her beautiful face and the wonderful times we spent together!

Unfortunately, at the end of that summer I received orders to report for active duty at the front and I never was able to see or speak with her again or say good-by. I was unable to get in touch with her; I did not know where she was staying in Berlin with her **Arbeitsdienst** unit, nor did I have a telephone number or her home address.

All that was unimportant at that time. We always planned our dates in advance from week to week. We had always known her time of arrival with the help of the railroad timetable at the Gatow railroad station. I always would pick her up and we certainly had a marvelous joyful time being alone together....

(Now today, 2004, as I reflect back to those tremendously happy times we were privileged to spend with each other I must really admit, that I dearly loved her and missed her terribly for a long time.)

.... Often times she took the last train back, departing at 1:05 A.M. But I still remember that last time I saw her off to leave and go back to her unit in Berlin. She smiled so lovingly and waved back to me through the window as I walked alongside the then moving train, we were throwing kisses to one another. Then I just couldn't keep up any longer running as the train slowly gained speed and so had to stop, I just stood there, watching the train go off into the distance as I continued waving back to her. Not knowing, that it would turn out to be the last time I ever saw her, I walked back to our base in happy expectation to meet her again the following weekend. We had planned to take out a paddleboat and paddle around to look for a good place to spend a quiet, romantic afternoon. Sadly it wasn't to be. Oh how I wished, that it hadn't come to this end...!

HAPPENINGS AT THE ASSASSINATION ATTEMPT ON HITLER'S LIFE

On July 20th 1944 the entire base was suddenly alarmed and at high alert. Security all around the base was increased. All personnel had to report for a line-up and roll call.

We were ordered to appear fully armed with live ammunition and stand at attention for an inspection. We all wondered what was going on and a rumor began to go around, that we were expecting an eminent attack... Attack ???? Who would attack us here, fighter-bombers? There was no air raid alarm, so what could it be? Well we soon found out what was happening when our base commander held a short speech informing us, that an attempt was made to assassinate Adolf Hitler in his *Führerhauptquartier* (Main Command Post) in Rastenburg, East Prussia.

The suspected assassin by the name of Oberst Klaus von Stauffenberg, was a decorated and trusted officer of the army. Stauffenbergs eye was covered with a black eye-patch as was mentioned by our commander to be an identifying feature. He had been wounded in battle on the eastern front, whereby he lost one eye and suffered other debilitating injuries, which made him unfit for front duty. He became a staff member of Hitler's entourage in the *Führerbunker.* (Hitler's bunker)

We were told, that he was on the run, possibly on the way to Berlin and that there were also a number of other conspiracies going on by more members of a certain clique who had secretly sworn to end the war by killing Hitler. The names of them escaped my memory, but I know that they were very high ranking officers, even Generals, who had formed a highly secretive group. They deemed Hitler as being insane and took it upon themselves to form a new government and sue for armistice and peace with the Allies.

Our commander informed us, that Hitler was only slightly wounded and was ok, giving further orders to take all measures to catch the conspirators and especially Oberst Klaus von Stauffenberg, who was believed to have fled to Berlin,-- (and that was confirmed)-- to contact his co-conspirators there....

We later found out, that when he got to Berlin to tell them that Hitler was dead (and he surely assumed that to be the case); that he couldn't believe it, especially when told that Hitler was alive and well. Actually two bombs were concealed in his big diplomat case which he had placed under the conference table next to Hitler, but he had time only to activate one of them before entering the room and seeing the guards there, feared getting caught. After placing the case containing the bomb, he left with the excuse of having to make a phone call, not knowing, that Hitler had then moved further down at the table to look at a map. (This actually saved his life)....

.... After our commander's speech we were ordered to march out of the base to form various roadblocks not only nearby, but also at other strategic points and crossings being transported by truck. We were to take charge to control and stop all traffic for inspections and identifications of drivers and passengers of all vehicles.

We were actually part of a tight security ring around Berlin covering all in-leading and out-leading roads and highways, including rail roads, with strict orders to arrest any and all of those named conspirators and other suspicious individuals.

By nighttime we were supplied with food by Red Cross nurses who volunteered to do that job, bringing us warm soup and bread from a nearby set-up field kitchen. We were also supplied with flashlights and red flares. Teams of three man patrol groups were formed among us. Each on watch duty for four hours, while the others from our truckload were resting or sleeping on the truck benches or on the side of the road in the grass, until it was their turn.

The next day we were still on duty and received additional meals from the field kitchen, which was all very efficiently organized. At several times during the night and day, field police stopped by to take reports of any suspicious happenings. All our reports were negative and all that we found was one driver who couldn't find his ID right away but with a further search he was able to produce it.

Mid-morning on the 22nd of July the alarm was lifted and we could return to our Air Academy. We surely were glad to be able to take showers and shave and got time off for the rest of the day to make up for lost sleep.

All the conspirators were caught and by military law as traitors, the High Commend gave the order to immediately execute them by firing squads....

.... As far as I recall, all this happened just before my last two weekends spent with my beloved Gerda, after which I was ordered to report for duty at a ***Jagdgeschwadergruppe*** (hunt-squadron group) of ***# 53 "Pik As"*** (Ace of Spades) near Aachen, in the NW of Germany.

AFTER THOUGHT NOW IN 2009

As I am writing this revised version of my book now reflect back to that wonderful time we had together, Gerda Meinert-Wunsch and I.

Being a melancholic man, I often had thoughts and also dreams about the possibility of us having a life together.

What would have been the outcome, if we had gotten married? Would we be today, as it is written at the end of every fairy tale? :

"And they both lived happily ever after"? ....

Well, here I am still living today thanks to Jehovah God's loving kindness, care and blessings. I am still in fairly good health just before my 84th birthday, despite having lost not only this, my first REAL love, but also my still GREATER love, my forever dearest Hedi.

(See chapter eight)

View of Camp Tennsee

Boarding Train to France

In Uniform, Arbeitdienst

Mr. Harlan and part of our Fiddle Group

New Recruit   18 yrs Old

With Three Of My Roommates

Marching to Rifle Range

Field Drill, Lunch Break

Eight Men per Room, New Recruits

Tents at camp, Glider Training

Evening with Music

After 1½ Hour Soaring with the Kranich

Sunning Myself,   Holding the Starting
At Corner of Barracks   Flag - Glider Training

Group In Training

We were writing letters home

Flak Duty MG 81

More Flak

On top of roof, relaxing at Uncle Otto's in Berlin

Lewetzostrasse No. 16

Cousins Gerda and Irma
working in office of
Gruber and Skopnik

FIVE

The Little Rabbit

Near Aachen on the northwestern side of Germany, north of Köln (Cologne) was the Air Field of JG 53rd Squadron called "Pik-As" (Ace of Spades). About five or six of us new Fahnenjunker (Cadets) from Berlin-Gatow were assigned to that Squadron. It was there that I was introduced into air combat. I was assigned a brand new Me 109 Gustav 14 A S. Originally it was intended to be sent to another group of JG 53 at the Italian battlefront as replacement for a badly damaged one. It belonged to another pilot who lost his in an emergency landing, but did not get hurt. That pilot, so I heard, was killed while flying a mission with a borrowed 109. He was shot down after achieving 15 air-victories. Before the new plane left the factory it was re-directed to our unit, since I was next in line to get a new machine. It had the factory-painted white band around the rear fuselage as all the planes of the Mediterranean front had.

Getting into the cockpit, before an assigned mission, I always had 'butterflies' in my stomach. The fact was, that in the back of my mind I knew there was a strong possibility that I may not return. Once I was active on a mission, all the negative thoughts disappeared and my survival instinct took over. I was called a "Häs-chen," meaning "little rabbit" until I had my first air victory. That was the established custom in the Luftwaffe's fighter units. As soon as a novice pilot had his first victory, he became a "Hase" (A hare). After ten victories he became an "Alter Hase" (Old hare).

I flew as a wingman, in my 109 Gustav, as sidekick (Katschmarreck) for an Oberleutnant (Second Lieutenant) who flew ahead, to the left side of me. As Cadet I was in the rank of Lieutenant (Leutnant). Our group, as part of the "Pik As" (Ace Of Spade) Squadron was assigned to engage the escort fighters that came in with the B17's from England to bomb Germany. Our group of ME 109s had strict orders to leave the bombers to the FW 190s. Our job was to take the escorting fighters away from the bombers by engaging them in combat. That way our neighboring Squadron of FW 190 type had a free hand at the bombers without being bothered by the enemy fighter planes. We took them 'out of their hair', so to speak. Their FW 190s were much better armed and equipped to attack the bombers. Using the newest attack technique to affront the bombers face to face, gave them the advantage of presenting a smaller profile to the defending gunners of the B 17s. Also it was the weakest defense for the B 17s because only the front gunner could actively defend his plane. Their top gunners could not reach them because the FW 190s came in at a somewhat lower altitude than the bombers, so the front portion of their B 17s blocked the defending bursts of their guns. Then the FW 190s as they flew close to the bombers, rose to the same altitude of the B 17s, and sprayed them with bursts of their cannons, often with deadly accuracy, and then sheared off to the sides or dove below them tilted 90 degrees, as such having a small profile, to avoid a collision. They passed the bombers with such a speed, that the side and or bottom gunners had little chance to effectively aim and hit them. This newest tactic was more effective, than the old rear-attack whereby numerous bomber gunners were needed to defend their plane.

My initial task and order as wingman was to stick with the Oberleutnant and observe how to attack and learn from his tactics of air combat. I was not to engage into combat on my own, unless I was attacked; then of course I had to defend myself and had to try my best to hit the enemy fighter first before he got me. I served as a second pair of eyes for my Oberleutnant. For example: I radioed: "Herr Oberleutnant at seven o'clock a Spitfire approaches you." Because I flew at the right rear side of him following his plane, he depended on me to be his rear shield.

As his wingman I followed this flight pattern for about one week, just observing the tactics, avoiding my own engagements as ordered. Then, at what I recall was my sixth or seventh mission, a Spitfire came at me from 3: 30 o'clock, (My right rear side), as I was alongside and just behind his plane. My 109 blocked his view and he wasn't aware, that I was being attacked. I radioed: I am under attack! That Spit-pilot probably took me for 'easy prey' since as a novice pilot I made no effort to actively engage in air combat. Now I really had to defend myself and engage that guy in my first air combat. I think, that he may have been bitterly disappointed, that I turned out to be his equal with my flying skill. For a good fifteen minutes, we curved back and forth; up and down in a dog fight trying to shoot at each other.

Again and again we were alternately behind each other, but too far apart for me to pull the trigger and have a chance to hit him without wasting ammo. He, in turn started firing from a farther distance and was successful in a few hits into the fuselage of my Gustav. Nothing vital was hit, as most of his rounds just went left and right by me. As I didn't pull the trigger, my opponent may have assumed that I was out of ammo or had jammed guns and so risked coming closer to me, but that was his fatal mistake as he soon found out....

I had heard earlier about Erich Hartmann's tactic: Never waste any ammunition. Get as close as possible to the enemy, on collision course, so that once you pull the trigger, you are sure to hit him with a short burst of the twin 20 mm cannons. The cannons were located atop the fuselage and they fired through the turning propeller by synchronized sequence, so as not to shoot your own propeller off. A single round out of the 30 mm cannon would be enough "to put his lights out". It had such explosive power that a single round was fatal once it hit any part of a plane. I chose the big cannon, the breach of it was right between my legs in the cockpit; and as it happened, all five of my total air-victories, were brought down by one round with the 30 mm cannon shooting out of the spinner, the propeller-knob of my 'Gustav' 109....

.... I made an immediate "Immelmann" maneuver....(During WW I air combat, Max Immelmann nicknamed "Eagle of Lille" was responsible for developing this dogfight maneuver. It was actually a clever way comprised of a simultaneous loop and roll designed, to allow a dive back at the attacker from his rear.).... By gunning the throttle forward, I gained the power to make an immediate upwards loop. While rising, I twisted my plane then came down, so I was up above and behind him.

As I was diving, 'hanging on his tail', I was still too far from him to accurately aim and pull the trigger. I gained more speed and came almost close enough to shoot and not miss but suddenly he maneuvered out of that dangerous situation. I followed him as close as I could but by his next sudden turn he again got away from me. His Spit could fly sharper turns than my Gustav.

Then I saw him again and the quick evasive moves he made. But then while coming at me from the right side with his guns blazing from afar, my rear fuselage later showed some holes in it as most of his rounds of that burst missed me. I heard the impacts that hit me. Shearing out to the right against him I got out of his line of fire. He then turned to his right, and I made a full loop towards him. I forced him to come from my right side, and he was close enough in front of me, flying right into my firing line. As he passed in front of me, the self-installed black dot on my front windshield pointed right into his engine, I pulled the trigger (Set to single round) and hit him. I saw the impact as I sharply pulled up not to collide with the Spitfire and passed over it. Circling back, I saw flames and black thick smoke trailing from his engine and then the pilot jettisoned his canopy bailing out, he jumped from the burning plane. As I observed the deploying of his chute, I was relieved to see him alive. That happened to be almost directly over our field base. I realized now, that I had just become a 'Hase' with my first air-victory!

His Spit dove nearly straight down in flames, trailing thick black smoke and hit the ground exploding into a big fireball just outside our field.

This was my very first "real" air combat and 1st Luftsieg made me feel so proud. I was also relieved and then calm came over me as I looked around for my Oberleutnant.

With all the twists and turns while in combat, I lost sight of him. But he saw my fight with the Spitfire and the actions I had taken. He himself bagged two Spitfires on that same mission, one of which I had observed earlier out of the corner of my eyes and could later verify as being his victory. That was at the same time I was 'busy' with my engagement with a Spitfire. I did however find my Oberletnant shortly after I downed mine and stuck with him again. I was not attacked again. The remaining Spits soon broke off the fight as we were all running low on fuel.

It was the policy in the Luftwaffe that a witness had to verify a fellow pilot's victory. In addition further proof was provided by film from the gun camera on the plane.

As mentioned earlier that entire scenario took place close to our own airfield and directly above it. I don't remember how many Spitfires and or bombers were shot down that day in our flight area. I do remember though, that the bombers continued on their way without their escort fighters, pursued by the FW 190s. I saw at least three go down in the distance and more may have been downed further away by those relentless attacks of the swarming FW190 bees.

I really admired the B 17 formations; they flew stubbornly straight ahead without taking any evasive action. They flew in bulks of about 50 as they defended each other from those 'bees' sticking tightly together. I saw what looked like a FW 190 going down trailing smoke in the distance and saw a chute deploying, so the pilot must have been okay.

The British pilot whom I shot down landed with his chute on a freshly plowed acre adjoining our airfield and was taken as prisoner of war by our field guards. Later that afternoon, after I had landed at my base, I met him:

His name and rank was: Lieutenant Fred Browning from London, England. He was interrogated at our base headquarters before I had returned from the mission. Evidently he was told, that it was I who downed him. As he saw me he walked towards me and with a smiling gesture he said: "So, you are the chap who got me, a jolly good fight! He also patted my shoulder while saying that, repeating the same phrase. So he and I were allowed to chat with each other and share our combat and training experiences. He confirmed, that he really thought I was a novice pilot, and had jammed guns when I did not pull the trigger for so long in our dogfight. That evidently fooled him. He had gotten careless and paid the price.

I found him to be a better skilled pilot than I. What he did with his Spit I never thought possible. Again and again he evaded my efforts to get to him by what seemed to me to be impossible turns and loops. If not for his carelessness, I must have gotten him due to the fact that I had the better plane and a deadly 30 mm cannon. I believe if we were both flying a 109 Gustav, he would have shot me down with the snap of his fingers. I was amazed that he mastered his Spit in such a spectacular performance to comprehend what he achieved. Unbelievable!

He was one year older than I; he was twenty and I nineteen, as I found out in our friendly conversation. We had no animosity toward each other. He was doing his sworn duty as I was mine.

His flight training took a much longer period of time than mine did and that resulted in his superior ability to fight so well in combat.

Fred Browning was 'happy' that the war was over for him, even though he became a P.O.W. and had to serve his time and wait for the day of his liberation. I regret that I never came to know of his whereabouts. We were comrade's in-arms, doing our duty as soldiers. Recently I tried searching for him on the Internet but was unsuccessful in locating him.

On those clear days when we had to fly several missions, we were encouraged to take "energy tablets." They were made from dextrose fruit sugars and were called: Dextro-Energen. They were shaped like wafers and were about one inch square in size. Being chewable and having a pleasant tasting citrus flavor they produced a lot of saliva as well. They did a remarkable job keeping me alert and focused with concentration. They gave us the necessary stimulation with the extra energy needed to sustain the various stresses we encountered while on combat missions.

Several days and missions later, flying as Wingman with my Oberleutnant, we once again became separated in combat when I became busy with other enemy planes. We broke up our fight without hitting each other because of low fuel levels. Over the radio there came a command to head home as we were nearly out of gas. While flying home I saw in the distance another plane heading in the opposite direction. I asked myself, "Is he friend or foe?" To make sure, I swung around out of his view getting behind and below him. Then I could identify it as a Spitfire.

Knowing that the Spitfire had a rear view mirror I made sure to stay below and behind him while I caught up to him. When I was less than ten meters (Thirty feet) away I quickly pulled up and with one round out of my three-centimeter canon shot his entire tail section off. Immediately it was blown off of his plane. As I flew by him, it almost hit me.

To my left I saw the forward tumbling Spitfire and it's Pilot exiting the plane. His chute opened and as I circled around him he saluted me and I returned his salute. Again I was relieved, because I did not have to take a life. The only witness for my 2nd Victory was my trusty gun camera. It was a foolish risk to take, being so low on fuel. I arrived safely at our base field with the last drop of "sprit" in my gas tank. Later I was able to review the film and was amazed how close I came to almost colliding with him.

At the end of one of those missions as I jumped down from the wing to the ground I felt a strange squishing in my boot. When I removed my boot back at the Base I saw that my foot was bloody. On closer inspection I saw a small hole at the shaft of my lambskin-lined flight boot. I found a fragment from a friendly-fired Flak that had hit my plane. It had penetrated the skin of the fuselage and then lodged in my flight boot. It hit my left shinbone and stopped right there. The wound was treated at the Infirmary with bandages and I did not require hospitalization. I was issued a new pair of flight boots.

After this 2nd victory, near the end of that August in 1944 I was lucky enough to get a few days of leave to be able to attend the 25th (Silver) Wedding Anniversary of my parents back in Fürstenfeldbruck. Unfortunately, I arrived two days after the celebration due to travel delays, like bombed out railroad tracks, etc. Nevertheless, it was still a happy occasion for the family. My younger sister, who was in the

Arbeitsdienst in another city, had also received leave to attend the event.

Due to the same delays, she wound up being one day late. A photograph of the joyous family gathering was taken in our backyard after the celebration occurred. I still have that picture showing us all together.

My youngest sister held her pet rabbit 'Schlusele' as we sat at the garden set that my Great Uncle Hermann had built for us years earlier. I had repaired that set prior to entering the service, as the years of outdoor exposure had damaged it.

A Day Of Miracles

On the way back to my field base from Fürstenfeldbruck, while traveling to get to our field near Aachen, I had a most unusual and miraculous experience. To this day I cannot explain it in any other way or form: "My Guardian Angel saved my life in a most mysterious way."

Let me begin to share this amazing story:

I had arrived at the Hauptbahnhof (Main Railroad Station) in Köln (Cologne) and was told, that there were no trains going to Aachen due to bomb damage to several areas of the tracks. I was directed to go to the nearby Oberkommando (High Command Office) of the Wehrmacht (Armed Forces) to find out how to get back to my unit.

I walked the street leading from the railroad station to a plaza where the building with the Command office was located. I was asked to show my travel order papers when I arrived there. They wanted to know why I had not gotten a stamp from the stationmaster. I explained that I did not know I needed the stamp. They informed me that I had to go back to obtain the stamp that verified the date and arrival time. I took the same street back to the train station. About half way there I heard the dreadful siren wail, in the wavy pattern signaling an air raid. I ran to the next Luftschutzkeller (Air raid shelter cellar), along with many other people.

That deep basement was entirely painted, ceilings, walls and floors with fluorescent paint so if the lights failed we were able to see one another. A person's shadow would remain on the wall when stepping away from it after having stood against it for a minute or two with the ceiling lights on. That was really weird but funny and the children that were present were busy playing lost shadow games laughing and booing, having fun.

The fluorescent paint gave off enough light to see where one was going in an emergency. It was an eerie strange feeling when the lights went off for a while and the entire room was aglow in a greenish / purple sheen. The dimensions of the room were not recognizable any more, because that strange glow felt like you were submerged in water and could walk unaware right into a wall. One had to walk like a blind person with hands and arms stretched forward as feelers to find the way. You could never imagine that something so strange and spooky existed until you were there, experiencing it firsthand. Spooky and even frightening, one was so unsure to walk, really like being blind.

During the air raid we heard and felt bomb hits nearby. The floor and walls seemed to vibrate; the lights flickered a few times but stayed on. After about half an hour the 'clear' signal came, (a long un-interrupted siren tone), and we could all leave the shelter.

As I went up to continue on my way to the train station. To my surprise I saw a huge blockbuster bomb in the middle of the street. It was about three feet thick and ten feet long. I had never seen anything like it in my whole life.

It made quite a deep indentation on the cobblestone pavement as it hit the ground flat on its side. Not aerodynamic in form and without fins, it looked like a large cylinder with rounded ends, so it must have tumbled over and over coming down.

Upon closer examination, I saw, that it had a crack in its side near the center with a trace of smoke emitting from it. I realized, that if it had exploded as it hit the street we all would have been buried in the shelter, as the building surely would have collapsed on top of us in the basement. Thanks to the Lord, it did not happen. So I went on my way, reached the Bahnhof (Train Station) and got my papers stamped.

I came out of the Station to go back to the Command Post, and saw that a bomb had knocked a chunk out of the tower wall at the base of the famous Cathedral of Cologne during the raid. The cathedral is located right across the street from the train station and I walked over to examine the damage.

A smaller bomb than the huge blockbuster I had seen on the street had hit the tower base. While looking at the stone debris, a fellow soldier came over and asked me for directions to the Command Post.

Before I could answer him, another man appeared standing next to us. He was dressed in a long black coat and wore a hat he had pulled partially over his face. I don't remember seeing his face. He exclaimed: "Oh, just follow me, I am on the way there too!" So we followed this strange man and exchanged info about our units and why we came to Köln.

As we were talking, I told him about the monster bomb I had found ahead on the street about fifteen minutes before. I noticed that the strange man was leading us through a parallel street in the direction of the C-Post. It was at a higher elevation than the lower street where the bomb was.

I asked the stranger who led us: "Don't we have to go along the lower right street to get there? "No, no he answered, this upper street is much closer and safer." So we followed him further, strangely putting complete trust in him, while we continued to talk about the big blockbuster bomb.

We came just about parallel to the big blockbuster bomb laying on the lower street when suddenly we were blown to the ground by an enormous ear shattering explosion… It knocked the breath out of us. Immediately I thought "w-h-e-w!"…..That was the "monster bomb."

It exploded at the same moment that we would have been passing there, had we been walking on that lower level as I had originally intended to do. We got back up on our feet, saw and felt that we were still in one piece, and were glad about it. We looked for the stranger but were unable to find him. Where had he gone? … He seemed to have disappeared into thin air…

As we looked around searching for him to find out if he made it through the explosion unharmed, we saw nothing but the brick-rubble from the collapsed buildings on both sides of the street. They remained the same way as they were from earlier bombings than were caused by this new explosion. He couldn't have gone and hidden anywhere, because there were only huge piles of building debris all around and along the street.

The former magnificent old houses were no longer standing nor were any recognizable entrances to cellars. He was gone, but my newly acquired friend and I were safe. We shook the accumulated dust off our uniforms and started walking to the plaza of the Command Post.

Then suddenly it dawned on me: "My God!" That was my Guardian Angel who had prevented me from going back to the bomb. We surely would have been blown to bits had we gone there as I was so determined to do. Cold sweat came over me, as I realized, that my life could have ended right then and there, if it wasn't for this divine intervention. Nothing of us would have been left, had we been scattered into unrecognizable fragments spread all over the neighborhood. A shuddering thought! We would have disappeared just like my Guardian Angel had and nobody would have known about it as we would have vanished into oblivion.

Back at the C-Post my newly found friend and I said our good byes as arrangements were made for me to ride along with a truck delivering a load of flour to our airfield near Aachen for the field bakery that was located next to our base. On our way a few kilometers out of Köln, on a raised tree-lined country road we suddenly saw a fighter bomber coming at us from the left side at ground hugging altitude with guns blazing.

We stopped quickly, tires screeching and jumped down the embankment to our right and laid flat on the soft ground. Not more than ten feet away from me a bomb hit the soft soil. Booooom!!! It exploded deep inside the ground creating a large crater and scattered soil.

It almost buried me alive! Wow, I thought, that really was a close one! That was the third time in one day that my life was spared. My Guardian Angel was still with me and had saved me again. I could feel the protective shield of the Guardian's wings wrapped tightly around me. Fortunately the plane kept on going and did not return for a second round of attack.

Shaking the dirt off, we went up to see if our truck was still useable, and miraculously it was still in working order. Some flour sacks had received a few bullet hits but that was about it. The motor was still running and the doors left open from when we had quickly jumped from the truck. So we kept going and by nightfall we arrived at our base.

What a day that was, I never in my life could forget those miracles that I was privileged to live through. From then on always, I felt safe, knowing that I was steadily protected by my Guardian Angel. I really believed that I would survive through "thick and thin." My time was not up, and I had a long life ahead of me, I was sure of it! Thinking back to that remarkable day of miracles, I still can't fathom how I made it through all those strange calamities without being harmed. It was a perfect and convincing example of God's mysterious ways and His protective help….

…. The daily routine continued after I returned to my JG53 airfield by way of that "flour truck." Almost every day in-good weather we had to take off to "welcome" the bulks of B17's and their fighter escorts. Again I flew missions as wingman and we did our best to keep the fighters "busy" and away from the bomber formations.

That way the Fokke Wulf 190's could do their jobs and try to shoot down as many bombers as possible by frontal head-on attacks. But because we were always so overwhelmingly outnumbered, we all knew that we were fighting a losing battle, but we had sworn duty to our country. I was not able to add more victories in the next couple of weeks. Their escort fighters were "tough cookies,". They were much better and better trained than our group of young novice pilots. -

At the beginning of October the greater part of our group received orders to re-locate to the Russian front at an Airfield near the North of Budapest, while the rest of the group remained at the area near Aachen. We received replacement ME109 G 14's for the "fresh pilots" who came right out of flight schools. These new "Little Rabbits" were then introduced to air combat by the "Alten Hasen," (Old Hares).

While there in Hungary, at the end of November I received a letter from home telling me that my older sister would be getting married on December 12th. I applied for leave to be able to attend the wedding. Since the weather was mostly unsuited for flying and the front was more or less at a standstill, I was granted leave for one week. I rode on returning supply trucks towards Vienna. Once there, I took a train from Vienna then changed over to another one about half way due to bombed out tracks. We finally got to Munich by taking a bus around the damaged tracks.

My sister was in her early twenties and was marrying a Doctor. I wanted to be there on time, but because of the train delays caused by further bombed tracks, I missed it by two days. We celebrated all together once my younger sister and I arrived. She also arrived late for the same reason after taking her leave from the Arbeitsdienst. Nevertheless it was still a happy occasion for us, and it was the last 'togetherness' with my entire family for many years to come.

It was also during that time that the German people experienced extremely rough conditions. The constant bombing took its toll on their patience and tolerance to endure this seemingly never-ending war. There were hardly any food supplies and all food was rationed. Meat was very sparse and the daily diet consisted mostly of half rotten potatoes. The potatoes, which had been kept in cold storage, often got frozen and when stored in a thawed condition they began rotting and then stunk. Because of the starch in them the freezing process made them excessively sweet as the starch turned into sugar and that was almost sickening when cooked and eaten.

I clearly remember that last furlough when I came back home to Fürstenfeldbruck and all too soon had to return back to the war. It seemed like such a long walk to the train station accompanied by my father. First I kissed my mother "Goodbye" and she stayed back at the house. That felt almost like a last "Goodbye." They never knew if I, their son would ever set foot back in their house again.

At the train station my father said to me: "I am proud of you my son!" That remark brought me to tears. For we both knew that indeed, this could be the last time that we would be together. It could have also been the last time that he would see me alive. This was finally, his way of proving that he really loved me. Words cannot describe how touching that moment was for both of us.

It was during that walk to the train station that I revealed to my father the truths about my involvement in the war. I was told earlier by my commander not to reveal too much while on leave. It was all to be kept a top secret. But then, I was walking a fine line, so I guess I broke down to give my father some indication as to what I was up against and how we at the front knew, that we were fighting for a lost cause. He was not surprised.

Most Germans already felt that the war was lost. But they were afraid to talk about it. There was already a strong resentment in the German population as the war lingered on and on. That was resentment against those who kept the war going, and I was part of it. Because of that I decided to be dressed in my civilian clothes, while on leave.

I returned with a heavy heart to active duty, and reported to the area just North of Budapest, where our flying field was located. We had a new Group Commander Hauptmann Helmut Lipfert because our former one had transferred to the new Messerschmitt 262 jet-fighter outfit located in Bavaria. To our surprise, rank was of no importance with our new Commander. He was just one of the 'boys.' We addressed each other by our first names, since we were all in the same boat.

Helmut was quite a few years older than most of us. He had a kind, caring and fatherly manner and never pulled rank. He taught us new tactics that were extremely helpful in our future missions. We flew only in good weather because most of us had little or no instrument training, which was really vital to navigation. Especially in the vast farm and forested regions without any recognizable landmarks flying VFR was very difficult and it was really easy to get lost. But we managed with our compasses that everyone knew could provide us with basic directions.

At our section of the front, the opposing Russian enemy to the South of Budapest flew the Polykarpoff I-16, the "Ratas." They were older planes that had already fought against the early ME-109's during the Spanish Civil War (1936-1939). They were developed further just as the 109. The new ME-109's like the one I flew, proved to be superior in combat as were newer developments in previous models compared to improvements the Russians made on their 'Ratas'. Our planes were designed better overall and could definitely outmaneuver the Ratas. Nevertheless, in combat a good experienced Russian pilot could give us a lot of trouble. That was evidenced by some bullet holes in my plane.

Often we could not fly for days because of inclement weather so we went hunting for hares. Most of the pilots were billeted at nearby Hungarian farm homes and we had time to spare while waiting for better weather....

.... It was a Hungarian custom to greet new houseguests with special baked muffin-like breads accompanied with salt. When new 'guests' arrived, they were always welcomed in that old tradition and invited into their homes. At first when we arrived and were offered bread and salt, we had no idea about their ancient custom. We gratefully accepted their offerings along with a glass of homemade wine. Later we got more familiar with this friendly gesture....

...At the farm fields after the corn was harvested the dried stalks were bundled and placed throughout the field; upright in bunches of eight or ten and leaning together forming a tent-like space in the center. My buddies chased after the hares while I hid in one of those bundled stalk piles. The hares outsmarted them by returning to their preferred places after the hunters were far away.

One hare came running and hopping from right to left about one hundred meters away from me. I took a potluck shot at it, aimed and pulled the trigger of my Karabiner. I did not expect to hit him. But low and behold, I caught him in mid air and he fell dead to the ground. I ran up to where he fell, picked him up and saw that I had struck him right through the heart. Then I went back to hiding in one of the stalk bundles in hopes of bagging another hare.

After a little while I heard a noise beside my hiding place. Within two meters a hare was slowly hopping along, facing away from me. My gun sight was still set at one hundred meters; I did not expect one at such close range. The hare hesitated a moment and looked from side to side; I aimed a little below the white cottontail and pulled the trigger.

Upon impact he was immediately tossed head over heals before landing on his front feet, while his rear feet were stretched flat on the ground. He was crying like a baby and I felt so sorry about what I had done. I never knew that rabbits were capable of making any such sounds, for that matter, crying. I felt so guilty for harming that poor animal.

I made the decision to put him out of his misery by a quick blow to his neck with my gun butt. That killed him instantly. Then I took a look to see where I had hit him. It seemed that the bullet entered into his rear end and traveled inside his right upper thigh and exited at his knee. No wonder he could not hop away from me and must have been in great pain, that poor thing.

From that moment on I swore to myself to never ever hunt and kill any animal again. That piercing cry from the hare was so touching and made me feel so guilty, that I certainly was not proud of what I had done. But being a soldier I did not dare reveal my true feelings to any of my buddies or the farm people. God only knew how sorry I was killing His creatures.

Later I brought the hares back to the farmhouse and the lady of the house prepared them to be cooked for the next day's dinner. I proudly told the farmer how I hit my target from one hundred meters away while the hare was running. Of course he didn't believe my ability to do that with a Karabiner. He said: "Come on, don't tell me such an unbelievable story!" So I asked him to show me a nearby target to aim at and hit to prove to him that I could actually do it. He lead me to the back door and told me to look across the farm courtyard behind the barn where an antenna pole was standing for his radio. That pole stood about one hundred meters away from where we were at the back door of his house. Its wire was attached to a porcelain insulator, which was about one meter from the pole connected by another wire. He pointed to the insulator that was about the size of a chicken egg and told me to hit it.

He surely thought that I would miss that tiny target. But, since the wire was hanging directly above us curving down towards the house it was directly in the way of my sight in front of the insulator. So I told him, that one way or the other, the antenna will come down because aiming directly at that porcelain ball I would hit the wire first. But if

I barely missed it I would still hit the porcelain ball. I also told him to not be angry with me when the antenna came down.

Oh, go ahead, "It's alright, you will miss it anyway!" So I took aim, and fired…promptly, the antenna came down, while the porcelain ball dangled on the pole. When I saw the expression of disbelief on the farmer's face with his mouth wide open, I smiled at him. He swallowed and couldn't say a word, and I knew he was angry with me for what I had done. I had warned him that I could do it!

The next day the farmer and his wife had Mittagessen (Lunch) on the table for our group of six pilots. The farmer's wife told us that one hare weighed in at six kilos and the second one at slightly over five kilograms. (Twelve and ten German pounds). The wife was an excellent cook and her meals were always plentiful. She baked the hares and served them with potatoes and red cabbage as well as green peas. Home baked farmers bread was also served at the meal.

For me it was impossible to eat any part of the poor hares that I had killed the day before and was satisfied with just potatoes, peas, cabbage and bread and passed the plate with the 'meat' along to my table neighbor. My conscience bothered me for having taken the lives of those poor animals without thinking of the consequences, that still to this day I cannot forget. I can hear the echo of the hare's crying ringing in my ears as I reflect back to that day of hunting. I stuck to the promise I made to myself, never to hunt again and I never did in the future. The enormous guilt I felt for killing those pour animals will probably be never forgotten. I kept those thoughts to myself, so I would not be taken for a 'softy.' ….

….But, as it happened in the following three years, I would pay a dire price over and over again as punishment for the sins I had committed: And this was merely one of them. Maybe those years did chalk up some credit for some future misbehavior; well, only God the Almighty knows!

I surely did not have the slightest idea of what was waiting ahead for me. If someone had foretold me what I would have to go through, I would have deemed him crazy. No human being could withstand all that suffering and come out alive, - - - impossible!" As it turned out, I was ninety nine percent right….

The weather improved and we resumed combat flights with search and destroy missions. During the wintertime there were not many good days for us to fly. We flew in "Rotte" meaning, pairs. Whenever we spotted Russian planes we attacked and engaged in "dogfights."

One day towards the end of October I shot my first Russian down, and he too bailed out. It was merely due to the fact that my aircraft was far more superior to his. He was fortunate enough to have been 'downed' on his own territory, so he was spared from becoming a prisoner of war. That downing became my 3rd Victory. At the same time, my partner shot down two, and was also my witness as well as the recorded film in my gun camera.

My 4th Victory occurred on another good flying day early in November where we had high visibility. Once again another pilot of a Rata bailed out, this time on our territory, and he was probably taken as a prisoner of war. I never found out what had happened to him. On yet another good flying day we again engaged in a dogfight with more Russian Ratas. But this time we were eight planes. After some tricky maneuvers I achieved my 5th Victory resulting again in a bail out. A fellow pilot and my gun camera film confirmed it. Later I was able to view that film clip and it clearly showed the impact of the single 30 mm cannon shell right in the engine just behind the propeller as it burst into flames followed by the bail-out of the pilot and at the end of the clip the opening of his parachute was visible. Proof for another victory, but no "kill".

After this 5th Victory I was recommended to receive a medal. Paperwork was submitted to the Luftwaffe headquarters in Berlin for me to receive the Iron Cross, better known as the EK 1 (Eisernes Kreuz), First Class. It's design was about a 2 ½" Black Maltese Cross which was edged in silver. It had the raised numbers of the year 1939 on it to distinguish it from the WW I medals which had 1914 on them.

Two mechanics were always permanently assigned to each pilot and his plane. The one pair that was assigned to me way back in August near Aachen, were still with me and the Messerschmitt 109

G14 AS (Gustav) I was still flying thanks to the competent blackmen, as our mechanics in their black over-alls were called. Their names have escaped my memory. This was my aircraft for the entire time I served in the Luftwaffe until I either lost it in combat, had to bail out and let it go, or in an emergency landing it was damaged beyond repair. Then its undamaged parts would be salvaged and re-used to repair other planes. Getting spare parts from the factory was almost impossible at that time; railroad tracks, transport trains, and trucks were increasingly and constantly bombed and attacked by strafing Allied fighter planes and never made it to their intended destinations. There was turmoil everywhere. I was lucky that I never had to make an emergency landing during that time. But later in 1945, I did.

From then on we had inclement weather with some heavy snowfalls. The front was almost at a standstill. For quite a while there were many uneventful days and weeks. In January, at the beginning of 1945, we finally had a few days with good visibility to fly. Most were uneventful but I do recall a few skirmishes without success from either side. Some of my comrades and also Helmut Lipfert downed a few more Russian planes in skirmishes; at a few of them I served as his wingman. On other rare fine weather days that January, I was unable to down any more Ratas in combat missions.

February was another rather uneventful month with more bad weather, so most of my group decided to spend their spare time going hunting for rabbits, deer and or pheasants, but without me. I kept myself busy with other things, like taking care of my gear and helping my mechanics to keep my Gustav in shape. I had a persisting problem with my radiator flaps; they eventually located the cause of it and fixed it…. Towards the end of February the weather improved and we resumed flying missions over Russian territory but there was not much action.

On March 4th just before daybreak we were waken by an alarm sounded by a hand-cranked siren that we better get moving fast! We were outdoors sleeping in our tents, which were built over trenches. Potbelly stove heaters kept us warm.

During the night we could hear the quiet r-a-t-a-t-a-r-a-t-a.... of what we called the "sewing machines." They were the open cockpit biplanes that Russian female pilots were flying and dropping small bombs by hand from, just like it was done in WW I.

Those machines must have had "rubber bands" for engines; they were like the early flyers from the First World War. It seemed as though they flew just about anything that could take off and stay in the air! The Russians were "scraping the bottom of the barrel, just as we were. Their mission was to disturb our sleep so we would be too tired to fly our missions.

That day turned out to be a brilliant day with exceptionally clear visibility. We had increased the number of our planes to a group of twelve and took off. There was also a new shipment of replacement planes that had arrived from the Messerschmitt works to have some in reserve. My good old "Gustav" held out, served me well and never failed through it all. It always started up even in the severe cold weather. My two mechanics often worked through the night fixing any and all things to keep my beloved Gustav in shape. My life depended on their expert workmanship....

We took off and met the incoming Russian planes, which flew into our territory. We immediately engaged in dogfights.

A short time after being in combat with another Rata, my aim was a little off target, but I managed to damage his gas tank. He immediately "showed the white flag", as the jargon goes and dove down. He was losing gas but was not on fire and trailing behind him was a white stream of evaporating gas that created a long flag like image (similar to skywriting).

He dove down to tree top level in the direction of the front to get home. I followed him down but did not shoot at him because he would not have had a chance to bail out at that low altitude at treetop level, or for that matter, while at a steep dive. The fast slipstream would have hurled him against the vertical rudder while trying to leave the plane and he would have certainly gotten killed. I was not out to kill him. I wanted to get his forced landing into my gun camera as proof of another victory. I was hoping he would have to go down in our territory but he kept going, hedge humping with evidently enough gas to go on. I suddenly realized we were on the Russian side of the front.

Without warning, I saw tracers of machine gunfire shooting by me from the ground coming at me from the forward right direction.... at two-o-clock....

To explain what that means: When flying we always were heading from the center of an imaginary clock in the direction to 12 o-clock and while in combat or on any other flight we warned each other which direction an enemy plane was approaching using the imaginary image of the clock face. That way everybody knew instantly where to look to take evasive action. So, if an enemy plane came from behind, the warning from a fellow fighter would be: "Number 6 (my plane) a Spit' is coming at you from 6 o-clock!"....

My Parents Celebrating
Their 25th Wedding Anniversary

The Dulias Family. Our last get-together.
My Youngest Sister with "Schlusele"

Six

Captured, Becoming A Prisoner Of War

As I was passing over the frontline with tracers flying by right in front of me, I had no time for evasive action and I heard loud pings hitting my engine and saw the impacts and some debris hitting my windshield. The engine started to sputter as the cockpit immediately filled up with smoke, and I knew I was doomed. The first thing I did, was to jettison my canopy in order to be able to see and breathe. I quickly searched for a suitable spot to make a belly-landing. Luckily, I found a clear opening in the forested area and set my mortally wounded machine down on the snow covered flat ground.

Coming to a stop, I made a quick exit, ran away from my beloved "Gustav," and within split seconds it blew up. Immediately, I headed towards the nearby woods to hide. Following my training of the procedures for bailing out, I used my survival knife and dug a small hole in the forest ground to hide my documents, including a photo of me in civilian clothes from my last furlough wearing the party pin. I intended to hide in the woods until nightfall and hoped to make it back through the nearby front line. I still heard the crackle of exploding ammunition from my burning ME 109; it was my beloved Gustav's goodbye call.

I started walking by feeling my way through the forested area's thick underbrush. I did have a survival compass which had glow-in-the-dark directional points for N. S. E. W. and a glowing needlepoint top indicator. Besides that, I had my survival pocketknife and my Luger with thirty bullets. I continued to grope my way through the forest and it never seemed to end.

It was now beginning to dawn. I remained in hiding there in the forest when I heard some voices. Russian was being spoken. I found a secure place, and hid in the underbrush. I peeked through the branches and saw a group of six drunken Russians passing by. They passed perhaps twenty feet from me. I saw that they were soldiers, not civilians and they walked along a narrow path and I carefully observed their movement and then managed to advance forward on my way back towards our side.

As I kept stalking in the direction of the front following my compass direction and snuck past them, another troop came along and they spotted me. They yelled: "Stoi, Stoi!" meaning Halt, Stop! Unfortunately they spotted me before I did them. I guess I was better at navigating up in the air than on the ground! I had to hold my hands extended and outstretched above my head. They shouted commands in Russian to me that I much later got to know as derogative, dirty curses.

They were a mean bunch and I knew that they hated the *"Luftwaffe"* because of the great damage that was done to them by us. It was known that downed *Luftwaffe* Pilots were executed on the spot. They all pointed their Tommy guns (machine pistols) directly at me. Then one started talking and sounded as he was giving me orders.

I knew he was extremely angry as he was shouting at me, obviously due to the fact that we had a language barrier. I couldn't understand a single word. He began hitting me in the chest with his gun butt. I almost fell backwards and his stroke took my breath away. He motioned for me to walk and pointed to the direction they came from. As I passed him, he kicked me hard in the back and I almost fell forward. As I stumbled, the others cursed me too and then hit me with their gun butts. Finally I got knocked to the ground, yet they continued hitting, kicking and trampling me so hard, I almost passed out.

They probably would have killed me for sure if a Russian Major had not come up and stopped them, maybe it was their commander. He was a most impressive character. To my complete surprise, when he and I met face to face he spoke and addressed me in fluent German without the slightest accent. At the same time he spoke Russian to his soldiers. Thanks to God he appeared just in time to spare me from certain death.

The first thing he asked me was: "Are you the pilot of the plane that went down?" Confirming with a: "yes," he stretched his arm forward with an open hand and he said: "Give me your gun!" I handed him my belt and holster containing my *Luger.* He slid the holster off my belt and handed the belt back to me!

I believe he was from the same troops that were doing the ground fire that shot me down and now had searched and finally spotted me. I acknowledged his questions and was really impressed with the Major's command of the German language.

He asked me my name and rank and saw that I was a *Leutnant.* He also asked what type of aircraft I flew, although it appeared that he was knowledgeable about that already. He ordered me to march ahead of him to their field command station, which was just beyond the forested area, to the North. I walked ahead while the soldiers still continued cursing at me but the major gave them orders to stop that.

Later, at the farm house which I correctly assumed to be their post, one of the Russian soldiers approached me, pointed towards his wrist and shouted: "Ura, Ura." He pointed to a chain hanging out from my pants pocket. I happened to have my grandfather Dulias' open pocket watch on me. It was of a copper-golden tone but without a cover. So I had to give him the watch. He held it to his ear, listened to it tick and shouted: "Ura, Ura." with a smiling face, obviously happy to get that trophy. In return he gave me a piece of bread. He was friendly, not too demanding, not stern, but just had to have my watch. Perhaps it was a novelty to him that he had only heard about.

At that station I saw several German infantrymen also held as prisoners of war. They were guarded by a few Russians and were not mistreated in any way. For the first time I saw a few female Russian soldiers holding their guns. When they saw me they shouted out: "Fritz, Fritz", that was their nickname for any captured German soldier, as I found out later. In turn, the German nickname for the Russians was: "Ivan."

The major went into this main field post command, a farmhouse. One by one all newly captured POW's were called into the post be interrogated by the major. I was asked if I knew of any more German outfits (Tanks, artillery and so on) at or near the front. I couldn't answer, due to my real lack of knowledge. Basically all I revealed was the fact that from the air I saw some German tank columns approaching the front.

I was then asked if I was able to draw maps. I replied: "Yes." I knew I was skilled in doing that because I had already been copying maps for our own pilots because of a shortage; supplies had dwindled fast and replacements never made it to our field base.

So he led me to an empty desk in the room where Russian soldiers were busy working on copying maps and showed me what he wanted me to do. So now, I had to do for the enemy what I originally did for my fellow pilots; I had no choice in the matter.

Finally toward evening they gave me something to eat, as it was their suppertime.

A bowl of cabbage soup was my first meal as "guest" of the 'Russian workers paradise.' They called it: "Kapusta." I welcomed that warm soup, especially after not having had any food at all since leaving my base the day before. In the rush of leaving my plane I had forgotten to take my emergency rations with me. The "Kapusta" was rich with lots of green cabbage leaves and included some potatoes and a few other vegetables along with some morsels of meat. It tasted really good and reminded me of the good **Kohlsuppe** (cabbage soup) we had often at home as my mother had cooked it.

Looking into the bowl there were even big fat-eyes (circles of fat) floating at the top, that is what gave the soup substance and it felt so good to have this warm meal after the cold night I spent in the forest. I was happy to receive that along with a hunk of bread.

The bread was quite familiar to me as being **Komissbrot**. I believe this German army-bread was among one of their captured supplies. After receiving this welcome nourishment I had to go back to the "drawing board." I continued to stay there for the remainder of the day, as it was already getting dark. Later that night I was led to the adjoining barn where I joined the other POW's. I was shown the floor as my place to sleep. It was rather barren except for some straw and I fell asleep in my flight suit. It was not torn as I walked in the dark forest and had remained intact. I slept all through the night; I was really completely exhausted after that "busy" day. In the morning my whole body was hurting me from the gun-butt blows and kicks I had suffered.

The next morning, March 6th, the soldier who took my watch came back to me and said: "Ura kaput, ura kaput!" He showed me what he thought the watch was broken. He looked at me with a sad face as he handed it to me. I quickly realized that he didn't know that he had to wind it to make it go on ticking. So I wound it for him and handed it back. He held it to his ear and smiled and grinned and looked like he was dancing for joy as he shouted: "Ura karascholl, ura karascholl," meaning, the watch worked again and that it was okay.

Then another guard came and motioned to me to come out and walk ahead of him while he remained about ten to fifteen feet behind me, pointing his gun at me and swung it in the direction he wanted me to go, towards an open field. While stalking in the snow covered field, I wondered why he walked so far behind me and also noticed that he followed in my exact footprints along the open field, like Indians did on a warpath. At any moment I really expected to be shot from behind; was this now the end of my life? As I glanced back at him he motioned to me and shouted: "Edee, Edee,"---- meaning that I should keep moving and so I was wondering when the end for me would come and walked on, saying my prayers in my mind, asking God that it will be quick without suffering pain.

I kept walking but nothing happened until we reached the obvious intended destination. To my great relief we came to another farmhouse that maybe was another such office post in a small village across that long stretched out open field. Once there I noticed a group of about eighty German prisoners of war, all were infantrymen. There were no recognizable men from the Luftwaffe. One of those Germans pointed to the field and asked me if I had come across it to get there.

To my horror and sudden realization of the danger I had been in, he told me that I had crossed a minefield. I almost passed out from that shock, that came right after I was so glad I did not get shot in that field by that Russian soldier. I was used as a "guinea pig" without knowing it and surely had expected to get shot from behind!

Now I knew why the guard was so far behind me, stepping into my footprints. Once again my life was spared My Guardian Angel led me through that minefield without harm. It was another "miracle" that saved my life.

Those German prisoners increased to way over one hundred as more POW's were herded into our group. For a roll call we had to form three lines. We were then counted two and three times over, as a guard walked down the lines counting and writing in a notebook. Then we were ordered to march towards the South, away from the front. Following our column were four horse-drawn supply wagons loaded with kapusta and captured German ***Komißbrot*** (Army bread) and other supplies that were covered with tent-canvas sheets. Following those wagons was another team of horses pulling a very familiar and surprising for us, German ***Goulaschkanone*** (Field-kitchen a.k.a. Goulasch cannon). It was comforting to know, that we would get warm soup on our way, at least once a day, as it later turned out.

Those infantry POW's each had their army-issued ***Kochgeschirr*** (Alluminum-kooking- eating dish) and their army spoon / fork combos, which were not confiscated from them as were most other things they carried when they became POWs. Also they could keep their army ***Brotbeutel*** (Bread-sacks with shoulder straps). I did not have any of that equipment and was hoping I could borrow that from one of those who were fed first whenever we stopped to eat, or I would go hungry. Being fellow comrades, I did get to borrow that. Back at that first farmhouse –Command post I was given my kapusta soup in an enameled tin-bowl and a spoon, but had to give that back after eating the soup.

Among us were many untreated wounded soldiers, most of them were sick and feverish. It turned out to be the beginning of a "death march," as we continued until nightfall. Then we were herded together in an open field and we stayed there overnight sleeping on the cold ground.

The German field kitchen that came along with us was cooking kapusta soup.

It was nicknamed: ***"Goulasch Kanone,"*** because during World War I, as the French looked through their binoculars to observe German troop movements from a distance, something looked unusual to them. But what they saw were these rolling field kitchens going back and forth with their chimneys tilted down to intentionally fool those observing French soldiers; they really fell for that fake 'cannon parade'. They really took them for strange looking new cannons and reported back to their Command that the Germans now had new artillery. Hence the name *"Goulasch Kanone,"* that stuck with the German Army to this day. Those WW I field kitchens were still the same design and then used in WW II with very minor changes. Actually they were huge pressure cookers with 5/8"thick aluminum kettle walls and bottoms, hermetically sealed covers on hinges were equipped with safety valves and could be locked in place. It did not take long to cook a meal in them and easily could feed two hundred men. Those kettles were enormous.

THE DEATH MARCH

The next morning the guards shouted: "Payjom, Payjom!" Get up, let's go, let's go! Three or four of the wounded and sick POW's did not get up--- they were dead. The guards just left them there in the field. After being counted again several times over, we marched on the partially muddy road. The snow was melting and mud-puddles were everywhere. Our march was leading us back farther into the hinterland, the area far beyond the front. While underway, some of the sick and wounded were unable to continue or had passed out. They just dropped where they were in the marching column and were dragged to the side of the road by a guard and categorically shot with several single rounds on the spot and were then further kicked off to the side of the road to make sure they're dead.

From one of those poor dead fellows I took an Army issue bread bag. It had a looped strap to easily sling over my shoulder across my chest. Inside the bag I found a shawl, a pair of socks and some Army newspapers. The shawl and socks came in handy for the cold nights and windy days. We continued marching all day long without food. At nightfall there was another roll call, as our numbers got smaller by the dead ones left behind. Each morning and evening they held roll calls. We were counted several times over and registered in a notebook. In the evenings we got our now familiar kapusta and bread. That kapusta soup was about the same quality as what I was served the first time at the Command post, not bad! And the thick slice of German *Komißbrot* was welcomed as filler.

On the third or fourth night of our march, the guards happened to find an abandoned farmhouse with a barn and stable. That was the first night we found shelter with a place to sleep under a roof. It was a welcome relief after so much marching and sleeping out in the open. I was lucky to be assigned to stay in the main farmhouse and it was still fully furnished.

We slept on the floor and while I was lying there I looked around the room. My eyes gazed upon a collection of books on a bookshelf right by my head and that sparked my curiosity. I was able to read the spine from one of them printed in gold letters, it looked quite familiar to me: *"Altes Und Neues Testament Die Heilige Bibel,"* (Old and New Testament the Holy Bible).

I slipped it off the shelf and opened it up. It was completely printed in the German language and on the first blank page I saw a handwritten dedication by a father to his son. I don't remember their names, but as I recall, it was in a neat handwriting in the old German *Sütterlin* type, that I had learned at public school. The pages of the Bible were rather thin and were edged in gold. So I decided to keep my find. It fit nicely into my bread bag. The size of the Bible was about eight inches wide by ten inches in length and had a spine about two inches thick. Besides that, I found a small black and white photo picture, which showed a quaint town with its church tower with an arched gate, along with a few blank pages of paper from a notebook, I took those along too. Some of the men collected old newspapers lying around and kept them as well. They were old German papers, so I took some too from a pile in the corner.

The next morning, after only one night of shelter, there was the usual roll call and then we continued marching on. Every day more and more men died of their wounds; some of the weak guys who couldn't go on were shot where they dropped. Some were bleeding to death. Others who were never treated for their injuries had developed gangrene and died. It was a pitiful sight but there was no turning away from it, and I cooperated in every way, just to survive. The fallen wounded and or deathly sick comrades each received a "mercy" shot in the back of the neck. The guards made sure they were dead, then left them there. They couldn't be buried. The ground was still frozen hard underneath the melting snow and thin layer of mud.

On our way we saw here and there bloated carcasses of horses lying frozen on the side of the road among burned out Russian and German tanks, trucks and other vehicles. Frozen soldiers both Russian and Germans were sticking out of the melting snow. It was a gruesome sight as we marched on and more of our sick and wounded fell victim to the same fate.

One of the guards pulled me out from our group and motioned me to sit down at the side of the road. I surely assumed again that it was the end of me and I would be shot, like so many of the wounded POW's. He pointed to my fur lined flight boots and said something in Russian, gesturing by pointing to himself. Much relieved, I realized he only wanted my boots. He removed his well-worn ones and slipped into mine. Satisfied with the obvious fit, he handed me his pair to put on. Surprisingly they fit me too and I was glad that this exchange was all he wanted and he wasn't going to kill me. "Edee, Edee!"… He shouted and I got up and re-joined our marching column. I didn't mind the holes in my 'new' boots because I was still alive and not dead on the side of the road. Instead, later on at a short rest stop he came to me and handed me a big piece of **Komissbrot** and a handful of machorka. Pointing to my "new" boots he smilingly asked: "Karascholl?" (It's OK?) I nodded and smiled back at him, so glad and relieved to still be alive.…

All this reminded me of when many years ago, in school at English class we learned a song that now came to me. Our English teacher also served as layman in the Lutheran Church and was very religious. He chose that English hymn to teach us the language, as well as Religion. That song is still sung in churches today. It is called "Onward Christian Soldiers." The words go something like this: "Onward Christian soldiers, marching on to war, with the cross of Jesus going on before."------ So, I kept marching on…on to a victory, because I was determined to do it with God's help…

…Some days we were given a small portion of tobacco about the equivalent of a heaping tablespoon. It was called "machorka" and yes, we were permitted to smoke. In Russia, machorka was the poor man's tobacco. It consisted of dried tobacco plant stalks that were ground down to resemble leaf tobacco, which was seldom, if at all affordable by the poor of the Russian population and the lowly soldiers. Our guards were puffing this machorka constantly. They self-rolled their reefs using rough Russian newspaper pieces and to me, a non-smoker, that stank to high Heaven.

The men who had earlier collected newspapers were able to roll their own portions too. I did not smoke at all, but I had a different idea. I thought if I traded my portion of tobacco with another prisoner for his piece of bread or for "another tin-can of Kapusta" I was able to enrich my own food ration, which in turn, was an important factor for my continued survival. My tobacco-addicted comrades were more interested in smoking than eating. I thought to myself that it was not very smart of them, but it was to my advantage, so I kept quiet… it was their business, I did not want to discourage them..

…The "Death March" lasted about a week, maybe even more, I can't remember.

I did not recall exactly as the days were repeating themselves day after day with roll calls, more men dying as we marched on and eating the same food, Kapusta and bread. Finally we arrived at Jasbereni, a town approximately sixty to eighty kilometers south of Budapest where the Russians had changed the width of the European rails to their wider Railroad system.

At the railroad station was a long train of cattle cars waiting for us. We found many hundreds of other German soldiers already loaded into it. The empty train came from Russia and when not in use to transport prisoners, it was used to re-load and transport dismantled German and Hungarian factories that came by freight trains of the European type and size to Jasbereni. The machinery, parts and supplies were loaded onto their trains to be transported to Russia. I noticed that many of the machines on those trains parked on sidetracks at that train station, were not properly stored or protected from the weather, they lacked waterproof coverings and were totally covered in rust. What a careless waste that was! Those machines were surely completely useless once they arrived at their intended destinations.

Each of our cattle cars had been loaded with one hundred soldiers. We entered them from sliding doors that were in the center of both sides of the cars. As you looked in, to the right and to the left, there were wooden platforms, or berths built about four feet up from the wooden car-floor. All four berths had a thin layer of straw as our "mattresses". The upper berths were centered between the floor and the eight feet high roof-ceiling. Twenty-five men were packed in each berth, fifty on each side of the car, counting the car-floor as berths too. The younger more agile of us POWs had to take the upper ones, the older and or wounded ones had difficulty climbing up those high platforms, there were no steps or ladders.

In the middle space, about eight feet between the two sides with the berth stood a potbelly stove that had a chimney pipe going straight out through the roof. A small metal bin filled with black coal was near the stove and a small pile of firewood next to it. Through an opening of about six inches width of one sliding door was a sort of gutter mounted in a downwards angle, sticking out a few inches from the side of the car, but on the inside was protruding about two feet in and a little over two feet above the floor.

Believe it or not, that was our toilet! Of course there was no privacy whatsoever. For the human excrement to be disposed of, you had to use a wooden stick to push that slush out down that gutter and let it spill onto the side of the tracks. To take "a leak" one had to stand and aim right but for the other bigger "business" one had to half squat and straddle that gutter and aiming was more difficult and often 'accidents' happened. Each 'perpetrator' had to clean up his mess. There was no such thing as toilet paper! The few of us who had collected some papers on the way to that village of Jaspereni , realized that our find was too valuable to use for that purpose. They used it to smoke their machorka, so other solutions had to be found to take care of that 'business'. We used some of the mattress straw. Also whatever else suitable could be found outside at the frequent stops of our train. Ten men at a time were allowed to leave the cattle car whenever stops were made to do their "business" at the sides of the tracks and whenever possible scavenge for more coal and or firewood as well as something to "wipe". That stick of wood being used to push the "big businesses" down the drain eventually ended up in the stove to burn when nothing else was left and available. It had to be replaced at the next stop, along with more burning material for the potbelly stove.

Each cattle car had one guard riding along with us. He of course had his sleeping place next to the warm stove and also had blankets to keep him warm. We in our car were always glad to get an older more compassionate guard, while in several other ones they had a few younger fanatic guards who were often cruel and used their gun butts to kick the poor fellows indiscriminately to let their anger out and steadily cursed at them. But most of the guards were much older men, perhaps they were unfit for front duty, they treated us kinder and more humanely. The train also had a passenger car for the guards who were routinely changed to give them rest. Sometimes we were not so lucky and got one of those communist trained bestially youngsters instead. Next to the passenger car there were three flat bed cars each loaded with a *Goulaschkanone,* a German field kitchen and a built-on shed for the cooks and supplies. Whenever our train stopped for the night we were fed our familiar kapusta and bread.

In the meantime I had 'acquired' one of the German *Kochgeschirr* containers and also a set of the spoon/ fork combos from one of the poor dead fellow POWs. I could now stand in line and get my Kapusta without having to ask someone to lend me his set.

And so the days and nights went by. We had long lost count and track of time and now never knew what day of the week it was....

JUST ANOTHER DAY AT THE GULAG

Along the route you could see more and more transports of factory equipment passing us on the way deep into Russia. We rolled mostly at night, because during the day our train was held at the stations sidetracks so that those 'priority' transports could go ahead of us. While we were waiting, parked at selected stations, more wood and or coal were given us to keep our stove warm and going. Because of all the delays I estimate that the trip took about six to eight weeks.... We really had lost our sense of time.

Every day several more sick and wounded died and simply got kicked off the moving train by the guards. No one ever knew what really happened to those poor souls!

We POWs counted ourselves lucky to get a steady diet of **Komissbrot** as well as Kapusta while on that transport. It must have been the very beginning of May when we reached our destination. The train was unloaded at **Grüntal** (Greendale) near Penza-oblast (Pensa) a town and big railroad station located at the Volga **(Wolga)** River in the Kazan region. We were marched to the POW camp known as the "Gulag," just outside town.

A Gulag was a forced labor camp where prisoners were held under inhumane and very primitive conditions. A high barbed wire fence was the boundary line of the prison camp. Our living quarters consisted of a stable-like post and beam structure, located half way underground in dug out trenches about fifty or sixty feet long. They were about six feet below ground level and about fifteen feet wide.

A roof starting at ground level and angling up at an about thirty-degree angle was built over them with tree trunks packed closely side by side and the cracks between them were stuffed with moss. A layer of straw and leafy thin branches of birch had been placed on top of that roof. It was then finished off with a layer of topsoil about one foot thick or more that came from the trench dugout soil. That 'bunker' was in a style similar to a root cellar or potato winter storage shelter. The disadvantage of this style of structure was that during a heavy rainstorm some water seeped through and you became often soaked with mud from the droppings. In the wintertime the roof became frozen and was therefore watertight. At that time large plastic sheets did not exist as they do today. That would certainly have prevented those leaks.

At both open ends of the trench there were steps leading down into our 'bunkhouse'. Heavy canvas sheets hung as end-walls and 'doors.' Inside on both sides of the 3-foot wide middle isle, there were posts carrying girders supporting the roof logs. Large two-story bunks made of wooden planks and crosspieces had been built between and attached to those posts accommodating about ten POWs on each story and were separated by two feet wide side aisles. Straw-filled mattresses covered each bunk.

The straw in them was already pulverized from the use of previous inmates. That of course didn't provide much cushioning so you felt the wooden planks under you as your weight pushed the 'straw' aside. There was no provision to heat our bunkhouse, so we had to rely on our own body heat. Each platform bunk held about ten men packed like sardines, and at first not more than three army blankets were provided to cover all. About one hundred men filled that entire "barrack" or bunkhouse. Later, one blanket could to be shared between every two men. Five Russian army blankets on each lower and upper bunk.

The latrine was located close to and along the edge of the barbed wire fence, about 50 feet away from our 'barracks'. It was built of a primitive open framework, (not sheltered with a roof like an "outhouse"). It was made of four to five inch thick logs and formed an "A" frame like structure. A thicker horizontal log fastened across the "A" frame was the toilet "seat." This "A" structure straddled directly over a large rectangular deep hole in the ground. The dimension was about ten by fifteen feet rectangular and about ten to twelve feet deep, possibly even more; it was impossible to tell, you couldn't 'look' through that "soupy slush" that also contained rainwater in the warmer times.

You had to climb up by way of several thinner horizontal logs, like a chicken ladder onto the thicker, fairly level and somewhat flattened log to sit down to do your "business". One had to lock ones feet behind the next lower ladder rung to keep your balance and not fall backward into that bottomless pit.

It had happened, that a guy fell down into that slushy mess and if nobody saw him to help pull him out, he came to a wretched end. I remember witnessing how one fellow prisoner, while sitting on that very primitive "toilet seat" excreted his entire intestines into that hole. He had become so emaciated from over-work and starvation that his insides just fell out, dropping out of him, like a string of rope. Crying and moaning in pain he tried to come down from the seat, but lost his hold from weakness or passed out and fell in and drowned there. That poor man just fell into a pile of shit, (pardon the expression) but as he was crying out in pain there was nothing anyone could do to help him. Especially not after he had submerged completely in that cesspit like into quicksand. What a dreadfully tragic death! They just left the body in there and I often thought that it could have happened to me! Every time I had to use that "facility", I was reminded of it.

That is how another soldier became "missing in action." His family never ever got to know what happened to him. He just vanished. I do not remember his name. I had to just deal with it, and be strong, think positive and continue trying to survive!

I still had my bread bag with the Bible and a few sheets of loose papers. Everything else got confiscated as we were '*filzed*' (searched) after entering the Gulag, including our **Kochgeschirr** and spoon / fork sets. The Russian guards just took a liking to them, perhaps perceived as 'fancy' utensils; better than what they themselves had. Instead we were issued tin cans and primitive wooden spoons. Whenever I had a rare chance, I would take the Bible out and read a few passages. My favorite book of it was the Gospel of Luke because it had that beautiful Christmas story in it and also because I was more familiar with it from school. I treasured that Bible and often reflected back to my being a young boy in **Osterode,** East Prussia attending religious instruction classes. It was a comfort to read it helped me to clear any negative thoughts from my mind. Prisoners were allowed to keep a Bible or prayer book but if they found us with any other written material, it was promptly confiscated, so we had to think of clever hiding places.

In the mornings our breakfast consisted of about a half tin filled of 'kapusta' that was nothing more than greenish water, you were lucky if you found a leaf of it in there, and sometimes a portion of Kasha. The

Kasha was made from barley and was more like a soupy puree, nothing like the way it should be, as a heaping spoon full of hot cereal.

The heads of cabbage that were delivered to the camp for our consumption were stripped of their limp outer green leaves and that was what they used for our soup. You were lucky if you occasionally found a leaf in your tin of Kapusta. The 'clean' heads of cabbage less their withered outer green leaves, ere regularly sold on the black market by the Russian camp personnel.

At night the piles of cabbage heads were loaded onto horse drawn wagons and taken from the camp. The camp personnel and guards were the ones benefiting from this deed of deception and theft. Those skimpy limp green leaves that we got to eat for lunch, if we were lucky to find one in our tins, were not nourishing at all especially if we were out doing hard labor. This starvation diet caused us to lose weight very rapidly.

The men smoked their machorka while I continued trading my portions for someone's bread, kapusta or Kasha. The guards also smoked and the prisoners copied their 'technique' of rolling their (reefers) cigarettes in newsprint. The reason smoking was allowed was to help keep up "morale." The men were willing to work with more effort to accomplish their daily workload and tasks if their addictive habits were satisfied.

Our workday began at five o'clock in the morning. Our first assignment was in the local Textile factory. They manufactured brownish-gray woven fabric, the type used for Russian uniforms. My first job was to pull apart the freshly sheared fleece of sheep and goats and sort them by color tones. Next we inserted them into a machine that converted the fleece into particles that would be spun into thread and then into cloth.

The final products were bolts of woven woolen uniform cloth fabric. An advantage of working there was that we were served lunch because we were working with civilians. They were mostly women of German descent from the local Volga *(Wolga)* region. Some of the women had young children with them.

I was able to speak with one little schoolboy who was maybe six or seven years old. I asked him if I could have something to write on. He gave me several small notebooks. Among them was one with graph paper which had squares less than one quarter of an inch in size. Another had a hardcover, and along with it a small colored red lead pencil. We all spoke with each other while working together but everyone was very serious about getting their jobs done, as "norms" had to be fulfilled. We were allowed to keep a swatch from the scraps of the newly produced fabric. I also was able to take a sewing needle and some thread that they used in a sewing machine.

For lunch we were served Kapusta in a bowl because we didn't have our tin cups with us. That Kapusta was definitely a better staple than the one given to us at the Gulag. Russian bread called "Kleba" was included with our lunch and it seemed to be from the same bakery that served our camp.

The flour was a mixture of mainly rye, barley, oats and wheat, which was ground together and included everything. All the waste of shells and spiny ends from the kernels (especially from the oats and barley) were included in the so- called "flour" mixture. That was then poured into oil drums about one third up. Then water and some salt were added almost filling the drum. The mixture was then stirred with a large wooden cooking utensil that looked like it was possibly an ore from a Volga River boat. Some sour dough that was kept from a previous batch of bread making was serving as the leavening for the new batch. This mix was constantly stirred and it looked like soup, with bubbles forming from the sour dough.

Once thoroughly mixed, they took bucket-like ladles and scooped the mixture into round conical shaped tin forms, filling them about three quarters full. Those tins were then shoved into brick ovens and baked for about three hours. Those that were filled too much ran over from the rising "dough." When done, after all that time baking, there was only a thin crust on top as well as the bottom and round sides. When the tins were emptied the bread was flipped upside down to cool and then cut into slices.

The inside of the loaves remained doughy and it must have contained about seventy percent water while the crust was of more substance. You could take the inside and squish it together. One guy even said: "Look at what we eat, clay!" So he squished it and threw it onto a wall and it stuck like a ball of wet clay.

Later on, when the effects from starvation began, you started to develop a condition called "scurvy." Your gums began to recede and your teeth loosened and could easily be pulled or fall out. Those spiny prickly pieces from the shells of oats and barley got stuck in your gums. Besides that, as those same particles traveled through your digestive track they caused more problems irritating your bowel movements.

The men moaned whenever they were on the "toilet." It became a sad daily reminder of that dreadful tragedy of the man who drowned in the hole full of shit. It was such an agonizing experience from "one end to the other" and there was really nothing you could do about it except to eat what they gave you and to do the work, just to survive! It seemed to take a harder toll on the younger ones because young Germans grew up during food-rationed times in the earlier War years. It was a fact that the older ones were able to hold out longer and remained somewhat stronger because of having had a more substantial diet before becoming POW's.

For another job assignment we went to the local forest and had to fell trees. We needed a lot of energy to work the hatchet and swing the axe. First we had to secure the cut-off long logs into a horizontal position clamped to two cross cleats of wood. Then we took a chalk line and snapped it twice directly over the log to create two lines of approximately one foot apart marking a beam to be hewn out of the log. Then we had to straddle that log and with a hand hatchet chopped grooves into the sides ending at the chalk line, straight down, spaced every six to eight inches.

By making grooves when the hatchet hit the wood vertically it snapped off and so created beams from the raw logs. I believe that in medieval times and also in the 1880s by the American settlers, beams were chopped in the same way for their log homes. These one-foot thick beam-logs with two flat sides were then transported by horse drawn wagon to the Volga River, (The Volga River empties into the Caspian Sea at the far away delta).

At the local riverbanks we later had to build box like honeycombs with those log-beams that were later to be filled with rocks. The purpose of that project was to prevent further erosion to the already eroded uneven shoreline that was destroying farmland, where the river sharply curved.

By continuing that project we had to build a movable platform so that eight men could stand on it to drive tree poles, like pointed telephone poles, into the sandy ground to secure the five foot high box structure. A ram, consisting of an oak log of four feet in length and two feet in diameter, with eight handles attached around it, was used as a "Jackhammer." It drove the poles into the sandy shore. Each of the eight men grabbed a handle to lift and then pull the ram down onto the tops of the poles. Working in unison the foreman started singing a type of Lumberjack song and we all tried to join in. That boosted the morale, well just a little.

It was all such a complicated and primitive way of getting the job done, especially to get the twenty-foot pole driven into the shore ground. It took almost all day to drive a pole but the honeycomb structure proved to be effective against further erosion and shore damage. As the poles were driven down, the platform had to be lowered step for step from a height of about fifteen feet and secured at the next lower level and that's what took so long. The eight foot square platform was secured to four double poles at each corner that were connected to each other by ladder rungs, allowing the platform to be lowered step for step on those rungs as the pole was driven lower and lower. Crossbars connected and braced the four ladder posts together to keep them steady.

One can imagine that this primitive procedure took a lot of time to accomplish our goal of driving those long poles down to the five-foot high level of the box structure to be even with its top. Each pole about every eight feet apart had to be driven into the ground along the length of the entire structure. Depending on the length of the river curve the boxes were built up to five and six hundred meters long, (eighteen hundred feet).

For each and every job there never was a fast or easy way to get it done. Everything was so primitive and old fashioned. We were working two men per log beam with one starting on each end to chop beams out of logs…

While grooving the beams with the hatchet, my partner who was about the same age as I was, made a wrong swing and the hatchet landed diagonally into his right leg and cut his shinbone apart, just below his knee. Because of the frosty nights, the trees remained somewhat frozen. It seems that guy didn't have any experience about how to handle the hatchet. His leg dangled away from him and a couple of other POW's and I had to lift him onto a horse drawn wagon to a hospital in the town of Penza. He remained conscious but was moaning in pain. A guard was driving the wagon and I had to accompany the poor guy, and sat next to him while securely holding his leg up, which we had temporarily bandaged and braced. His muscles remained in tact. He was hardly bleeding but his bone had popped out from his skin and I could see the bloody bone marrow. There were no words to describe what I had seen and I never found out what had happened to him.

After delivering him to the hospital, I was driven back to the work site and continued chopping because I had to fulfill my daily "norm" in order to earn my five hundred grams of "clay" bread. I did not receive my bread that day because I was unable to fulfill the 'norm" without my partner.

Back at the camp at night we were supposed to get the promised ration of five hundred grams of bread. Instead, we were told we did not fulfill our required tasks, so we only got one hundred and twenty five grams of that lousy so called "bread." But we considered ourselves lucky if we got a nice crusty end piece. Each portion of bread was actually put on a scale for exact weight. Supplements were attached if the portion was under the required weight. The daily ration was exactly one hundred and twenty five grams, a quarter of a pound.

It was more than enough to endure the agonizing hardship of living in a prison camp as a Prisoner Of War and being forced to fulfill daily tasks of hard labor with very little nourishment. But there was also the darn fact that I had to earn that food!

Worse than that, was the fact, that the daily constant reminder was right before my eyes, it was the worst possible scenario: That death was final and there was no coming back.

I was already living through a hell on earth. The grim and gruesome site that was most upsetting was right before my eyes every day....

On May 10th, 1945 when the European part of WW II ended, a speech was given at a roll call held by the Russian Camp Commander. The resulting count: <<<< 4864 >>>> prisoners present at our campsite. "The war is over!" He called out and promised us that we would be returning home soon. ***"Scora Damoi"in Russian.*** This "good news" turned to bitter disappointment as days became weeks and weeks became months and months eventually turned into years without any action or intention of sending us home. ... No wonder, that in the spring of 1946 only >>>> 348<<<< POW's were left in our camp.

Starvation and illness took its toll on the majority of the prisoners in a very short period of time. Each and every day forty, fifty or more of our fellow comrades were found dead in the morning. All were victims of the severely harsh and inhuman treatment we had to endure. The slightest onset of an illness overpowered the already weakened immune system of the overworked POW's, resulting in death.

I remember, as I was lying next to an older comrade, (my blanket partner), on the crowded multi-occupied bunk and trying to get some sleep, that he just kept coughing. I had to turn my face away from his constant coughing, while I held my breath so that I would not inhale any of his germs. I was terribly afraid that I would also get sick. When the coughing finally stopped, I fell asleep.

In the morning, there was his cold and stiff body at my side, a victim of pneumonia. It was a horrible sight seeing him there with a wide-open mouth and open glazed eyes. Just terrible! This was happening all too often throughout the camp.

The piece of scrap material that I could keep from the textile factory I wore wrapped around my chest, over my shirt. Every day it was of great comfort and kept me warm.

I continued to trade my portions of Machorka for either a piece of bread, another 'bowl' of Kapusta or some Kasha. On day I considered myself lucky for finding a small bone in my Kapusta still containing some marrow in it and sucked it out. It could have possibly been part of a leg bone of a sheep or goat. It was extremely rare to find a morsel of meat or bone in the 'soup', so I kept my find because I thought it might eventually be useful for something.

I read my Bible every day, especially my favorite Books from the New Testament: Matthew, Mark, Luke and John. The Bible and all my small possessions that I had acquired over time were kept in my canvas bread bag.

By the late Spring (early Summer), we were assigned to work on the "Kolchose," it was a state owned farm. The land had been confiscated from the former owners of those farms. They were allowed to keep their farmhouse and a small parcel of land as a backyard. And then they were forced to labor at their former own land for the state and for the "common good".

Our job was to plant seed potatoes. To start with, huge bulldozers had plowed the wide spread fields. Each of them pulled a thirty-foot wide multi-plowshare assembly. Then each gigantic bulldozer pulled an arrangement of harrows about thirty feet in width over the plowed fields to rake them loosely smooth. Our work group consisted of about one hundred men. We were ordered to form a wide line shoulder-to-shoulder. Each one of us had a shoulder bag (sack) of seed potatoes that had to be planted. We worked in unison stepping forward foot by foot in a straight line and deposited a seed potato into the ground

We used a wooden cone-shaped two-inch thick stick to punch a hole into the ground. Then dropped a potato in and used both hands to cover the hole making a small hive of soil above it. While we were working in that way, the guards were facing us from about fifteen feet in front of us, shouting commands and cursing at us. They were watching us closely to make sure that we didn't dare eat any of the seed potatoes.

When some guys indeed ate some, they were struck hard with a gun butt and knocked down, kicked and cursed at. They angrily yelled things like: "Edee na chui jobt foju maat,"(but that is certainly not suitable for me to translate here), and other such obscenities including one with utter disrespect to the mother of Jesus, Mary. This went on continuously all day long, day after day.

Those guards were a bunch of "Barbarians!" Mostly they were young Russian soldiers, fanatic communists, thoroughly indoctrinated into their system! We were always glad when we had older Russian guards and considered ourselves lucky. They had more compassion for us and even gave orders in a friendlier, humane manner. Guards were constantly rotated in their assignments. This potato planting took a few weeks; and later we were assigned new tasks. Where any slave labor was needed, we were sent to do it.

One very strange incident I do recall while we planted those potatoes during the many bright sunny days. On one of those days, all of a sudden it got strangely and gradually dark and darker; we experienced a *"Total Eclipse Of The Sun."* That was on July 5, 1945.

(My co-author Dianna Popp researched that occurrence in that time and particular region of Russia)

It was an eerie, almost total darkness that lasted for quite a few minutes and then gradually it became brighter again. We were all awed and wondered about that occurrence.

One of our older guards was evidently scared by that happening, pointed up to the sky shouting something in Russian, obviously frightened. A fellow POW who was fluent in Russian started to laugh hysterically and told us what that guard was shouting: "Look, look, the Moon is eating the Sun!"

This surely was a once in a lifetime occurrence for all of us and we later often spoke among ourselves about how that day became suddenly a night for a while.

Once a month we were marched to a de-lousing facility. There we had to strip naked and put our uniforms and underwear in a bundle onto a metal hook. Footwear was lined up on the floor, but I no longer had the pair of boots that I had to "exchange" earlier, during the Death March.

Now most of us had a pair of canvas shoes with wooden soles. The canvas top was nailed to the sole and since the stiff wood could not bend, eventually the canvas separated at the heel and often had fallen totally apart from the stress of walking. So, for a while I had to walk barefoot, until later when I received a replacement.

I recall that at the potato-planting job site there was still rye stubble from the previous year's harvest on part of a strip of the ground that had not been plowed. Those rough, sharp and pointed stubbles pierced the tender parts of the soles and tops of my feet. To avoid more punctures from stubbles while walking to the freshly plowed side of the field, I did not lift and place my feet down.

Instead I dragged my feet while at the same time pushing those thorny-like stubbles down flat to avoid being poked deeper. That reminded me of seeing British soldiers parade-marching in a movie in that style. It was agonizing and my punctured and sore feet became infected. Still today one can see traces of remains from the infected sores on my feet, as a result of it…

BACK TO THE DE-LOUSING DAY:

The bundles of clothing were hung up in rows in a hot-room where the temperature was raised to a degree that could exterminate lice. While that was being done, we walked into the large shower room where pipes hung across the ceiling with numerous showerheads attached. We all showered simultaneously in a fairly warm water stream, and occasionally got a small cube of gel type soap. When done, we drip dried because towels were unheard of. We received a clean set of underwear, but before putting them on we had to search all the seams for lice and eggs. If we found any, we squished them with our two thumbnails, and they popped.

The under garments were not of a soft quality. They were made of a cotton bed sheet material. You pulled the long sleeved undershirt over your head and it had an opening at the neck and one at the ends of the sleeves that you would tie-close, as there weren't any buttons. The under pants were the length of long johns and they also had a slit at the calf with laces to tie.

I was fortunate enough that lice never took a liking to me, so I never needed an in-between de-lousing, and never picked lice up from anyone else either. Also during this process our heads were shorn to the skin. Those who had a lot of body hair had to be clean-shaven over those areas.

In addition, everyone's pubic hair had to be shaved off. As time went on I felt a completely bald spot on the rear top of my head. I asked the other men to take a look and it was confirmed that an area about the size of a dollar coin was indeed bare. Our fingernails did not present any problem because they were worn down by hard labor and they were anyway thin and brittle from malnutrition.

Once all of this was completed, you then put on a clean uniform. You never got the same one back that you came in. Each time it was mix and match, bits and pieces, diverse uniforms were constantly being changed and exchanged. You never knew if you would receive something, which had been worn by the Hungarians, Polish, Germans, Yugoslavians, Finns or even the Italian or Spanish prisoners. 'We were all in the same boat' whether dead or alive. One time I was given a German uniform; its jacket had a bullet hole in the back of it and bloodstains that had resisted numerous washings.

The next work assignment was going back to the same forest area that we had been working in before, when we cut down trees and chopped beams from. Now we were given new work assignments and being paired in two men teams. They assigned a staked out piece of land for us, roughly about six by six feet, about two meters square. Using a pick and shovel we had to dig straight down, to a depth of about four feet, there was a horizontal layer of granite-like stone. It was about two to three feet thick and with the pick and also fist-hammer and flat stone chisel we had to break the layers apart, then excavated the loosened flat granite-like slabs-chunks to the ground level.

They had to be stacked up into cubic meter form and we had to pack them tightly with very little space between them. The 'norm' for the two-man team was to produce two individual stacks of one cubic meter each, side-by-side. The guards checked to see if each pile was properly stacked up, if not, they knocked it over and we were ordered to re-pack it tighter.

We were constantly strained to achieve our daily norm to earn five hundred grams of Kleba, but could never reach that goal. When a team almost came close to it, the daily "norm" was immediately raised to an unreachable level, thus condemning us to subsist on only a one hundred and twenty-five gram doughy, wet slice of the so called " bread" and the greenish water, called kapusta. No wonder our slave-laboring work force dwindled to smaller and smaller numbers. Also the long workdays of up to nineteen hours sped that pace up.

While at the Gulag, we often talked among ourselves. Some men had heard rumors that there possibly had been some sort of pact/ agreement among nations establishing Prisoner's rights. If that was the case, we certainly had no such rights! The five hundred grams of bread was not supposed to be earned by hard labor, it was to have been issued as a standard fare for the day. Whether we worked or not, it was to keep us alive in a humane way. Also we were supposed to get a daily ration of sugar.

The Quakers from America had been sending vast amounts of gift food shipments to prisoners all around the world. I know this for a fact because I saw the empty cartons and read the printing in English saying so; I could interpret it, because having learned that language at school. We never got any of it, yet those cartons were lying "empty" on the garbage piles. They used those gift-food shipments for themselves and or sold it on the black market. The Russians gave us only the sugar as our 'regular' ration and not as an extra supplement as it was meant to be by the Quakers. All that happened due to the corruption going on within the individual camp managements.

Perhaps to some extent the Russian government didn't know that was happening in the camps, we never saw any inspectors who could have kept that corruption in check.

If they in fact had sent inspectors, they ignored it because it was a common practice throughout the entire system and we got caught on the short end of it. Of course, that resulted in the POW's suffering and ultimately death caused by this wide spread greedy, tolerated corruption!

I also saw large empty wooden barrels of curded butterfat that was also labeled as given by the Quakers. The individual camp personnel deprived us of what we were supposed to be given as humane gifts. As I told that to my fellow sufferers, all then knew what was shamefully going on here.

One of our comrades was a History teacher before he was drafted into the **Wehrmacht,** he told us that in 1864 there was a Geneva

Convention in Switzerland, establishing the rights, rules for and treatment of prisoners of war. Also in 1899 The Hague, Netherlands Peace Conference established a Permanent Court of Arbitration for the treatment of prisoners of war and was further defined in 1907. But the Russians didn't care, they exploited us in any way they pleased.

It was about that time; maybe after about five months of camp life, that I was approached by some of the smoking addicted fellow prisoners. They had noticed me reading my Bible and they wanted me to part with a few pages from it to roll their machorka into 'joints'. At first I was reluctant and didn't think that would be a good thing to do. I gave it a lot of thought because I cherished my Bible and prayed about that as well. But driven by hunger I finally gave into them. Slowly I sacrificed a page or two from the Old Testament part of my Bible. I did not quite understand it at that time and took that part mostly for a conglomeration of unintelligible sentences that made no sense to me. So since it was obviously useless to me to try to understand it, I thought it would be a good idea to trade a page or two for a portion of Kapusta, a piece of bread, a spoon of Kasha or spoon-full of sugar to stave off some of my constant hunger.

I prayed for forgiveness to God as I watched page after page from my Bible actually "Go up in Holy Smoke!" I was so happy to get that extra nourishment and in this way to sustain my life along with the additional trade from my issued portions of machorka. In fact now I was running a mini barter system of a trade business and at the same time playing a game of strategy to stay alive.

I felt so guilty about taking food from my comrades because I knew what their ultimate fate was. But after praying for forgiveness, I felt, that God gave me that opportunity, because as a non-smoker I was not abusing my God-given body. After making these trades, I must admit that the quality of paper from the Bible was far superior to the newsprint and packing paper they had been using. It produced a more preferred aroma (almost like a pleasant smelling incense), from the burning hand-rolled Machorka joints, than the stinky others.

We estimated that in the Penza region alone there were at least twenty-five separately operated Gulags. Each one originally held between four to five thousand prisoners. That gives one some idea as to how many men the Russians actually had to feed. But for their cost of that "food" they got way more than a hundred fold returns in accomplished slave labor.

Among us we discussed the various facts we knew or heard from others regarding these numbers. When a prisoner was transferred from a hospital back to a camp, it was not necessarily to the same one where he came from. This way we were able to find out more about what was really going on in the other camps and places.

A few prisoners who were transferred to our site came from the Moscow area. They shared information with us about where they had been and what went on there. Around Moscow the Russians had set up so called "Parade Camps," for inspection purposes by dignities and or foreign reporters so the rest of the world got to know how "well" the prisoners in Russia were treated. In those camps the POW's were served better food, and received better care and treatment.

It is my belief that the top "Ace of Aces," Major Erich Hartmann, with his confirmed three hundred and fifty two air victories was able to survive ten years there only by being in one of those camps. For example, in the Gulags where I was confined in, he could never have survived for that long....

Later, when by the Grace of Gad I had returned home, I got to know how Erich Hartmann became a POW of Russia: Fearing that he surely would be executed for the anger he caused the Russians of having downed three hundred fifty two of their planes, he deliberately surrendered himself together with a few of his group to the American forces.

The unbelievable fact, that they turned Hartmann over to the Russians, was for the German people and me an unfathomable act of cruelty. But the Media kept that quiet and even today, when I mentioned that to my friends here in the USA, I saw utterly surprised and shocked faces; they absolutely could not believe that. But by researching this fact it has been proven to them by accurate History books and documents. That's politics for you. Who was actually responsible for that? I have never been able to find out and now all that is forgotten, as if it had never happened.

…As in time the real truth about that cruelty became widely known to the German people. That act certainly didn't earn the United States any roses in the eyes of most of the older Germans. Despite the Marshall plan help for the hungry, the enormous shipments of food and the humane help by various organizations, like Caritas Church groups, etc., that resentment took a long time to eventually be forgotten.

The relentless bombings left much of the older population homeless and for a long time they could not forget the senseless losses they had suffered by the "***Ammies***", as the Americans were called. In contrast, the younger generation of Germany easily made friends with the American soldiers. The older generation held Erich Hartmann in their memory as their celebrated hero, he was the Ace of Aces. Nobody in this world had achieved more air-victories, than ***Bubi*** Hartmann (their nickname for him) because he looked much younger than he really was, he was their boy hero.

Another "task" of ours was working in a stone quarry, or a better description of it would be: Stone Processing Plant. Earlier I mentioned that we had dug up layers of granite stone in the area where we felled the trees and also made the hand-hewn beams for the reinforcement along the Volga River bank. Following that, we had to load those "harvested" stone slabs onto trucks to be transported to that plant....

Those "trucks" were all American Studebakers, given to the Russians by the Lend / Lease agreement with their then American Allies. The help they received with that agreement was a tremendous military advantage for the Bolsheviks. The thousands of tanks, air planes, trucks, jeeps, ships and weaponry enabled the Russians to gain time to replace their losses the Germans had afflicted them with. So they could continue their offensive and kept advancing towards Germany.

....After they were transported to that processing plant the slabs were unloaded to form huge piles. A huge stone crushing machine that produced gravel to be used as roadbeds was located there. But the machine could only accommodate stones no larger than the size of a man's fist. So, our job was to take those slabs and by using a three or five pound fist hammer, knock those slabs into smaller pieces and then load them onto rail carts that could be tipped and unloaded into a pit at a lower level.

At the bottom of that pit was a conveyor belt that 'fed' the stone crusher. Chutes of wood planks guided the dumped stones onto the moving belt and it transported them up to the crusher machine's holding bin. From there another chute dropped them into a rotating crusher.

At the other end of the crusher were huge rotating sieve drums that sifted the gravel and sorted it according to size. One quarter inch pebbles, one half and three quarter to one inch were piled by yet another conveyor belt onto separate heaps, each in it's own bin. Out of the end of the rotating sieve drums the larger stones up to two or three inches in size dropped into a larger collection bin. So there were five different sizes of pebbles besides finer sand for the roadbeds and asphalt production.

Next to the crusher plant was an asphalt plant that received the sand and finer saved fragments, produced by the crusher as well as the quarter to one half inch pebbles. They were turned into asphalt as topping to the layers of ***"Schotter"***, the German word for the rough stone bed material of the newly built roads.

THE WAY ROADS WERE BUILT IN RUSSIA "(VERY INTERESTING)"

First the grading of the general straight staked out dimension of the road being built was done by us slave laborers with picks, shovels and rakes. A leveling-plank that had   attached handle bars and was resting on imbedded level wood rails along the side edges of the new road, was shoved back and forth across the width of the road while slowly moving in the direction of the yet unfinished part, pushing the access of the sandy soil forward in the same direction. Thus a fairly smooth and level base was created in this primitive way.

The leveling plank's bottom edge had an imbedded upside down steel T-bar so it would not wear out as it was shoved back and forth along the wood rails. If too much of the pushed soil slowed the process down, than some guys with shovels had to lighten the load by removing enough of it to enable the 'shoving' crew to work the leveling plank forward.

Road-grader machines as we know them here in modern times, did not exist way back then. Occasionally, when some hilly sections in the mostly very flat and vastly treeless land were hampering our way in the already slow paced advance of building the road, some of the big farm bulldozers were put to work. They helped us to roughly push the bulk of soil out of the way and the rest had to be done by our men with shovels and rakes in the described way above.

That road base as well as all following layers of the roadbed material, the diverse Shotter layers starting with the two to three inch stones and gradually smaller ones and also the two layers of asphalt were "steamrolled"…. And now comes the unbelievable funny part:

Well, it may be funny for the reader of the description of this primitive work and equipment in Russia, but for us "Voina Plenies" (Russian, translation: War prisoners) it was a bitter reality to endure all that slave labor and especially the constant hunger.

The " Steamroller "

The special "steamroller" was a huge heavy-duty steel drum about four feet high and six feet wide, it was filled with water for weight. A moveable long shaft was attached to the axle of the huge drum. The shaft was equipped with ten attached handles that made it possible to pull the roller by ten POW's. By the "steam of the sweat" of those ten POW's they pulled that 'thing' back and forth over each applied layer on the roadbed.

An open trough attached above the drum of the roller had to be constantly filled with water that then dripped onto the roller, as an attached scraper kept the drum wet and clean while rolling asphalt. What a "modern" contraption that was!

Later, after other crews from neighboring camps worked on that road, our group was again assigned to continue building it. I was then part of that ten-man steamroller crew. Believe me, our own sweat that was drenching our shirts really evaporated fast from our bodies in the form of steam as we rolled that monster to flatten each layer of the road material. We kept our shirts on, not to get sunburned. From time to time, large ladles were passed from man to man filled with the same water that was used for the trough above the roller. That was for us to drink, so "we would not run out of steam!"

On a hot day we had to change crews every hour, as we were quickly exhausted from this strength-sapping task. I forgot what the set "norm" was for a certain length of building roads that our crew had to produce. But you can be sure that we never were able to "earn" our five hundred gram portion of "Kleba" each day and had to make do with only one quarter of a pound ration each night. The Russians made sure of that, those bastards. I can't say it often enough, it was constantly on our mind, even in our dreams we were slavering and longing for more 'bread'.

So we were "involved" in every step of building roads, from mining the granite stone to the finished "product.". The only fairly modern devices at that time were the stone crushing- and asphalt plants, possibly counting the asphalt spreading machines and the huge bulldozers. All the rest of the work was accomplished by slave labor in a most primitive way.

In case one of our men dropped dead on the job, (It happened quite often), the guards would yell "Nitchewo, Nitchewo," (It doesn't matter). When we wanted to tend to the fallen comrades, the guards pointed their Tommy guns at us. They shouted "Edee, Edee," "Rabota!" which meant: "Go ahead and work!" It became harder and harder to endure the long hours of slave labor on empty stomachs and many POW's often passed out. Myself included, from pure exhaustion.

Our bodies became more and more emaciated from the radical "weight-reducing diet" of hard labor! In the late evening we had to march back to our camp. Often it was way over an hours march, depending on the distance we had to march to work each morning. There we received our "hard earned" ration of a tin of Kapusta and the doughy Kleba. We quickly ate it and totally exhausted we fell asleep on our bunk for the few hours of sleep they allowed us.

The "Payjom" call (Wake-up call) came much too soon, way before sunrise and the whole routine of another torturous day began all over again. We were so glad when Sunday came up, our day of "rest." But even then we had things to do. Like cleaning our barracks, and washing our sweat drenched shirts and underwear.

Late in 1946 we were allowed to write our first postcard home. We were supposed to get and send one per month, but often a month was skipped. We could only write exactly twenty-five words or less, we were told, or else it would never make it home. Those post cards were pre-printed double cards with the senders- and return address. One side of it was blank for the twenty-five words to write to our family and an identical one attached as an answer-return card for our loved ones to use in reply, also with only twenty-five words

We didn't have a pen or ink and only the rare pencil that one or the other had, made the rounds among us. Once again I had one of my "brilliant ideas!" Why not make my own ink and writing stick? From the workshop at our camp I obtained some iron file dust and mixed it in a spare tin cup with the juice from 'gall-apples'; those walnut size 'apples' were ball-like growths that could be found under numerous oak leaves. The grown oak trees around our camp produced quite a good number of those "acidy apples" and I had no trouble finding green and juicy ones, suitable for my new project. The acid juice mixed with the iron file dust resulted in genuine, nearly black ink. It didn't even smudge after the writing dried if it had accidentally became wet from spilled water. I used a dried oak twig with a carved point as my writing stick for my first card home….

I still have it today and display it attached to my picture poster that I always have with me at events I am attending and where I sell my book and autographs to the public visitors.

….At a later time I traded a page or two from my Bible and some of my ink for a penholder and pen from the metal worker that he had made at the camp workshop.

But at first I tried to fashion my own "pen" in a similar style from a thin stick of oak wood, which I carved with my homemade knife. I hammered the pen out of a sliver from an old shovel, a blade of steel, on one Sunday in the camp's workshop, but I was not too happy with it, it didn't quite work to my satisfaction. The pen that the metal worker made was perfect and I could write with it in a very fine print into my 'home-made' booklets.

Since I was making a good amount of ink I managed to trade some of my supply to fellow prisoners for some of the usual foods: Another 'bowl' of Kapusta, a piece of Kleba or a spoon of kasha or sugar and so saved my Bible pages for later trades.

At the tool shop there was a foot-operated grindstone stand. The rotating stone wheel was half submerged in an attached trough, creating a whetstone affect for sharpening our tools. Some of them were spades, shovels, picks, and yes, even knives as well as cold chisels that we used to separate layers of granite stones in our "quarry holes," as well as picks' points that needed sharpening. Our hatches and axes got sharpened as well when they got dull from use.

Come Monday, the workday routine started all over again. The only reprieve we got was when there was an extremely heavy and steady downpour of full day rain, which we welcomed. Then we could stay "home" in the camp, although we had to deal with the "mud" flopping down from the ceiling of our underground "barracks." And at each end of our 'bunkhouse' where steps led down to the floor level of our living-quarters, the rain collected when the gullies at the bottom were overflowing. We had to bail the water out up to ground level or we got mud floors inside, there was no wooden flooring installed.

The good thing was that we got "lunch" on those days, "a bowl (tin) of Kapusta." Green water or not, it was something to warm our stomachs, we didn't need spoons, sipping it out of the tin can did the job. The quarter pound of Kleba we got only once a day, after we returned from our workplaces, and in evenings on rainy days.

But on those rain days we were not as exhausted as on those hot sunny days when sweat soaked our clothes during those long hours of hard labor. During our march in the evening back to camp, the cooled down air did dry our shirts and pants, so we didn't take them off before going to sleep.

I remember one hot day, while laying asphalt on the new road that we were building; one of our fellow prisoners became seriously injured. For the two layers of asphalt of the road building we had a spreading machine. It distributed the asphalt evenly over the entire width of the road and rolled on rails, temporarily placed at both sides of the road. At the front of it was a long open trough in which a rotating worm-screw type of gear was located. It moved the hot asphalt from the center toward the sides of the trough, evenly distributing it. The worm gear was so constructed that one half of it spun to the left and the other half to the right, while the single jointed axle turned in just one direction. Studebaker dump trucks brought the asphalt and dropped the mixture slowly into the center of the trough. Thus, the machine spread it evenly over the entire width of the road because at the bottom of the trough was an open slot that by hand control widened and closed depending on what thickness the layer had to be. The machine rolled slowly forward on its rails as the asphalt was laid down in a controlled thickness. Before each truck dumped a new load into the machine two men had to shovel and scrape some misplaced asphalt back into the trough. I was one of the two men team assigned to do that job this particular day.

On this hot day my partner collapsed and fell rear-end first into the rotating worm gear. The machine operator stopped the gear in an instant. But unfortunately not before he could prevent the sharp worm gear from cutting deep into the poor victim's left buttock. It was almost severed from his body. It also tore his hipbone bare. This was an extremely gruesome sight! Not much blood came out of the wound but the terrible sight of the reddened flesh and the exposed bone was sickening, to say the least! We lifted the unconscious victim onto an empty asphalt truck that brought him to the prison hospital in Grüntal (Greenvale).

As a result of all the hard, physical labor, I developed a hernia in my lower abdomen. It was the size of half an egg and it had popped out from my lower right groin.

Building the road between Moscow and Stalingrad the lifting and placing those heavy iron rails for the asphalt spreader took its toll on me. Yes, that was my reward, something to take home with me!

You just had to accept and deal with those unpleasant realities in your own personal way. What a life we had, it was just "Another Day At The Gulag!"

JUST ANOTHER DAY AT THE LAZARETT (PRISON HOSPITAL)

With the continuation of those long days of hard labor along with the bitter cold of the winter I found myself physically getting weaker and weaker, although mentally I remained strong. The living conditions were extremely poor, and it continued with more men becoming sick and dying every day.

The standard fare of the same bland almost poisoning diet, was taking its toll on my health. When I say, "poisoned", I mean it literally! Sometimes we got rotten fish or almost decomposing, and stinking meat and bones in our daily portions of Kapusta. One time I fell ill from fish poisoning and felt so miserable and seriously ill. I was doubling over, as if I had to crawl on my hands and knees. For sure, I thought I would die from it and wound up once again back in the hospital to recuperate.

Usually during the de-lousing a doctor came around making inspections. It was at one of those days that the doctor pinched my skin, noticed the condition I was in and had me admitted to a hospital.

There occurred a series of 'ins' and 'outs' between my stays at the Gulag and hospital. Whenever I gained some strength back I was sent back to the camp, only to become weakened again in a progressively shorter span of time. I could not endure the constant fourteen to nineteen hours of slave labor. Sometimes only one week after returning from the hospital I fell back into the same situation of becoming weaker

and passing out. Sooner or later I landed back in the hospital.

At one of those stays in the POW hospital we were put on a scale to determine our weight. I arrived there weighing only 31 kg; that is 62 German pounds, the equivalent of about 67 American pounds (and I was six foot tall).

My muscles were so shrunken that just the skin was loosely hanging around my leg bones and arms. When I walked on the wooden floor, it sounded, as if I had wooden shoes on my feet, but it was the "klickety-klackety" of my foot bones, that had no more meaty cushions on them and it really hurt walking barefoot. Out at the Gulag I had stuffed some straw into my shoes to ease the pain of my bones carrying my weight on those hard wooden soles. When I laid flat on my back, I could count all my ribs easily and when I pushed my stomach in with my hands, I could feel my spine bones. I was a walking skeleton and I felt like a zombie, my memory was failing me. Sometimes I didn't know who or what I was and couldn't count one and two together. Later, after my return home I looked at my old school books and did not remember ever having seen them before…

By October 1946 we thought that we were going home. The Russians, (so the rumor went), had orders to clear out all the prisoners of war that were beyond the region of the Volga River. On October 17th the sick ones were put into a military prison hospital.

The others were spread into several camps. I counted myself as one of the "lucky ones" and was admitted to the hospital again. Unfortunately I was again completely malnourished and even had dystrophy, so I was to be admitted. Another year of hard labor and poor nutrition had finally taken its toll on my health. But being admitted to the hospital had its advantages and it gave me a few new possibilities. I was given some more freedom while I recuperated. I could roam from room to room visiting other comrades and also do things for myself.

So, using the few things that I had acquired earlier that I kept in my bread bag I was able to start a few projects. One that occupied much of my free time was creating small miniature notebooks that became my journals, as well as prayer and recipe books. I used what little paper I had, including the papers from notebooks that the schoolboy gave me when I was on my first work assignment as a prisoner working in the textile factory.

I cut the papers up, also the hard cardboard type covers and created miniature notebooks that measured not more than two by three inches in size. Some had graph paper and I wrote as tiny as I possibly could in the **Sütterlin** (German script), squeezing writings into the limited spaces. Those projects allowed me to be creative and also kept my mind active and working. My ink and the fine pen I bartered from that metal worker in the camp came in handy for my tiny lettering.

The hospital was a former schoolhouse, and the former classrooms were converted into wards. Some rooms had wooden bunk beds; others just had straw mattresses laid down in rows close together on the floor. I was assigned one of those mattresses alongside a wall. Each of us was issued a large warm blanket and a straw filled pillow. What a pleasure it was, to lie down on a mattress with lots of straw in it. Unlike the powdery filling of worn out straw we had in the camp.

Can you imagine, we even had our own blanket for the first time since becoming a POW? The pillow was also a first-timer! The big problem that existed was an abundance of bed bugs. Unlike the lice, they did take a liking to me when they came crawling out at night, I decided to protect myself against them.; it was another invention of mine.

I devised a way to remedy that situation: I folded my large woolen blanket in half and sewed the two open sides together, creating a sleeping bag. After I slipped into it, I pulled the third open end inwards creating my cocoon and tied it inside together with a string. That knotted end also cushioned my head, like an extra pillow. I was able to sleep undisturbed by those nasty bedbugs throughout the night. In the morning I came out of my cocoon without any bites of those pasty bedbugs. To the envy of all my fellow roommates, I was free of those swollen red welts that the bugs had caused. The idea of my invention caught on, and was then copied by many others.

Each room had a tall tiled heating oven. It was almost identical to the ones we had in **Königsberg** while in the lower apartment of the **Werkstättenstrasse**. Each day a wood fire was started for about two hours and the oven never got cold. It gave off twenty-four hours of heat continuously and its ashes remained hot and glistening. So we were in a comfortable warm environment despite the forty something below zero temperatures outside.

The food was by far so much better than what we had gotten at the Gulag. Now our bowls of Kapusta really had substance. Plenty of cabbage leaves along with potatoes and vegetables were in it. Even morsels of meat we found along with more (eyes of) fat looking out of the bowl than looking into it. That was just the reverse of the Kapusta we got at the camp. Also, the Kasha was of the right consistency, not like the watery spoonful we got at the camp. The Kleba (bread) was still the same but we got it twice a day and in larger portions. Combined it was almost a pound. Patients with digestive problems received white wheat bread instead of the doughy rough rye mixture. Three meals were served daily and on Sundays we sometimes received a small portion of pudding. Each day we received a heaping tablespoonful of sugar and an equal portion of Machorka. An old German saying went: ***"Wir leben wie Gott in Frankreich,"*** (We live like God in France). It's meaning:

We are living a life of luxury! All of this without having to earn it with hard slave labor!

Two doctors were always on staff. One was a Russian Medical Army Major and the other was a female Doctor. I recognized her from the camp inspections and at the de-lousing facilities. She and two other Doctors had to evaluate the health conditions of the POW's and made the decisions as to who needed the hospital stays. She had previously chosen me out of the twenty to thirty prisoners to be brought to the hospital. She was rather fluent in speaking German and listened to our complaints and showed compassion towards us, she really cared.

While I was visiting another ward I came across the fellow who had the accident with the asphalt spreader. I noticed that his wound was still open, and saw how the Doctor changed the inserted gauze bandages every day to absorb the puss that was still developing. Evidently there was a lot of septic matter remaining in the wound since the day of the accident. The Doctor rinsed the wound with saline solution before filling it up again with more gauze and then applied tape to hold the wound closed.

For nurses we had two German **Mediks** who also were POW's. There was even a German Army Chaplin who took care of our spiritual needs. He visited the wards every day and on Sundays he held a non-denominational service for all those who were able to participate. Whether Catholic or Protestant we were all the same, and he was a POW just like the rest of us.

One cold frigid and snowy day the Russians decided to select some able-bodied patients to go out on a job. Our assignment was to march to an abandoned house in the next village to pick up some frozen potatoes. Each of us had to pull a sleigh with a few empty burlap sacks tied up on them. To get there we had to stomp through deep layers of freshly fallen and sometimes frozen layers of snow. We were dressed fairly warm with the exception of what we wore on our feet. We wore a Russian winter cap that had earflaps. The usual issued shoes were not suitable for that weather. They were of the same make that were issued to us in the camp, with wooden soles that were nailed together with the canvas tops.

The wet snow and constant walking took its toll on them. The heels separated from the soles and snow got into them. Within a short time my feet became completely numb. It felt as if I was walking on a sea of cotton, I lost all the feeling in them.

The weather was much colder than we expected with the wind blowing and snow falling like in a blizzard.

When we arrived at the village and the abandoned house it was totally frozen inside. Frost completely covered all walls and ceilings. The huge pile of rock-hard frozen potatoes was in the middle of the floor. We filled our sacks by hand as if we were picking up stones. Two men had to drag out each potato sack and load two onto each hand pulled sleigh. On the way back, not feeling my feet, I was afraid that I was suffering from frostbite.

We wore German Winter Military reversible camouflage jackets, which were warm. What was unfortunate; was that we did not have socks, boots or protective foot coverings. Instead we wrapped our feet with strips of the bed sheet type cotton cloth.

When we pulled the sleigh back through the snow we had to take many small breaks to catch our breath. Our group was only five or six men, chaperoned by one guard. Upon our return back to the hospital I removed my shoes and foot wraps and noticed that my feet had turned completely white. They looked like those from a dead man!

Our friendly German *Medik* knew exactly what to do. By starting to massage the feet and then submerging them into luke-warm water, circulation slowly returned. I, as well as the others suffered excruciating pain, as if we were on fire! My nose was also white. The insides of my nostrils were frozen. As they also slowly defrosted I was in more pain. To this day I have an impaired sense of smell as a result of that.

Most of the frozen potatoes were then actually used to make Vodka for the guards. A few were cooked for us in the Kapusta but they didn't have the right taste and the consistency was more like a gel.

Frost turned the starch of the potatoes into sugar. When thawed the sugar turned into alcohol and that was distilled into Vodka. We had all of the work, but none of the rewards! Just more uncalled for pain and suffering.

I became friendly with one of the patients who came from the camp I was in. He had worked as cook in the kitchen of the Labor Camp. Well fed as he was, he had a large and burly stature. Unfortunately he was afflicted with epilepsy and had frequent seizures. During all of his seizures he got "out of control." His arms and legs flailed about. It took about six other able-bodied patients to hold him down. The ***Medik*** would put a wad of gauze into his mouth to prevent him from biting his tongue. His condition worsened and he never got out of there alive. A fatal seizure took his life.

One of my new duties was as an Orderly, and I also tended to the burials of the deceased. The "Cemetery" consisted of deep trenches that were dug out by bulldozers in the fall. It was located about one half mile away from the hospital. We transported the corpses by a large hand wagon when the weather allowed. In the winter a sleigh replaced it. When a body was heavy, like the man with epilepsy, a team of four men was needed. Normally there were just two men for the job.

Arriving at the trench we had to lift the body off the wagon and then lay it on the ground. I said a prayer while standing by him. Then the four of us grabbed each of his limbs and swung him down onto the bottom of the trench. Beneath him were already dozens of others, and hundreds to follow. The hospital staff attached a small label to his big toe and his underwear remained on him, unlike the corpses along the camp fence. Before we left the hospital, the Chaplain gave him his last rites. That was comforting to know because at the camp that was never done.

As his lifeless body hit the bottom of the pit a grunt escaped from his mouth when his lungs compressed as he landed hard on the bottom. It was a most unexpected, startling and at the same time grotesque sight and sound! Then we had to shovel lime powder over his body followed by dirt to cover his remains, in preparation for the next burial above him. I believe that during my entire stay at the ***Lazarett*** I must have participated in at least fifty or more such burials.

During my stays in the **Lazarett** I continued reading the reduced contents from the Old Testament of my Bible. As a consolation, with the help of the Chaplain I started creating a small personal prayer book. It was also written with the homemade pen and ink and I named it: **Promptuarium** (meaning in Latin=A Ready Book, For All Occasions). My entries into it were Bible scriptures that I remembered from my childhood, along with prayers and quotations from the Bible, and some writings especially for me by the German Chaplain.

I managed to save some pieces from my issued as well as traded bread supplies, ate the crust and then mixed the inner parts with some liquid from my tin of Kapusta. I had enough to create dough to be kneaded into a couple of small loaves enriched with my portion of sugar. I placed them into the ceramic heating oven close to the glowing ashes. When they looked browned and crispy I removed them. As soon as they cooled I anxiously sunk my teeth into my homemade cakes. After others saw what I was doing they also copied my "recipe" and the oven in our ward turned into a bakery oven.

One Christmas when I was still in the hospital, I believe it was during the second year that I was there, the Chaplain trained a group of ten men who had exceptional good voices and talent to sing. Together they formed a choir with bass, baritone, and tenors. They hit all the octaves in a most harmonious way as they sung songs that were composed right at the hospital site. One in particular, was so very touching.

It was sung in German, and I can't remember the words but the melody of the refrain plays over and over in my mind. It drove all the men to tears. Hearing it sung brought back my own childhood memories of the beautiful Christmases I shared with my family. There was no means to have any musical accompaniment. The singers stood there holding their hand written musical notes.

It was comforting for us all hearing them perform. It was so gripping and moving; it brought tears to our eyes. I never heard that beautiful musical composition ever again. There was no way that it ever made it beyond the boundaries of the prison hospital to become published in the outside world.

> *You just had to accept and deal with those unpleasant realities in your own personal way. What a life we had, it was "Just Another Day At The Lazarett."*

MY FIRST LETTER HOME

Creating my little notebooks gave me inspiration and I started to record some information about myself in a series of mini journals and in the form of letters to my family....

You have to remember that at the camp anything in writing with the exception of Bibles and Prayer Books, if found, would be confiscated. I managed to hide all well.

Being in the hospital also gave me the opportunity to acquire little stacks of Russian cigarette paper for rolling Machorka. Since I had already enough for my booklets I traded my portions for more food supplements. I was writing my journals in hopes of being able to eventually send my recordings back home with one of the prisoners who would be lucky enough to be released and sent home with the occasional transports.

I wrote to my family that I had a fever and compared myself to some starving soul from the poorer caste in India. My recovery in the hospital was not the greatest but I could slowly gain some weight back. In addition to malnourishment and dystrophy I got sick from some type of Malaria, but it was not the familiar tropical kind. In fact, once you got over it you were not immune from getting it again. But unlike the tropical type that stayed with you, this non-tropical one occurred only by another bite from some kind of insect. But this type of Malaria caused a higher fever that could be fatal. I contracted that three times and got over it, thankfully. But as was later discovered, my heart was affected and enlarged and that caused it to develop an irregular heartbeat.

The *Lazarett* was located in the Village of Nischnie Lamow, near Penza and it was as I mentioned earlier, a converted school that was then used as a prison hospital.

By February of 1946 I had the opportunity to give this first Journal to a fellow Prisoner who was a Czech. He was supposed to be on the first transport home and so I asked him to keep it, hide it, and when he reached the Homeland to please send the little Journal to my parents. I wrote their address on it for him. I sent two other journal booklets with released POW's returning home, but only this first one made it through and my parents saved it for me, I still have it today as part of my display on visited events.

....The following, for the first time after almost sixty years, is what I am reading and translating today. It is very painful for me to reminisce over these sad but true facts, but at the same time I am finally able to share my story and release what I had hidden, even from myself for too long....

... As written in my cigarette paper booklet:
I withheld to my parents the more unpleasant happenings; it could have caused me   repercussions and punishment if the booklets ever would have been found and confiscated...

... *"Meine Lieben* (My Dear Ones)... Paper is scarce, as is the case with everything else here. Up to now writing to you was impossible. I want to give you a small review about my past here. In March of 1945 I became a POW at Naggi Sallo in Hungary at the River Gran, not far from Budapest. We marched many kilometers until we were loaded into Railroad cattle cars. At Jasbereni (Hungary) there were wider railroad tracks for our transport to Russia. Once in Russia we had to pass through numerous temporary campsites and were interrogated and everything we had was confiscated. The train made many stops and we were de-loused and so on. By May 9th we arrived in *Grüntal,* near Kasan (Kazan) at the Volga River, West of Moscow. There we worked on the *"Kolchose"(*Farm). It was hard work for sometimes sixteen to nineteen hours with very little food. Many of us became sick, many died. In October 1945 there was a rumor that the zone behind the Volga had to be cleared of all POW's and the sick were put into the **Lazarett** and the others were dispatched to a Camp in the vicinity of Pensa. I counted myself as one of the "lucky" ones and was admitted to the Hospital" …

I continued writing and telling my parents that I had a job at the hospital doing errands, such as picking up potatoes and helping the **Mediks** to take care of the other sick and wounded comrades. I guess I was something like an Orderly. I was also told that I had to stay until the last Prisoners would be transported home and that it wouldn't be in that same year. I continued writing in that first Journal: …

….."You will be astounded about what I will personally reveal to you later when we are together again. My future is all set." I am very anxious to see how my sisters look. (My two younger sisters would be nineteen and seventeen). I don't have my photos any more because they took everything away from us. Only in my dreams can I see all of you.

Soon I'll be making it to my twenty- first year of life and I'll be of legal adult age. Can you imagine that? How fast time goes by? Hopefully things are not too rough by you? For all the time that I have been away from you, it can be made up, well, mostly in reference to the food. I am also curious about what happened to my dear friend Irmi, I'm sure that she stopped at the house to inquire about me. Please convey my "Heartfelt Greetings" to her and tell her that soon I will be home. Here in the hospital

(**Kriegs- lazarett**) and so far throughout my stay, I was together with a comrade who is also from Fürstenfeldbruck. His name is Hans Weber. Please contact and let his wife know that he is still alive and surely will come home soon."

In March Hans was fully recuperated and was sent back to the camp. "If he comes home first, he will visit you and tell you about me. Once we are both home then, that day will be celebrated every year as a "New Birthday" and that will be the right thing to do. So now I close for today and God willing, we will see each other soon, healthier and happier. My "Heartfelt Greetings and Kisses" to all of you, and my friends, relatives and acquaintances, Gottfried."

...I continued writing July 2, 1946: ...

My Dear Ones... "It turned out differently than we had expected. Until now, no more transports left here. But now in July there are supposed to be some more returning home. Sorry to say, that I got notified that I was to be dispatched back to the camp. It seems they need more men to finish the new road between Stalingrad and Moscow. They wanted to have it completed by October. Everyone who was capable of working was required to go on this project. Therefore, that's how we became involved. All the patients from here are supposed to be sent home within a short time, but those of us left behind have to get stuck with it once again. So we are being promised that by the winter we will be sent home. Let's hope so! It looks like tomorrow we will be sent to the camp. Therefore, I am writing these few lines quickly and will leave this letter behind as well as two more. Whoever is able to get on the transport back I will dispatch these letters to you in hopes that you will receive at least one." There were rumors and more rumors and one disappointment after the other....

Actually the German Chaplain at the hospital has been a wonderful man and most inspiring. We were able to spend quality time together in discussions as well as with prayers. My friendship with him strengthened my spirituality. Actually he helped me in finding the fellow patients and prisoners who would be going home so that they could carry my messages with them.

I lived with the positive hope and outlook that not only my parents would know that I was indeed still alive, but also the fact that one day soon I would rejoin them.

About that same time in camp we were issued our first postcard, which was given to us by the Red Cross. Finally, we were given permission to write one card home. The card had a return portion on it with our address. I decided that I would hold on to the postcard until a later date because I had no idea what my new location would be and if I was moved from one place to another, they would not forward it. So, instead I stuck to my original plan of sending my own messages home along with men who would be released soon.

Continuing with translating my Journal Letter: …

"I heard that the new Camp where I am supposed to go to is much better managed than the one I was in earlier. Some of our patients came from there and told me that they got more to eat than at the hospital.

All I can say is, who knows why it's good that I am being sent back to the prison camp? The good Lord will lead me the right way and not forsake me. Some day He will lead me on the road home. So let us not lose our faith and courage and let's keep hope for finding freedom."

Greetings and Kisses, Your Gottfried."

N.b. (nota bene): additional thought: "By the way, I am here with the former top Pastry Chef/Baker **Herr** Maschinski, now called 'Maschner.' He is from Osterode and had his business across the street from the Catholic Church. He was there to the last days and reported that Osterode was surrendered to the Russians without a battle and that it seemed that most of the city appeared undamaged."

On July 8th I continued writing…

"My Dear Ones, until now we did not yet leave the hospital. It looks like it will not happen because the Doctor said that now in July the transports leaving here are leaving directly for the Homeland. If there are not enough passengers then maybe we would have the possibility of being one of the 'lucky ones' to be part of it. Here anything can happen! The Russians are in every way 'unpredictable.' Therefore, let's hope for the best. If I should not be one of those lucky ones, we have to console ourselves with Gods word.

The good Lord has so intended and He knows when it is time for me to be sent home. I remain in Gods Hands; He will lead me and guide me when it will be best. The Bible verse at my Confirmation is again and again my consolation. "Do not be afraid, because I freed you, fear not, because I redeemed you. I called you by your name, you are mine." "I belong to Him and He is in me and beside me, what should

I be afraid of? The Lord is my Shepherd I shall not want." 'Better to go through Gods school than be forsaken by Him" ….

I continued writing by telling my parents that these nice scriptures I remembered were embroidered and hung framed on the wall over the sewing machine in our home. "I am clinging to these scriptures and again and again they comfort me. Therefore, the good Lord already knows when it's my time to be sent home and He will lead me to you, now we just have to patiently wait."

…."It is a precious thing to be patient and hope for the help of the Lord." Yes, to be patient we shall and must be in His hard and tough school of life. The good Lord kept me alive through these very bad times, and will continue doing so, and lead me to you, being healthy. This Prison is a very tough test I had to undergo and have to pass it. It is also a punishing mercy that He let me go through this but I learned a lot and I matured.

The word of God always comforted and helped me with an awful lot. I have a better trust in Him; that He will protect and keep me safe like a good Shepherd does for His sheep. Therefore, don't worry about me. He will make everything all right".

Originally I made this booklet for myself to write some poems in. Other booklets I made for various things. The Poem: "The Secrets Of The Flowers" I composed during one of those nights when I could not sleep. My thoughts are always with you and I often dream about my homecoming. Therefore, we will not give up hope and I will trust God further. Keep on trusting God. Be patient in times of sorrow and persevere with hope and hold on to prayers."… These words are really meant for us!

Here is the German version of Gottfried's Poem in Rhyme:
"The Secrets of The Flowers"

Blumengeheimnisse

O lasst die Blumen zu uns sprechen
Denn sie geben weisen Rat,
Wenn ein Herze will zerbrechen,
Weil liebend es geschwiegen hat.

So die Rosen uns von Liebe künden
Von der Sehnsucht klagt das tränend' Herz..
Gelbe Blumen von der Falschheit Sünden,
Die dunkelroten von der Liebe Schmerz.

Tulpen, Nelken, Lilien und Narzissen
Sie belückten gestern uns und heut,
Als shienen sie genau zu wissen
Was ein liebend' Herz erfreut.

Der stolze grossgezackte Rittersporn
Erzählt von der Helden Sagenborn.
Ein kleines Blümlein immer zu uns spricht
Von seinem Namen: Vergiss-mein-nicht.

Des Blattes Grün verspricht uns Hoffung:
Von Treue raunt der Blüten Blau.
Das Weiß von Reinheit, edler Lebensführung
Und Lebensfreude schenkt die blum'ge Au

Das rote Blühen gleich der Liebe ist
Doch das gelbe warnt vor Neid und List.
Eingefang'nes Sonnenlicht ist der Blüten Pracht
Vom ewg'en Werden kündet's und von des SchöpfersMacht.

GD

Here is the English Translation of Gottfried's Poem: (not rhymed)

The Secrets of The Flowers

O' Let the Flowers speak to us.
Because they give wise advice
When a heart starts to break,
While in loving it remained silent.

So the roses speak of love and,
The tearful heart proclaims a longing.
Yellow flowers speak of sin and deceit
The dark red ones speak of both pain and love.

Tulips, Carnations, Lilies and Narcissus
They bring good tidings for yesterday and today
It is as if they exactly knew
What brings happiness to a loving heart.

The proud flower, the Knight's Spur
Is telling us about
The Legends of the Medieval Knights.
A tiny flower forever speaks to us
Of its name, Forget-Me-Not.

The green of the leaves is promising us hope,
The blue of the blossoms whispers about faithfulness.
The white ones portray purity and noble behavior.
And life's happiness is given to us by the fields of flowers in bloom.

The brilliant red ones are equal to love
But the yellow ones give warning of envy and malice.
The beauty of the flowers is a result of catching the rays of the sun
It tells us of the ever rebirth and of Gods power.

GD

I wrote another poem that was included on the first page of my Journal from Russia. It has a special meaning, as a remembrance of my "Goddess." Here Is the Poem.

Gedenken An Meine Göttin.

Wer geliebt kann nicht vergessen.
Wer vergisst hat nie geliebt.
Wer geliebt doch hat vergessen,
Hat vergessen wie man liebt.

So auch du hast mich vergessen,
D'rum vergessen kann auch ich,
Kann vergessen Dein Vergessen,
Dich vergessen kann ich nicht.

Here Is The English Translation:
(It's exactly the same and rhymes too)

Remembering My Goddess

He who has loved cannot forget.
He who forgets has never loved.
He who has loved and still forgot,
Has forgotten how one loves.

So you too have me forgotten,
And forgetting I am too,
Am forgetting your forgetting,
But never am forgetting you.

Here is the German Version of Gottfried's Poem: The Tear

Die Träne

Macht man im Leben kaum den ersten Schritt
Bringt man als Kind schon eine Träne mit.
Und Freundentänen bringt als ersten Gruss
Dem Kind die Mutter mit dem ersten Kuss.

Man wächst empor dann zwischen Freud' und Schmerz
Da zieht die Liebe in das junge Herz
Und offenbaret das Herz der Jung- frau sich,
Spricht eine Träne; "Ja Ich Liebe Dich."

Wie schön ist doch die Träne einer Braut
Wenn der Geliebte ihr ins Auge schaut.
Man schlingt das Band sie werden Weib und Mann
Da fängt der Kampf mit Not und Sorgen an.

Und wenn der Mann die Hoffung längst verlor,
Blickt noch das Weib vertrauensvoll empor
Zur Sternenwelt zum heit'rem Himmelslicht
Und eine Träne spricht: " Verzage nicht."

Der Mann wird Greis die Scheide- stunde schlägt
Da stehen die Seinen um ihn tief bewegt
Und aller Augen sieht man tränenvoll,
Die bringen sie als letzten Liebeszoll

Doch still verklärt blickt noch umher der Greis
In seiner Kinder, seiner Enkel Kreis
Im letzten Kampf, selbst schon im Vergehn'
Spricht eine Träne noch in seinem Aug:
"Auf Wiedersehn"

GD

Here Is The English Translation:

The Tear

In your life you barely made your first step
As a child you already bring a tear along.
And tears of joy bring as a first greeting
To the child, its mother's first kiss.

One grows up and between Happiness and Sorrow
There comes Love into the young heart,
And reveals itself to the young woman
A tear says: "Yes, I Love You."

How pretty is the tear of a young Bride
When her loved one looks into her eyes.
One ties the knot and become wife and man.
Then starts the battle with distress and worries.

And even if the man has long lost hope,
His wife looks up in trust and faith
To the world of stars, to the bright light of heaven.
And her tear says: "Do not despair."

When the man gets old and the hour of parting is near
His loved ones stand by him deeply touched.
One sees all eyes filled with tears,
They bring to him as a last sign of Love.

But quietly the old man looks at the circle
Of his Children and Grandchildren
In the last battle almost in leaving
A tear in his eyes says: "Until We Meet Again"
"Goodbye

So, I continued writing in my Journal, sharing whatever I could… day by day, week by week… ***I added more to my Journal in hopes that my parents, or loved one could read it…***

"Being here I learned a lot and I'm fully realizing why I've had to go through all of this. In earlier times I did not have respect for bread and often I let it be wasted. Now I pick up the tiniest crumb with my wetted finger in order not to waste. Even with a small piece of bread I wipe my tin cup and spoon clean, so as not to waste any drops or morsels of food. I'm eating with thanks (being thankful) for what God has given me.

In earlier times I was too fussy and picky. Now I eat everything and don't complain." "Being here I also learned an awful lot about human behavior. I saw and also realized how stupid and bad some men were. Once I saw two older prisoners who were also fathers of children. They were fighting and cursing at each other. I told them: "If your children would be here to see and hear you, they would be ashamed of you and would want to disappear in the ground!" If it isn't so, that the apple didn't fall far from the tree?"...

When I am home, I will tell you about how bad these fights were. "This prison is for me, in every way, a 'form of higher life education.' Also in this time of need I learned to know God, how He really is, and I heard His thundering voice. I opened my heart to Him that He could live within me. Many of my comrades never heard His thundering voice, and lost their faith completely. Many of them didn't have it so bad. They had good workstations, with enough good food to eat. But, to help them get those posts the Devil must have been working within."

"You will never see the old Gottfried again, who left you December 26, 1944. But you will find a new Gottfried, a scholar who went through the High School of the Lord and carries Christ in his heart, who proudly carries His name rightfully, 'Gods Peace.' (**Gottfried**)

This Prison is a big turning point in my life. Like a newborn, I will lead my life striving to seek the heavenly homeland. When I come home I will draw a line under the past. I will begin a new life according to Gods plan. He will be at my side and guide me."

"Therefore, I am closing for today. May the good Lord bless you and keep you and may He shine His face upon you and give you His holy peace into your heart." Therefore, don't let your head hang down. Soon we will greet each other, God willing...

Those were my words, and it was "Just Another Day At The Lazarett!"

THOSE DR. ZHIVAGO RUSSIAN WINTERS

We were in the middle of a severely cold winter with temperatures of forty to forty five degrees below zero, Fahrenheit. The ground was frozen five to six feet deep. If you have ever seen the movie Dr. Zhivago, that would give you the best idea of what those dreadful Russian winters were really like for me.

Looking back, I'm not sure how I endured it, but I survived through three dreadful, bone chilling cold winters in Russia before being sent home. Finally, because of my constant passing out, I was useless to them as a slave laborer and being too tough to die, they finally decided to let me go. That was the only way to get home, if you didn't die on the way, which also happened often.

Day by day, each morning, we marched the same route to our worksites along the barbed wire fence. Each day of slave labor lasted as much as eighteen or nineteen hours. Looking out and through the barbed wire fence I saw an eerie sight.

Stripped naked corpses were piled up about six feet high in that freezing air. To me, in sad realization, they didn't have an identity. Not any more. Their clothing had been removed, it had more value on the black market. Ice-hardened limbs often broke off as if they were made of glass.

During the nights, packs of wolves and wild dogs made a meal of them, feasting on the human flesh, ripping with their fangs large chunks of "meat" from those corpses. They didn't have to fight for that "privilege" among themselves, as often is the case out in the wilderness. Here they had an abundance of food to their hearts content. Their "dining table" was set with such huge amounts of "ready to eat delicacies," that night for night, as they came to feast, they found an unending supply.

No Human Being Ever Deserved To End Up That Way!!! That Was The Lowest Of The Lowest, Just Horrible!!!

Any human being would find that sight to be a scene from a horror film, evil and unimaginable in the civilization we are living in. But there it was the bitter reality and each day we saw the pile growing higher and longer, as more and more bodies were put into this "storage."

Of course, it was impossible to bury the poor souls in the cold of the Russian winters. The ground was hard as a rock for a depth of at least five feet. Trenches could not be dug until it was Spring when the hard ground had thawed. By then the corpses were reduced to skeletons; the bulldozers came and pushed all into the trenches.

As I saw this sorrowful pile of humanity growing larger each day, I often wondered if I would eventually become part of it some day. But I quickly pushed these negative thoughts out of my mind. I was still the confirmed optimist that I always had been. I felt that I should never ever give up hope, no matter what my odds were or how hopeless my situation appeared to be. With God's help, I knew, that I could make it and with my strong will to live; I did indeed succeed in the end.

Come Spring, the stench of decomposing flesh was constantly present and permeated the entire camp area and well beyond it's boundaries. Flies laid their eggs in the decomposing pile of bodies and soon maggots were crawling all over an in the rotting flesh. Soon we got used to the stench and gruesome sight and were less and less conscious of it as time went by. One can get used to just about anything, if a situation of 'discomfort' lasts past a certain threshold and or time-span.

Seeing how fellow inmates ended up, after perhaps we had spent and shared part of our lives together, did at times get me depressed. I constantly had to compose myself and take a deep hard look into my psyche. I continued to endure it all and never once did I think of taking my own life, but many of us did.

Earlier, in combat over Germany and later on the Russian front I had many close calls where I almost lost my life, yet I was spared. Knowing that alone gave me inner strength. I was more and more convinced that my Guardian Angel, whose wings I imagined were wrapped tightly around me like a shield, was protecting me. So I kept marching on, as a Prisoner of War, as a Christian soldier, on to victory! I lived with the strong hope and the real dream that one day soon I would be going home. Nothing could deter me from this belief!...

Goulasch Kanone - Traveling Kitchen

A Pen and Ink Drawing
Done by a fellow POW

Just Released,
(Former POW) 1948

Wooden Box
and Pen I made

Wallet made from Woolen
Fabric from Textile Factory

Souvenirs I kept (while being a P.O.W>)
Mini Notebooks and Journals

SEVEN

Alive And Free, Friedel Is Finally Home!

I was too tough to die and too weak and sick to do slave labor work, so I was no longer of any use to the Russians and finally, I was sent home. That was of course long after the War had been officially declared "over," in the European part, in 1945.

I took memories with me of that gruesome "Horror" film scenario of "Another Day At The Gulag." But I was still not set free, not until I could finally reach home and once again see my mother, father and sisters. I bid the Chaplain a farewell and gave him what remained intact from my Bible, just the books of Luke and John and a few pages from the other Gospels.

It was a long train ride home. The ride in the cattle car back to Germany took about three weeks. We traveled only by night. By day freight trains passed us in the opposite direction. They were still transporting the dismantled factory equipment, machinery and other goods to Russia after the nearly three long years since we first became POW's. I already began to feel freedom being without any armed guards. Only a couple of un-armed guards as "tour guides" were with us.

I remember a sad incident at an overnight stay in a rail yard somewhere on our way home. It was left to us to collect (steal) wood and coal to fuel the potbelly stoves in our now unlocked cattle cars whenever we had the opportunity. At night, when we were "parked"

in one of the rail yards, we explored in pairs the respective locations for anything usable as fuel to heat our potbelly stoves. Other freight trains were parked at both of our sides. We had to crawl under them to cross the numerous tracks of the rail yard where we could hopefully find material to burn, preferably coal, which took less storage space and burned longer and also gave off more heat.

I just cleared the last track under a train, when it slowly started to move. My buddy following me was caught by surprise and at the last second pushed himself away with his right hand on top of the rail. The wheel of the boxcar rolled over his hand severing all four fingers and part of his thumb. He was lucky, that he was able to clear the track without being killed. Of course he was in shock and stared at the stump of his hand, not believing what had happened and at first probably didn't feel any pain. But then he screamed and shouted: "My hand, my hand", and promptly passed out.

Poor fellow, having that happen to him after years of prison life and of all places on his way home to freedom. I crawled back for help and together we dragged him back to our boxcar and called for one of the Russians who accompanied us. He in turn contacted the stationmaster, who called for a truck to bring the still unconscious comrade to a local hospital after temporarily bandaging his injured hand ….What ever became of him, I don't know.

An hour later, almost at daybreak our train resumed its journey to Germany and we talked among ourselves about this accident. We felt so sorry for this poor soul.

A few days later, it was all but forgotten, as we grew increasingly excited with anticipation of arriving home and reuniting with our families. The food that was provided for us was more plentiful and much better than the one we got in the Gulags; even better than in the hospital. Again, as it was the case when we were transported to Russia, there was a German field-kitchen aboard the train, so we were served warm, healthy soups with plenty of meat and vegetables, as well as "fat-eyes" floating on top and we even could go back for seconds whenever we stopped for the night. Maybe the Russians figured it would be a better idea to bring POW's back to Germany, that were in somewhat better shape, than the ones who had left from the camps and or hospitals from way back in Russia. With this better food and nourishment, we gained some weight, but there also occurred some water accumulation in our bodies that made us look fuller. That, of course, was a clever deception to fool the German people at home.

It was a surprise to me that Germany had been divided into four zones. They were the Russian, American, British and French. Once we reached the Leipzig railroad station in East Germany, in the Russian zone, we were free to go. I sent a Telegram home, notifying my family, that within several days I would be arriving. Along with our discharge document we received some East German money, I forgot how much, but it certainly wasn't a "fortune", just enough to be able to buy some food for the few days it might take to reach the American Zone. Those of us whose families were living in the Russian Zone, were given transportation to their hometowns. I was put on another train (no cattle cars) on my way towards South Germany, occupied by American forces. I was running a somewhat high fever and had dysentery and now was up to about 70 kilos/140 pounds mostly due to water retention.

The Infirmary personnel at the Border to South Germany where we home-comers had to go through a medical examination, wanted to keep me for a few days until I recovered. But I was determined to go home, and I wouldn't allow any unnecessary delays preventing me from crossing the border and continuing my way home. But I was delayed anyway by being held at ***Hof-Moschendorf*** at the pass-through camp in the American zone, in the Southern Region of West Germany. Their medical personnel examined us too and wanted to keep me there for a few days. But again I was too impatient to be delayed and just asked to give me some medication to get me going to Munich by a more comfortable West German train.

I finally arrived in Munich and I looked for the local train to Fürstenfeldbruck. Getting to the right platform I was waiting on a bench for the train to arrive. I noticed a man staring at me; he looked like yet another "Russian." I was stunned; here, was a "Russian?" I certainly did not expect that unpleasant surprise. He was dressed like the Cossacks, wearing a fur trimmed flat top cap on his head, a form-fitted jacket decorated with rows of buttons and stitched trims, and a pair of knickers and high riding boots.

His appearance was rather striking to me, as I guess mine was to him. I wore a Russian winter cap with earflaps and a military German camouflage winter jacket and pants. I felt rather uncomfortable until he broke the ice by speaking to me. His comment was: "I can see that you are coming home from a Prisoner of war camp in Russia?"

My reply was yes, and so we continued our conversation, got on the train that was just then coming in slowly and came to a stop. He was very friendly and expressed, how sorry he was that his countrymen had treated me so miserably. During that half hour trip to Fuerstenfeldbruck we kept up our conversation until we reached my stop. Upon my exiting the train he shook my hand, said goodbye and I felt something slipping into my hand as he was shaking it. When I had stepped onto the platform the train started to move, we waved to each other as he continued to his destination. I took a quick look and saw that he had given me fifty *Marks*. I was filled with thankful emotion as I started to walk from the train station to town and the new location of my parent's residence.

It was January 4th, 1948 when I finally walked down the *Angerstrasse* where my parents then lived. They resided at that location since being evicted from our Villa at the start of the American occupation. I already knew that from the letters they sent me, yet they spared me from some of the not so great news.

As I approached the house *Angerstrasse* 5, my mother saw me through the ground floor window and promptly fainted. I saw her sinking to the floor disappearing behind the windowsill.

That was the moment when my Guardian Angel decided to release his protective wings from me, telling me everything was OK, that now I was set "free." Just as I was a Pilot and had my wings, so did this particular Angel and it flew up and away. But he let me know that he would still be watching over me, since now I was in a safe place. What I had finally earned was "A Passport To A New Life," and that was all I had!

Getting into the door of the apartment I was greeted by my father and my sisters with hugs and kisses, laughter and shouts of happiness.

My mother, who was helped by my older sister, had come to and they joined us all in the happy celebration of my homecoming. ...

I had managed to sneak those mementos I had made in the POW camp and hospital along with me without being caught. They were tucked into a small camouflage canvas bag

(I had made from tent material) that contained all the mail that I had received. Also the billfold that I made from the woolen cloth that came from the Textile factory. It held the several small booklets that I had fashioned from the little boy's notebook and also from cigarette papers, part of a diary, and a handwritten prayer book. It also contained a calendar, written up names and addresses, as well as a booklet with recipes, and advice about cooking and preserving foods, etc. It also contained my hand-carved Machorka box.

Back at the hospital I was able to carve that small wooden tobacco box that I carved my initials into with the year 1947. The 'so called' intended purpose of the box was to hold Machorka. But for me it also served as a container to hide what I had written. I made it with a false bottom so it looked like it only contained tobacco. The Russians would have confiscated my most treasured written 'souvenirs' that I had. My canvass bag would have been discovered, had I been frisked. Luckily, I wasn't. But just in case, I had it hidden on the bottom of my bread bag under some extra underwear and foot rags we had received upon leaving for our trip home.

...As my family welcomed me, my eldest sister exclaimed: ***"Friedel, you're finally home!"*** That was always her nickname for me. She never addressed me by my birth name. They all saved their food ration cards

for me, and I also received a care package from a Charitable International Organization called "Caritas."

Their rations usually consisted of 250 grams (one half of a pound) of meat per person, and 100 grams (about one fifth of a pound) of fat / butter, weekly. But I was still not well, because I starved for too long, I experienced bloating with water retention. We tried to enjoy ourselves by going to the movies. But even that was painful on my bones. The seats were of hard wood, without cushions. It was difficult for me to be comfortably seated because I was just skin and bones, surrounded by water. I had to take a pillow along with me to sit upon, I lacked the "natural" cushion of "meaty" buttocks.

A Doctor made an evaluation of my health and decided to send me away to recuperate. Because my body was at first rejecting real and nourishing food I had to be treated at a Convalescent Home near the **Nebelhorn** Mountain, in the Bavarian Alps. My stay there, in the picturesque town of Oberstdorf (located near the borders of Austria and Switzerland), was for one month. The home was located in a high altitude and that along with three meals a day, snacks, and care packages from Caritas brought me slowly back to better health.

What was also nice about being there was that it was so peaceful and I was able to be in touch with nature by hiking and exploring. It was almost like I was refreshed and uplifted, closer to the heavens as God was looking down at me. The happy fact was, that I finally made it back home after all, and I felt "free."

About three weeks after I returned home I went up to Angels Mountain above the **Klosterkirche** in Fürstenfeldbruck because I wanted to see if the carving I made in the Beech tree in 1939 was still there. It was, but at the same time I found out that Sieglinde was engaged to be married. I accepted hearing that news without regret because we were never deeply involved or in love, we had always been just great "pals." Looking back, I guess I was just looking for the familiarity of being in a normal environment, and returning to the "civilized world," the way I had remembered it.

Another great pal was my friend Irmi, and she was still single. She became a Nurse working at Nannhofen Hospital, as an Assistant to the Surgeon in the Operating Room. Irmi lived in a nearby town called Olching. After I came home from the Convalescent Home and was feeling much better it was wonderful being able to spend some time with her for Easter. It was not a dating relationship; just a get-together and we had a good time being with my family.

We had originally become friends when the Boys and Girls of the Hitler Youth Groups were joined for various rallies. She wrote several letters to me while I was at the Gulags in Russia, encouraging me to hold onto my faith and to trust the good Lord to bring me home. She even sent me a little poem of encouragement: (translated from German):

"If you think you can't go on, a little candle light appears out from nowhere, so you can go on again and sing of the power of life, sunshine and happiness."

In the letter she even drew a picture of a lit candle amidst a shining sun. Of course, whether it was a card or letter from someone back home it always lifted my spirits, helping to re-affirm the hope and assurance that someday, with God's help I would indeed come home. Her mother was also a nurse but with the Red Cross. I knew she liked and approved of me and encouraged my friendship with Irmi and probably hoped that we would have married one day.

Also, shortly after I returned home, I did indeed need that Hernia Operation; the hernia I received in the Russian prison while building the new road. We had to constantly move the heavy iron rails for the Asphalt spreading machine as we progressed finishing section for section. Lifting those rails and carrying them to the new and not yet paved sections of the road was a task our weak bodies were not suited for, so something had to "give." In my case, it was my groin.

The operation was successful and Irmi was there for me. She not only recommended that I come to the Hospital where she was working, for my surgery, but she was also on Private Duty and could look after me as well.

My father was almost certain, that once I came home, I would want to become a Pastor or a Priest. That was based on the letters I wrote home, with such spiritual conviction. However, while in prison, what I was referring to was altogether different. My statement of saying "I had a plan," was something that the Baker from Osterode and I had many conversations about.

What would it be like, once we are out of Prison? At the time it seemed like a good idea that once free, we should get together and run a Bakery. Actually that dream was often what kept us going. We talked about the varieties of cakes and pastries that we could make and sell. But that dream never became a reality, and I never knew of his whereabouts afterwards or if he was still alive. We lost contact when he was transferred back to camp while I remained at the Hospital.

Almost everything and anything that I had ever owned in our original Villa in the **Pucherstrasse** was gone. While I was a POW I wondered why there was a change of address and my parents tried to explain a little bit about it to me. But once home, I faced another sad reality, that other than my family and friends, the things that I once thought were of value or importance to me were no longer there.

When the Americans took our house over to convert it into their headquarters, they emptied my room. The very valuable ancient coin collection that I had inherited from my Grandfather was gone. I clearly remember one very rare solid gold Roman coin that had the Greek Goddess Diana pictured on it. It was the size of a silver dollar, but twice as thick. It was my most prized piece of the entire collection (of valuable coins and paper money).

Another fact they revealed to me, once I was home, was that my youngest sister's life had been in danger, but by divine intervention she was spared dying young. She was in jeopardy while being in the backyard of our Villa, before the end of the War.

It was April 28, 1945 when out of nowhere, machine gunfire by a lone P 47 American fighter plane hit the house and bullets swished past her, within close range of her head. It missed her by only about two feet, or less. Big holes were blown into the stucco west end wall of the house and shrapnel landed in the attic.

She and my mother were really scared! Within minutes the same thing happened again. She saw a P 51 Mustang, American fighter plane dive down and heard shots. The gunfire even hit some people who were standing in line picking up their food rations at the local grocery. Several of them got wounded, but luckily none were killed.

It was generally known that lone planes were strafing the ground at unauthorized targets. It also happened, that children in a schoolyard during recess had to run for cover. The same was true for farmers out on the field behind their plows. It was always a single plane flying low, without having any witnesses. Pilots who had personal grudges let it out by attacking innocent civilians, and at anything they saw moving. Never was there anything known or written about that fact in American newspapers.

I heard from my sisters that my mother washed uniforms for the American soldiers. As pay she received coffee and cigarettes. Those items were traded with local farmers in exchange for farm produce, dairy products and meats. Those were items that were not readily available at the local grocery store even with ration cards. Many things became scarce because factories and food processing plants could not recover fast enough after the bombings. Food transports fell victim to bombings as well.

By 1947 my **Tante** Anna and **Onkel** Gustav were also settled in Fürstenfeldbruck. I heard from them that by 1945 they had fled their apartment and went onboard the Wilhelm Gustloff Red Cross Hospital ship. They legally exited Germany before Königsberg was going to be taken over. By being German citizens they became refugees in the neutral territory of Denmark where they were confined in an internment camp.

They were among the "lucky ones"; because at the next and last Russian submarine. trip departing from Königsberg going the same way to Denmark, the ship had been illegally torpedoed by a Russian submarine.

The Wilhem Gustloff sank with all onboard into the icy **Ostsee**, (Baltic sea) a total of over nine thousand civilians and wounded soldiers. Despite the fact, that the Wilhelm Gustloff was clearly marked as a hospital ship with a huge red cross on white background at both sides of it and was flying the Red Cross flag. Nevertheless the Russians sunk it, that was clearly against the rules of the International Geneva Convention. Another example of the blatant disregard the Bolshevik regime of Russia demonstrated to the civilized world.

In 1949 I had an accident. At work I fell from a hayloft all the way to the root cellar. While being an apprentice in carpentry, working for Lorenz Kiener, we had a job to build a barn for the Hotel Post in Fürstenfeldbruck. Through the middle of the barn a drive-through parted the horse stable on the right from the cow stable on the left, both of them had haylofts and root cellars.

I was to install flooring on the level of the hayloft, above the horse stable. I had gotten up there by ladder. The lumber truck was below me at the drive through of the barn. I was handed bundles of long wooden floor planks and had to pull them up to my level. I grabbed a bundle at its top and while pulling it up, walked backwards to stack them on the partially finished section of that loft floor. Not realizing that there was an opening behind me for a stairwell that had not yet been built, I fell down through that opening legs first and landed past the horse stable onto the last bottom concrete step in the root cellar.

My left foot hit the edge of the step at the bottom and all the weight of my body fell on my twisted left foot, breaking all eight bones of my foot joint including the heel. At first I was "stunned" and in shock as I sat on the second step and didn't feel any pain.

As I looked down at my awkwardly twisted left foot, the sole of my shoe was facing me. I realized then what damage had been done. I called for help because I couldn't get up by myself. The driver of the lumber truck came down and tried to lift me up, but he was not successful. Instead, he called for an ambulance. I was brought to the same hospital in Nannhofen where I had my hernia operated on earlier.

My stay in the hospital was for about three weeks before I could go home. A cast was put on and I was in a lot of pain while in an upright position, less so, while lying down. Even the strongest prescribed painkiller was not strong enough to take me out of my misery. Once I was discharged I went home with a pair of crutches and wore the cast for about another month, perhaps two, before it was taken off.

The Orthopedic Doctor who treated me at the hospital was excellent. I did not require any surgery. Instead, under continuous monitoring by x-rays he was able to manipulate the bones back into place, except one that had completely disintegrated.

Thanks to him, I was later able to use my foot and went back to work. I was declared twenty-five percent disabled. My left leg appeared thinner as the muscles had somewhat deteriorated from lack of use. At first I did not regain full movement but with practice and patience as well as continuing pain, I slowly was able get the full use of my leg back despite the one missing cube bone. Immediately I received monthly payments from the Workmen's Compensation for my partial disability.

My older and the youngest sisters were working for the American forces as Secretaries in the former Air Academy No. 4 based in Fürstenfeldbruck, now nicknamed: *Fürsty* Air Force Base. During that time my older sister was dating an American Air Force Captain and my youngest sister was dating a Chief Master Sergeant who was in charge of the Mess Halls. He was also the operator of the 'Link Trainer,' an early flight simulator for training pilots.

Her boss at the Housing Office / Replacement Center gave her things that he got from the BX. Items such as chocolates (like large

Babe Ruth candy bars), condensed evaporated milk, Lions brand coffee from England, donut flour mix and women's nylon stockings were all greatly appreciated by her.

One day my youngest sister was speaking with one of the American Air Force pilots. She mentioned to him the gunfire attack of April 28th. To her complete surprise he told her that he was the one who did it. He said he had orders to shoot whatever he saw moving. For her that statement was so incredibly shocking and unbelievable. For him to admit to her what he had done, and without any feeling of guilt! What a coincidence, meeting the man who almost killed her. He claimed that it was in the line of duty; and didn't even apologize to her.

My Hair was starting
to grow back

Oberstdorf, A Picturesque
Town in the Alps

A Little Writing,
Relaxing.

Mountain Climbing, View
of Nebelhorn Mountain

Sieglinde

Helmut Link

Werner Barthel, Girlfriend,
and Helmut

Irmi

Working, 1949, As an
Apprentice. Bottom picture
was where I had my accident

EIGHT

Finding Hedi, the Girl For Me

It was not easy starting over once I returned back home from the Russian Gulags. It was difficult to find some sort of 'normalcy' and fit back into a war torn, yet 'civilized world.' I did manage to put almost all my efforts and energy into continuing my education and finding work.

By late 1949, I was still working as an apprentice at the carpentry shop of Lorenz Kiener in Emmering, a small village next to Fürstenfeldbruck. The work took me into different homes on private jobs in and around the area.

Often I noticed a nice young woman crossing the street about the same time that I went back and forth by bicycle to and from my job. She lived in the house of Doctor Christ in Emmering. He was the Chief Surgeon at the County Hospital. I observed her daily routine almost every day as I traveled the same route, the ***Emmeringerstrasse.*** I was not interested in dating or even getting married for that matter, until I saw this girl. But I was too shy to approach or even try to talk to her. I just couldn't find any way or reason to do so. But I continued watching her and smiled at her as I passed by on my way and she smiled back at me.

One day, my boss informed me that we had a job at the Doctor's house to build a new wood storage shed. I thought to myself, that's just great, because now I would actually have the opportunity to finally meet the girl I had admired for so long.

While working there we managed to exchange glances at each other and she being employed by the Doctor as house-daughter served breads, cold cuts and beer to us on mid-morning and afternoon breaks.

Finally we could speak to each other. Once again I became interested in women, not any woman, just her! Something inexplicable attracted me to her. She was such a picture of innocence with her pleasant and Angel-like features, that I couldn't help being drawn to her.

You might say, it was the proverbial "love at first sight." Now, having reason to speak to her, I found the courage to ask her, if she would do me the honor of going out with me, maybe to a movie or a Café. She shyly replied in a smiling way, that I would have to ask the *'Frau Doktor'*, the wife of the Doctor.

In Bavaria the wife was usually addressed according to the title her husband had, that was the long established custom. Even my mother was always addressed as the *"Frau Reichsbahnrat,"* the wife of the Railroad Advisor, and so on… The husband's title was automatically used in regards to any married woman in this region of Germany. It was perhaps a strange custom, the women didn't "earn that title, they "acquired" it by marriage. I then asked the Doctor and his wife for permission to take Hedwig out on a date. They hesitated at first, but then said it was all right.

I met her and came into the Doctor's elaborate Bavarian style house to pick her up for our date. The house was most unusual yet quite traditional to the period of time and region of Germany that it was built. It had a "Storybook-like" appealing design to it. It blended in nicely with the surrounding landscaping, and was very charming. The house had colorful country styled paintings and old German sayings painted around the wooden beams and panels. They were located just below where the roof, doorways and windows came together at the second and third story balconies decorated with "gingerbread" trim work.

We decided to go to a movie and I think it was the one with Errol Flynn called "The Buccaneers". When I got to know her a little more I found out that the Doctor and his wife had originally given her a place to live as house-daughter under the Doctor's supervision. This was when she was recuperating from the dangerous illness of Tuberculosis. She was a patient of the Doctor and he didn't want her to go back home to the farm to do all the hard labor there. She needed more rest and medical care, and supervision to fully recover. So they kept her on to be their housekeeper.

None of that mattered to me, it was not important, only she was important to me. As time went on we felt more and more comfortable with each other. I did not question her at all about any previous dating or intimate experiences and she also did not question me. I couldn't help myself and fell in love with her.

I knew right away, that Hedwig Wagner was the girl for me. I remember one evening we had our first kiss while sitting on a bench beside the Amper River bank in the backyard on the doctors large property. It was at least after the fifth or sixth date. I didn't dare risk offending her. To my surprise and happy expectation, she kissed me back as I declared my love to her and she replied, that she 'liked' me too. She didn't say 'love', not yet, that came weeks later as I was courting this lovely girl.

One weekend we decided to go with our bicycles to visit her family at the Farm House in Gröben near Schrobenhausen; it was a three-hour bike tour away. I was officially invited to come with Hedi to meet her parents. It was the first time I met them and her younger brother and sister.

Altogether she had six brothers and three sisters; it was a family of ten living and growing up on that big farm. Two of her brothers and all of her sisters were already married and had moved away. Her older brother Bert was presently running the farm. Her parents had signed it over to him and then retired to the old folks part of the farm. He later changed his mind and married into a yet larger farm and so her younger brother Andreas inherited the farm. Hedi had another older brother at home who was a war invalid, brain damaged due to being buried under debris thrown up by a large bomb and rescued too late.

At first, the parents were reluctant to accept me as they realized I was born a Prussian and not a Bavarian. The Prussians in Bavaria were called **"*Saupreuss,*"** meaning Pig Prussian. That was since earlier times when the King of Prussia had defeated the Bavarians in a war.

We stayed at the farmhouse for a long weekend; I think it was at least three nights. After that long bicycle ride to get there, our legs were aching from pedaling up and down the hilly roads. I was given a guest room and I remember that the featherbed there was a darn nuisance. It was so stiff and puffed up and over-stuffed with goose down feathers. It was almost as if I had to wrestle with it.

Her parents lived in the older part of the house and her brother Bert had taken over the main part, he being the 'Keeper of the Farm' at the time we visited them. They showed me the grounds of the Farmland with pride. It was mostly agricultural with a large portion of it being a forested area. This was painstakingly tended to, representing the wealth of the family. When cash was needed for greater expenses, like paying a dowry for a daughter, some trees were felled and sold to a lumberyard for a very good price. Timber was very expensive; supply and demand set the price.

They owned a few animals including some cows, horses, pigs, chickens and adorable piglets. My first impression was that the entire place took me back in time. It was far from being modernized, yet it brought back fond memories of when I was thirteen and spent a month at the farm in Lubjewen, near Nikolaiken, in East Prussia…

…After the war, Lubjewen was in the territory given to the Polish at the Yalta Conference held by President Roosevelt, Churchill and Stalin when they divided Germany and took my homeland East Prussia and other parts of the former Germany away…

…There was a wooden outhouse on the second floor of the house that was attached to the end-gable wall. It was an unusual one, being a two-seater that had a chute that led the waste into the exterior septic holding bin that also was the place where the waste of the animal stables was collected. That was later used as fertilizer for the farm fields. Inside that two-seater John was a wire hook-like device that served as a toilet paper holder and dispenser. But at that time there was no rolled bathroom tissue available, so they used torn up newspapers or pages from an old telephone book.

Downstairs in the main middle room, the kitchen, there was a huge hearth. Water was pumped from a well at the kitchen sink, which was then heated in a reservoir by the steady ongoing fire of the hearth. If you wanted to take a bath, they had a large tin tub that had a high back to lean on and had to be filled by buckets with blended hot and cold water.

While there I wanted to make myself useful, so when I noticed a broken ladder, I offered to repair it, and I did. But because I was also a carpenter-apprentice, I built them a new one, using their tools and materials. I also helped pitch hay for the cow and horse fodder.

It was fun feeding the cute little piglets cut-up pieces of leftover homemade farm bread mixed with milk. They lapped it up making such funny sounds with their slurps, snorts, slurps and snorts. After that lovely weekend together, her family accepted me and then Hedi and I started talking about the possibility of getting married.

I made a watercolor painting of a brilliant set of red Poinsettias. I had copied it to scale from a picture postcard that I had. That was my very first Christmas gift to Hedwig because I was a little short on cash to buy her one. A gift made by a labor of love, from me to her. I also handcrafted the frame for it.

It was not easy at all breaking the news to my father that I wanted to get engaged. He said something like: "You, my son, want to marry a servant?" He did not approve because she was not of an upper class family. Personally, none of that mattered to me. At the same time I was certain that I wanted to convert from the Lutheran faith to Catholicism. We wanted to marry in the **Klosterkirche** of Fürstenfeld. I knew what I wanted out of life, and I was no longer going to live up to the expectations of my father. After all, it was my life and up to me to decide!

While I was in the POW Hospital in Russia I became intrigued with the concepts of Catholicism and of course, it was by sticking with my religious beliefs that I remained emotionally strong and alive. I had shared my innermost thoughts, my feelings and beliefs with Hedi and she introduced me to **Pater** (Father) Ludwig, a Monk serving as Priest in the monastery church Fürstenfeld. With her full support I began taking religious instructions, without any of my family knowing what I was doing. Within a short time I was christened "Catholic" in the **Theatiner** church in Munich. It was a special Mass for all those converting to the religion. My witness / Godfather was the father of my old school friends, Gert and Rainer Nolde. At that time they were living in Fürstenfeldbruck.

After absolving my test as carpenter-journeyman, I started as an Architectural student in the *"Oskar Von Miller Politechnikum."* It was a well-known and respected Institute for technical trades in Munich. I commuted daily by train.

One of my American friends asked me to exchange 500 script dollars for him on the black market there. Unfortunately it turned out to be something of a "scam" operation and I lost the money (1,200.00 Marks). Not wanting to lose my friendship with him, I dove into my own personal savings in order to give him the money he expected. That resulted in my own personal loss; my account went down to 169 Marks.

So, my dream of continuing at the *Politech* to become an Architect never came into being because I just couldn't afford it. I only needed two more semesters to complete my education. I just had to quit because the tuition for the next semester was due in two weeks and I was unable to come up with it. I went back to work as a carpenter for better pay than I had gotten at the carpenter shop as an apprentice. I started working at the U.S. Air Force Base, Department of Air Installation, Maintenance and Repair. I figured that once I saved enough money, I could go back and finish school. But that never materialized.

Hedwig and I secretly became engaged when I presented her with a gold friendship ring. She quit her job working for the Doctor and took a job as a waitress in the *Café Brameshuber.* Hedi lived there and shared a room with other waitresses. She revealed to me that had she not met me and become engaged, that she would have considered becoming a nun.

It took courage revealing to my father that I had become a Catholic. Earlier, after I converted I told my mother about what I had done and she was extremely supportive and agreed with my decision. She kept that information secret, as I asked her to. I had wanted my father to attend my Wedding but he was stubborn and kept rejecting the decisions that I made. I remember him saying: "We are Lutheran, our ancestors were persecuted by the Catholic Church and they had to leave their home and country. That was because they steadfastly clung to their belief." "So you want to give that up? You are not my son any more!"

All of my friends as well as my mother and sisters were constantly badgering him, trying to persuade him to change his way of thinking. Finally, after many weeks he rescinded. After all, I was his only son and it was my life.

Despite all the turmoil he created, for the first time in his life he attended a Catholic High Mass, to everyone's surprise, and also walked Hedi down the aisle, giving her away. Her own parents were not able to attend the wedding.

After taking our wedding vows on the morning of March 31, 1951, we then had a party luncheon celebration in the same mansion where my friends Gert and Rainer Nolde's family lived. Following that we were driven to visit Hedi's parents in Gröben, and my parents met hers for the first time. Her parents had earlier turned the reign of the farm over to their son, Bert. Her brother was totally against giving her a dowry because she did not marry into a farm family. To think of all things, I was a Prussian, not a Bavarian.

So, following that, we had to sue in court for the minimum dowry that Hedi would be entitled to.

By that time my friend Gert Nolde had become a Lawyer and was able to represent us in court. As a result we won and received the minimum dowry established by law.

With that settlement we were able to purchase our first set of new furniture. For the time we were renting a large room in my parents apartment and that was what we called "home." In one corner of the room we made a kitchenette with a modern stove that was invented, patented and designed by Gerts father. It was the first time that a wood / coal burning stove used for cooking featured a dust free ash removal system. But it was short lived in post war society and was soon replaced by gas and or electric ranges.

Hedi cooked many wonderful meals on that stove. We also bought a modern kitchen buffet cabinet unit for our dining table, yet another "new" invention. The table was the size of a cocktail table. The surprise was, that by lifting it up the legs extended, dropped and locked into place, creating a dining table after pulling out extensions at both ends. We also purchased a modern King size sofa bed that had storage drawers under it for the bedding.

All the searching and trying to find another bigger place to live that we could call our own, was futile. To our disappointment, nothing was available. It was post-war time. Many places were still in ruins and had not yet started to be rebuilt. We were told the waiting period could take seven or more years. More and more Eastern refugees entered the country and the housing shortage became worse. It was impossible to build to supply the demand.

The newly established German government enacted a ruling that anyone having a large apartment or house had to give up one or two rooms to a home-coming family member as well as to refugees, displaced peoples or a Jewish family.

Because of that my parents not only gave us a room but also gave up their parlor to a young Jewish couple. The main kitchen and bathroom was shared by all of us, the only area that my parents kept to themselves was their bedroom and living room.

Fortunately we all got along extremely well. The young couple even helped us out by sharing some of their supply of food. They had the privilege of getting extra supplies through their Jewish organization.

As a matter of fact, later when the young Jewish couple moved out to a bigger place, they purchased our Theden piano that had been in our family since we were living in Königsberg. (I believe that it was originally a wedding gift from my Grandfather to my parents). The wife had taken piano lessons so she greatly appreciated being able to get it.

Behind our apartment house in the backyard stood a small factory where they manufactured many things of different trades. They also had a knitting machine and produced sweaters. Hedi made a nice income selling sweaters door-to-door to American families who were living in the dependent housing at the now American Air Force Base

She did that in spite of the fact that she did not speak English.

I continued working at the Air Force Base doing installations, maintenance and repairs for the dependent housing. One of the biggest projects we did was extending the concrete runway so it could accommodate larger aircraft than fighters.

For yet another big project, bricks were brought in from the bombed out ruins in Munich. They were crushed down to pebbles in a special machine and then mixed with sand and cement and then poured into wire mesh forms for the exterior walls. Thus, porous walls were created in the construction of new dependent housing buildings. Openings for windows and doors were framed in wood and inserted in the temporary wire mesh wall forms. All exterior walls were constructed to be ten inches thick. The two sides of stucco enclosed the porous walls and so created natural air insulation. When the poured mix with the brick pebbles had hardened and the wire mash forms were removed from those new created exterior two story walls, one could see the rough building almost ready. Only the roof had to be constructed, windows and exterior doors to be installed and the exterior side of the main exterior walls to be fitted with a coat of coarse stucco, to have the total exterior finished. Then the interior walls were built of four inch thick, two feet by four feet lightweight foam concrete blocks. They were then stacked up together with mortar to build the walls. They could be cut with an ordinary handsaw into pieces to fit the intended walls that had to be built. Even grooves were cut with an electric handsaw for the insertion of the needed wiring conduits and also for the outlet and switch boxes before the walls were fitted with smooth stucco on both sides, including the inside of the exterior walls.

Interior doors and frames could then be installed in the designated openings, trimmed and finished, ready for painting. The plumbers and Electricians then did their jobs, the painters and other interior tradesmen, like carpet installers, etc. until all was finished for occupancy. With that technique the building took only four to five weeks to be completed from start to finish. Of course that was after the poured concrete foundation and basement walls were formed and cured. Even the two floors were constructed with pre-cast lightweight foam / tension tongue and groove two feet wide and 8 inch thick planks.

New facilities for the Air Force Troops, (kitchens), had to be built because the existing ones were infested with cockroaches. At the demolishing of the old buildings when we pulled the old flooring up, there were swarms of them running into all directions.

My pay was very good working at those jobs and once in a while when I was able to obtain script dollars I bought yogurt, my favorite dessert, in the Commissary.

At one time, we traveled by truck to an off the base job. While going there we saw a crate drop from an incoming food supply truck that was passing us by. We stopped and walked back to retrieve it. The supply truck kept going, not being aware of their loss. We lifted the crate into our truck and kept going to our assigned work site. Once at our destination we opened the crate and were surprised to find fifty dozens fresh eggs inside. Only a few were cracked in one of the paper mache' crush-proof 12 count containers.

What a treasure that was! We divided our trove among us, ten workers. Each of us was able to take home five dozens eggs, less the few that were broken. At that time as food was still being rationed. Two eggs per person, per week was the usual allotment. Once home, our wives were surprised at our good fortune and were able to prepare the meals that we had missed for so long that required eggs. Of course, most eggs were traded in exchange for other goods that were very hard to come by. So we all "lived it up" and celebrated our unexpected "special delivery" from Heaven.

It was June 7, 1952 when my close friend Gert Nolde got married. The wedding was held at the ***Klosterkirche*** and was most impressive. After we attended the Church Service, his College Fraternity brothers in full regalia like Musketeers, crossed swords and formed an arch for the newly married couple to pass through. The Reception was held privately in the three-story mansion that was owned by Professor Nübel, a widower, who was also a friend of my parents. Gert's family lived there, in the second story apartment. It was the same place where Hedi's and my wedding reception was held.

The three story high entrance hall of that building had a huge circular staircase along the four walls, giving it the appearance and atmosphere of a Ballroom. There must have been about one hundred guests. For entertainment, I brought my brand new Grundig console, stereo-record player / combination system having a long wave and short wave tube operated radio with enormous speakers.

From the selection of record albums I chose to play the wedding march from the Opera Aida. As the new bride and groom arrived and entered I 'blasted' the Wedding March, and that was the only form of entertainment that we had. The sound reverberated from the three-storied ballroom throughout the building.

Everybody joined in clapping to the rhythm of the March. The bass sound coming from the drums and string instruments was quite echoing and gave it the sound of a big orchestra playing live music. All the guests joined in dancing and celebrating. Unfortunately, the marriage of Gert and Maria lasted only a few years and ended sadly in divorce.

Finding Hedi, The Girl For Me.

"Just Married" 3/31/1951

As Newlyweds 1951

1952

Coming to America 1953
On board the Homelines.

Christmas At Our
Place in Germany.

NINE

Coming To The New Homeland On The Homelines

After the war Germany was still in a state of turmoil and destruction. This period of time lasted from the end of the 1940's way into the mid 1960's. Immigration to the United States was on the rise as an option for many German citizens who were able to make the move.

However, at that time the United States Immigration Services (now INS) put quotas on various ethnic populations. One good thing was that people who arrived in New York by ship no longer had to make their port of entry via Ellis Island. That way of entry to the U.S.A. ceased by the end of the 1920's or early 30's which made the immigration process slightly easier.

In 1952 my wife Hedwig and I decided to leave Germany. We had to wait until 1953 for the Visas. With a nation still in repair there was a lack of housing. As newlyweds we didn't have the choices or options available to find a place we could call our home. Coming to America would help me to provide a better life for my new bride and it was also a chance for me to start a new life, and forget the past.

Once we made the firm decision about emigrating to the U.S.A., I took a lump sum settlement from my Workmen's Compensation disability fund. First we bought ourselves new wardrobes. Mine included a Bavarian styled outfit of a Hunters (**Loden**) Jacket, **Lederhosen** (leather knickers), and a green velour hat with a feathered plume, mountain climbing shoes and a comfortable bathrobe. Hedi had a custom made **Dirndl** Dress and a new winter coat. I designed a wide brimmed hat for her that was also custom made of a burgundy colored velour.

When we received and accepted the offer from my youngest sister's parents-in-laws to be our sponsors, we applied for an immigration Visa at the American Consulate in Munich. As mentioned earlier quotas were in force at that time, we had to wait a year to get one. We were lucky that it came through that fast, because at first we were told that a two-year waiting period was the 'norm.' Maybe the fact that I was a skilled carpenter by trade, made the difference?

After purchasing our passenger fares for our journey to America by the shipping company Homelines we sent money (1,680.00 Marks) to our sponsors so that they could set up a $400.00 savings account for us. That way we could start our new life without being indebted as most immigrants were. Immigrants often had to borrow money for their trip as well as for their living expenses for the first few weeks in the United States until they got a job to be on their own.

As our ship, the Homeland from the Home Lines embarked March 5. 1953, I made the decision to leave all my bad wartime memories behind me. That month of March was actually the eighth anniversary since I first became a prisoner of war and "guest" of the "Worker's Paradise in Russia." But since I decided to forget that past, it didn't enter my mind as we planned for our immediate future.

Once I put foot in my new homeland, I also made the conscious decision to hide my past life. Both America and Europe were still working in the 1950's to pick up the pieces from the destruction of World War II. To think that I was once compelled to become a recruit into the Nazi party, without having a choice. I knew that this fact alone would not sit well with the American population. So, therefore, once I arrived in the United States I had to keep that my secret. Even my dear wife didn't have any clue as to what I actually had been through or what war memories I had kept bottled up and suppressed inside me.

Decisions had to be made as to what we would be transporting to our new homeland. As I look back, I guess we just didn't have any clue as to how different the new lifestyle would be. We brought just about everything that we owned.

We sold the new kitchen buffet and took only the sofa bed along and the table as well as our newly acquired chinaware set, books, and of course, our Grundig stereo-radio console and our record collection.

The voyage took us twelve days from Bremer Haven to Plymouth in England to Cherbourg in France, then over the Atlantic Ocean to Halifax, Canada and then from Halifax to New York. At first we were put in to separate double bed cabins we had to share with others of the same gender, for men and for women but with a little 'bribe' to the cabin steward Hedi and I got an inside cabin at the rear of the ship next to the stairway leading up to the rear deck. The service and food was very good and in the first ten days we had good weather and smooth sailing and spent most of the days on the rear deck in deck chairs enjoying the ride. Hedi was mostly seasick and despite not having to vomit, did not feel too well and ate very little, but was happy to spend the days laying down on the adjustable deck chairs in fresh air and sun.

The days went by very swiftly and I spent some time exploring the ship. I went all the way to the bow looking down to see the parting of the sea and also encountered some dolphins swimming along with us.

Just before we came to Halifax the weather started to change. It got windy and rough and a hurricane was coming up. Overnight we stayed in the harbor and it was not too rough there, but as we departed the next morning for the last leg to New York it got really nasty. Hedi and I spent most of the day in our cabin that was located right above the ships Propulsion screws. The high waves our ship encountered lifted the screws out of the water and one could hear them spinning freely and fast and then slowed down as they submerged again. It was a constant whirling up and down in measured sequence as we went along. A funny thing happened as I tried to climb the stairs to look out onto the rear deck, I had the feeling of stepping down as the next up-step disappeared under my foot; it was quite awkward managing those stairs to the top like a drunken sailor.

Looking through the rear door I saw the rear deck periodically swamped, the waves gushing over the railing. As I was standing there, I felt like being in an elevator constantly going up and down. I enjoyed that feeling, it was as if I was flying in my Messerschmitt roller coasting and was not seasick at all. The storm raged all day long, because evidently we were moving in the same direction and speed of the storm from East to West towards New York.

The last nights dinner was at the captain's table. Only eight people showed up because all the others were seasick. It was an elaborate fancy dinner we enjoyed with champagne and cordials as well as delicious deserts.

Eventually the weather changed to be a calm one and as we entered New York harbor I took pictures of the Statue Of Liberty as we passed by and then docked at pier 86 our final destination.

Upon arriving at the U.S. customs, the inspector/agent told us that we wouldn't need our down featherbeds. He said: " Because here, in America, we have electric blankets." That was the way I remember our "Welcome to America" after our long 12day voyage.

I also remember that Dwight Eisenhower was the President of the United States in 1953, and we heard about the death of Stalin while we were on our journey to our new chosen homeland. Another reason I personally wanted to leave Germany was because the United States was a "free country." By this I mean that it was not a police-run state where rules and regulations and particular political views were enforced. I knew that America was the land of the free and the home of the brave. I definitely felt it was a place to make new beginnings and another plan for our lives.

The In-laws of my youngest sister, who had sponsored our immigration, were living in West Englewood, New Jersey. They came to pick us up at Pier 86 where we disembarked in New York City. Riding with them on the way to their home, towards the George Washington Bridge we encountered a lot of heavy traffic. When we arrived, it was March 17th, St. Patrick's Day.

We found out that there was a big parade on Fifth Avenue, and we joked that it was for us, because we had just arrived. We stayed with my youngest sister's parents-in-law for about three weeks to get acquainted with living in our new homeland. We went shopping for some of our own groceries and they commented about what we were eating. "You eat butter? That's expensive, your savings will not last long doing that, we buy the less expensive margarine!"

For the first time I saw a wood frame house being built across the street from where we were staying. I thought to myself that American homes were built with "toothpicks" and I compared it to the ones made from heavier timber that I was used to working with while constructing homes in Germany. Later on I became acquainted with this new way of building homes and fit right in, as I eventually worked with an American partner.

Within a short time after our arrival we were fortunate to get jobs living with and working for a Jewish family, Bernard Cohen on Merrill Dr. Lawrence, Long Island, New York. That was actually arranged through my sister's father-in-law, Mr. Moneypenny. Mr. Cohen was a builder of big apartment houses in Long Island and Mr. Moneypenny was his production supervisor for all projects. Mr. And Mrs. Cohen and their two sons lived in an elaborate big home with attached twin garages and drove a late model Cadillac and had another sports car. There was also a huge backyard where parties often took place for Mr. Cohen's clientele in huge tents set up by Party House Caterers of Cedarhurst, L.I.

Hedi was hired as cook and housekeeper and I was the all-around handyman. Their gardener, a German man, had told me about a construction company called: "Lakso Brothers." that was looking for skilled carpenters to hire. I managed to get a full time carpentry job with them. We built luxury homes along Woodmere Boulevard in Cedarhurst, L.I., New York.

In the meantime, I took driving lessons from a retired policeman and was able to buy a 49' Plymouth Coupe from a German friend for a good price. Luckily, I got my license on the first driving test. I had practiced driving with my German friend who was a car mechanic for a Ford dealer in nearby Lynbrook where I had inquired about buying a car.

One day in the month of May 1953, the head of the Jewish family, Mr. Cohen, hired a carpenter contractor. The job of remodeling a bedroom for one of his sons was to be started. It was to include a built-in bunk bed, bookshelves, a desk with drawers and a Hi-Fi system. That was when I became acquainted with Clyde Fader, an independent contractor. While he worked there, we were able to talk "shop." I explained to him that I was a Journeyman-Carpenter by trade, in Germany. So, he made the suggestion to become his partner. He said that I should leave Lakso Brothers and that I was underpaid there, because I was not a member of the carpenters Union. I agreed and became his partner and of course bettered myself financially.

Being "Greenhorns," as the expression goes, we soon came to realize that Hedi and I were over worked and under paid in the Cohen's household. Although our employers helped us to apply for citizenship, and respected our religious beliefs, even driving us to the nearby Catholic Church on Sundays; they put more and more demands on us.

Hedi did sewing and dress alterations and made curtains for them with our electric sewing machine we brought along with us from Germany. Often she worked until very late at night without any extra compensation. The frequent and elaborate parties that were held by the Cohen family were always catered by Party House Caterers of Cedarhurst, (next to Lawrence). But when our employers found out that Hedi was capable of cooking all the food and hors d'oeuvres, the services of the Caterers were no longer needed. They just hired a few waitresses, a bartender, a large tent for the garden and I waited on tables too. So our workload steadily grew and the pay stayed the same.

Every Summer, the Cohen family spent two to three months in Europe. During that time, Hedi and I were "house-sitting." At the same time I became partners with Clyde. Together we went to Levittown, New Jersey where Clyde had contracted to frame Levitt Houses as our job; all the needed other work at those houses was completed by yet other specialized contractors.

We stayed in a rooming house in nearby Trenton. That was a most unusual experience for me. It was the first time in America that I lived in an almost commune-style habitat. We had to share a bathroom with the other tenants and it was located at the end of the hallway. After three weeks, the job was not yet completed but I did not like being away from my wife for so long. I returned to Lawrence, by myself, taking my first ride on a train back to New York and then on the Long Island Railroad to Lawrence. Somehow I managed to navigate my way back to join Hedi.

While I was away she was approached by Party House Caterers and was offered the job as Chief Chef with an alluring salary. It exceeded far over and beyond what both of us had been earning as employees working privately as domestics. It was an offer we couldn't refuse. So we rented a small apartment in Cedarhurst and when our employers returned from their trip to Europe we quit that job and moved into 526 West Broadway in Cedarhurst, only two blocks from Party House Caterers, so Hedi could walk to her job in minutes. From then on I was worked nights at those parties as waiter and days as a carpenter. Hedi was now the # 1 cook and managed all the cooking and baking for those parties and had command over several kitchen helpers.

When my partner Clyde completed the jobs in New Jersey he arranged for our newly formed "Ford Contracting Company" to frame fourteen houses in Copiague, Long Island, New York. They were located along a boat canal and we hired eight men to help us to get the job done. The foundations were in and we only needed to frame the new houses just as we did in New Jersey.

The builder hired us as sub-contractors and we were supposed to be paid one thousand dollars for each framed house. But when we had completed the work and wanted to get paid the fourteen thousand dollars, the builder had a different idea. He disappeared along with the down payments that had been made by the new homebuyers.

He left a huge bill behind, especially one with the lumber company that had all the lumber delivered to the jobsite. The carpenters we hired were entitled to their pay and of course, Clyde and I were responsible for their compensation.

Besides that fact, all of the builders' assets were in his wife's name. We were stuck and had to take out a loan to enable us to pay the men we had hired for the job. There was no other way to settle it. It was a deal gone wrong. We lost fourteen thousand dollars and never heard from him again.

Hedi and I worked extremely hard together for the first year of our new life in America in order to get ahead, and we strived to eventually purchase our own home. We were constantly on the lookout for a reasonable priced house we could afford to buy. That time enabled us to reach our goal of saving enough for a down payment so we could own our own home. Whenever we had an opportunity we looked all over Long Island for an affordable small house. We searched around Inwood near the then Idlewild Airport, but there was nothing we liked and the constant air traffic with all the noise discouraged us from settling there. We were unable able to find an affordable house anywhere in all of Nassau County.

We decided to look in Suffolk County that was much farther away. We found exactly what we were looking for in North Patchogue in the Canaan Lake area. There was a model house we looked at for a new to be built small home with two bedrooms, one bath, living room and kitchen, that came with all windows fitted with Venetian blinds, ceramic tiled bath with cast iron tub American Standard WC, a wall mounted sink and a recessed medicine cabinet with light. The kitchen came with base and top cabinets, Mica countertop and a Magic Chef gas range. In the small hallway between the two bedrooms and the bath there was a gas fired recessed floor heater, that kept the whole house warm, controlled by a thermostat in the living room. The kitchen had a ceiling light and a side door to the outside. The living and bedrooms all had several wall outlets, one that was operated by a switch at each entry door where a lamp could be plugged in, operated by that switch. The front door and side door had outside lights and switches, so the two step concrete stairs were lighted by night. We decided to buy one of these lovely homes and were asked for a $ 300.00 down payment as escrow towards the total price of $ 6,000.00 and a mortgage of $ 5,700.00.

Since we were not prepared to buy a house on that trip we did not have that much money with us. The sales man who drove us to the North-end of the yet unpaved Truberg Ave to show us the next available property of 60 by 100 feet size, was anxious to close a deal right then and there, since we also liked that property on the sloped down end of Truberg Ave.

He asked for a $ 10.00 down payment towards the balance of $ 290.00 to pay later at our next visit. We made several trips to see the ongoing construction of our home to take pictures and make sure that all was being done according to plan. It was indeed well constructed even the exterior sheathing was all done with one by six inch tongue and groove Cedar sheathing boards. Other homes that were built by other builders in the neighborhood had thin plywood- or composite board sheathing, so our builder didn't spare good material. Similar homes in the surrounding area had plastic tiles on their bathroom walls and cheaper steel tubs and the new owners had to do quite some work themselves to have it ready to move in. The wiring was all copper, while neighboring homes had aluminum wiring. The only thing we needed to move in was our own refrigerator; everything else was ready for us after the closing.

On our future visits to see our house being built we were never asked for he

$ 290.00 balance for the escrow and we figured, that perhaps at the closing we would have to pay it. But at the closing in June to which we went without a lawyer we only had to sign for a mortgage of $

5,700.00 and nobody asked for the escrow balance. So we actually got our home for a total of:

$ 5,710.00, so it was really a great bargain. We got our payment book for the thirty-year mortgage in monthly installments of $ 47.00....

On July 4th, 1954 we moved into our own new house. That was a little over a year after arriving in the United States. Friends wondered how we did it. Being in this country approximately one year, having bought a car, and now were able to buy and own our new home? A friend of ours said: "I lived here all my life, got married and live in a rented apartment, driving an old jalopy. We could not afford to buy our own home and you are here barely a year in the States and have accomplished all this?" Well, it was the fruit of both our toil and labor and many long hours of work in that first year in our new homeland.

Our new home address was at 246 Truberg Avenue (by Canaan Lake) in North Patchogue, Long Island, New York. According to the deed we also had "lake rights," for boating, fishing and swimming as well as the use of a clubhouse at Canaan Lake.

Using the Partyhouse Caterers truck we were able to make the move to our new home with the used furniture we had bought from a dealer in Cedarhurst.

We had to wait one month before we got phone service. The New York Telephone Company had not been able to install enough phone lines for the quickly increasing population in Suffolk County of Long Island.

When we finally received service it was a "party line." At times that became a nuisance due to the fact that about four or five families shared the same line. There was no such thing as privacy because you overheard other people's conversations when you lifted the receiver. A few times I had to break into a long conversation to let the other party know that I had to make an important outgoing call. But we learned to cope with it as just another aspect of starting our new life over here. About six or eight month later we got our own private line to our great relief. No more waiting for the long chatting housewives to get off the phone, it was such a nuisance.

At first, Hedi took a job as a health aide working in a Patchogue nursing home. She quit her job as chef in Cedarhurst because it was too far from Patchogue. Besides, she didn't know how to drive, nor did she have the desire to learn to drive. We had only one car, that black 49 Plymouth two-door coupe.

After we moved in we joined the local Catholic Church. Our Pastor, Father Cunningham of St. Francis De Sales Church, asked Hedi if she would like to become the Rectory cook and housekeeper, and I became the custodian for all the Church properties.

There was the Church and Rectory, a house next door to accommodate extra Priests, the Parish school on South Ocean Avenue, diagonally across the Avenue from the Church Building. Then there was the Convent for the teaching nuns and the Parish Hall next to it that actually was a large gym. The Parish Hall also served for some of the public Sunday Masses, and on Wednesday evenings for Bingo games and on other days as a gym for school basketball games and other functions for students of the Parish school. I had to set up the tables and chairs each Wednesday for Bingo and each Saturday the chairs and kneelers for Sunday Mass. The kneelers I built myself with attached foam-rubber kneeling pads, in the workshop that I had set up in the basement of the Hall. Each of the kneelers accommodated six persons. I also built the kitchen cabinets and countertops for the basement kitchen of the hall. When the Parish Hall originally was built, the kitchen was left unfinished for a later installation and since I was able to build them myself, that saved the parish the cost of hiring a kitchen cabinet specialist contractor.

There also were a lot of grassy areas on all those properties that had to be cut and maintained, landscaping to be kept clean of weeds and the raking of leaves in the Fall as well as snow shoveling in the Winter. Every school day the classrooms and halls in the school had to be broom-swept and cleaned. I did this, together with old Charlie, he was the sexton of the church.

Since my workload got progressively larger, the Pastor hired a helper for me, a retired NYC Firemen captain who had moved to Patchogue and became a parishioner.

At that time there were some renovations needed in the old school building. All the fascia boards at the roof edge were rotting and had to be replaced with two by ten inch planks to hold the gutters in place. In the basement the girders supporting the two-stories of classrooms were too weak to hold the weight and had sagged several inches. With the help of Clyde Fader, my former partner and his carpenter brother we installed a steel "I" beam under the existing girder and with adjustable screw-columns lifted the entire upper two floors to the former level position day by day a little bit at a time. That of course caused some of the plaster at the wood-stud walls of the classrooms above to buckle; the occurring cracks while the floors were slowly settling had earlier been patched up from time to time. Now, that the floors were being lifted to the original level, we had to replace large sections of loosened plaster in those walls. The plaster was held to the wall by the old fashion latticework, some of which needed replacing too. The basement had to be used as additional classrooms to accommodate the children of the new families that had moved to Patchogue, enlarging the Parish of St Francis De Sales.

We built an additional classroom in the Parish Hall at the upper open balcony. The three feet high end-wall of the balcony was closed up to the ceiling with sections of tempered ¼ inch plate-glass framed in wood. It had to be tempered glass that was especially ordered to the needed size because below at the gym-floor basketball games were played and the large sheets of regular plate-glass might have been shattered by errant balls.

The ceiling-mounted baskets and back plates had winches on the sidewalls to be lowered for the games and lifted for other activities in the Parish Hall. So Clyde, his brother and I once again saved the parish a good amount of money than if the Pastor had hired an outside contractor to do those jobs.

As we got somewhat "settled" into our house, and adjusted to life in America, my oldest sister decided to also come to America to make her home here. She arrived in December of 1955, just around Christmas time, and stayed with us shortly before getting her own apartment in New York City and taking a job as a Legal Secretary.

When she returned to Patchogue for visits on weekends, I taught her how to drive the new '55' Plymouth Savoy that we had just acquired. Hedi did not yet have a driving license nor did she make any attempt to learn. We spent a lot of time on the beaches of Long Island, and my sister thought that Rocky Point at the Sound and North coast of Long Island reminded her of the beaches of Samland, (at the Baltic Sea where we went as young children), because of the high elevated coast line in that area that had stairways from the upper properties down to the much lower beach. But most of the time we spent on the south shore beach at Westhampton beach on Fire Island. For my sister's driving practice I let her drive my car and she did pretty well with it and quickly learned to handle the driving. She is a very smart lady.

Within a year's time she became engaged to a man she had met in the city. Their marriage took place in Patchogue at the Town Hall and I was their best man and witness.

At that time we had a black Cocker Spaniel dog called Topper (we nicknamed him: Toppi). We got him from the caterer that we worked for earlier. He always came along with us to the beach and he really enjoyed running after the seagulls along the water.

At home for entertainment I loved playing records on my Grundig record player/ radio console that we brought from Germany. It was that very same one I used to play the wedding-march from Aida at Gert's wedding back in Fürstenfeldbruck.

I created a built-in cabinet / bookshelf combination wall unit that took up the entire area of the South wall of our living room, covering it from floor to ceiling. It also contained a built-in fold down desk and storage compartments fitted with louver cabinet doors. I really cherished that piece. Our television that we bought used from a dealer while still living in Cedarhurst was the centerpiece just above our Grundig console.

Facing that entertainment wall we had a newly bought sectional 90degree corner couch with a large throw rug in front of it on which our patent cocktail /dining table combo stood.

It was a real hot and sticky summer when I Ludi and I, including my older sister, drove in my car from New York to Harrisonville, Missouri. We must have been crazy because we drove non-stop taking more than thirty-two hours in that heat without air conditioning in my car; I drove the car all the way to and from our destination.

The purpose of the trip was to visit our youngest sister and meet her family. She had married a Chief Master Sergeant in the US Air Force, whom she had met earlier back home in Germany. He had a career with the Air Force as operator of the huge flight simulator there, and they were living at the Air Force Base.

Their first child, a son, had been born in Germany after Hedi and I had left Germany, and they had another son and also one daughter who were born here in the States. It was a pleasure to become re-acquainted with one another, now that we were all in our new homeland. We spent some pleasant days with each other and then drove back to NY's Long Island. On the way we saw an inviting lake and decided to go swimming to cool down on that hot day. It had a nice grassy beach where we spread our blankets to rest on and sunbathe. The big disappointment came, when we waded into the water to cool down. To our surprise the water was almost as warm as stepping into a warm bathtub, there was no cooling down. Only after we swam around a while and got out wet as we were, the gentle breeze of wind helped us to cool a little bit as we got dry in a very short time sunbathing. Long after we left that lake on our way home Hedi noticed, that she was missing her wristwatch that I had given her for her previous year's birthday. She remembered, that as we went swimming in that warm lake she placed it at the edge of our spread blanket. It must have slipped into the grass and she forgot all about it in the rush of packing up to get back into our car. Well whoever may have found it later was the new keeper of that watch, we did not turn back to go looking for it and waste time.

My other younger sister chose to remain in Germany, living with my parents and later got married to the son of the architect that designed and built the new house for my parents in upper Fürstenfeldbruck. The architect's family members were refugees from East Prussia and became friends with my parents.

When the Vatican ordered changes in the service of the Catholic Church were made, whereby the altar was brought forward and the priest was facing the congregation in performing the Mass, I was asked by our Pastor to do the needed renovations. At the same time I was also to renovate and enhance the entire inner church ceilings and walls. St. Francis De Sales Church's old Roman arch ceiling had a painted sculptured tin ceiling cover. With age the paint was peeling and flakes of it rained down onto the pews.

A re-painting would have been futile and eventually would have resulted in the same flaking, so I suggested we cover the entire arch ceiling and the flat ceilings above the side isles with 12" X 12" white ceiling tiles, that would give it a clean and smooth look.

I figured out how best to do it and then started the work with my new helper Salvatore Camarda, an Italian friend of mine whose wife was German. Salvatore and his wife also lived in the Canaan Lake area. To do the big job I needed a movable high scaffold to be able to reach all areas of the huge arch ceiling. I fastened long 2" X 12" planks onto the tops of the backrests of the pews in rail-like fashion so a rolling scaffold could move back and forth as needed for the progressing work. First I nailed 1" X 4" X 16 feet boards onto the arch ceiling starting from both side bottoms of the arch upwards every 12 " until joined at the very top of the arch and center line. The boards of course ran lengthwise from the rear of the Church all the way to the end wall where the altar was at the front.

The chandeliers over the pews had to be temporarily removed. All the electric work was done be another parishioner who was a licensed electrician.

After all 1 X 4s were installed, the work with the ceiling tiles could be started. Again we started stapling them from both bottom side edges of the arch, working row by row of tiles up towards the upper centerline. It was not easy to fit them following the curve of the arch and keep them in a perfect straight line and meet atop the centerline evenly. As the work progressed we had to move the scaffold forward constantly and slowly but surely reached the altar wall as the entire arch was finally covered. What a difference it made seeing a smooth white arch above instead of the old darkened flaky tin ceiling.

The side-isle ceilings were much easier and simpler to install and the whiteness of the new ceiling tiles reflected the lights of the windows and made the entire Church appear much brighter. The electrician installed new hanging chandeliers Father Cunningham had ordered and then we dismantled the scaffold and the plank rails.

Now came the work to move the altar. I completely re-built it and attached fine sculptured wooden ornaments as decoration on the front facing the congregation. As I remember I think I gilded those ornaments to stand out from the white background and as such gave it a pleasing artful look. The former altar wall was covered with sculptured ceiling tiles that formed a circle pattern by each of four tiles and the overall look with the shadowy indentations was a very pleasing sight.

In the center of it I attached the big life-size Crucifix with Jesus nailed to it. I felt like one of the cruel Roman soldiers, as I had to fashion a new long nail with which both his feet were nailed to the cross and hammer it in. With tears in my eyes I prayed for forgiveness for what I had to do, I felt so guilty and devastated. Still today I feel that guilt of being one of those who nailed our savior to the cross.

The edges of that big tiled area were framed in 3" base molding following along the curve of the arched ceiling. Yet another parishioner who had his own company of flooring and carpeting then installed new carpeting at the entire altar area.

Then I tackled the installation of new paneling along all insides of the exterior walls. Also the two side altars and the christening nave received their new look.

The last work was the installation of the new entry doors and changing the main entry of the front of the Church leading out to South Ocean Ave. Up until then we used the side doors from the front lobby. Other minor alterations in connection with the overall restoration were also finally completed and all that represented now my crowning accomplishment and biggest job at St Francis De Sales Church that saved the Parish a huge bundle of money.

I did not receive, nor was I expecting any extra pay for all the work I did and I saw this as my heartfelt thanks and good deed for the Good Lords help and aid I received and also for my safe homecoming from the three years in the Russian Gulags.

1954

That's Me and "Toppi"

1955 At Our House

TEN

Fifty Years Living In America (1953-2003)
(With Return Trips to Germany)

1953 to 1956 was a period of adjustment and getting settled. For the first five years we became familiar with the customs and ways of life in America. In general, back then people were much friendlier and open to learning and knowing more about one another than they are today.

We were able to form many lasting friendships, actually a few that have lasted a lifetime. One of the first couples that we met and became very close to when we first moved to Patchogue were Bill and Marianne Burns. One of the Priests from our parish at St. Francis De Sales Church had introduced us. He was the Assistant Pastor, Father Gorman, and Father Cunningham was the Pastor of that Church.

We made an instant connection after being introduced because Bill's wife Marianne originally came from Augsburg, Germany, in Bavaria (near Hedwig's Birthplace). That fact alone made my wife feel at ease while adjusting to her new lifestyle.

The Burns had their two daughters just before we started our own family. We joined them for get-togethers and later on vacations at Tupper Lake, in upper New York State. Later on they moved there permanently after purchasing "Lake Shore Cabins" to start a Motel-Resort business.

In 1954 I had my first opportunity to once again pilot an aircraft. That was by taking off from a small airfield that was located alongside Sunrise Highway, in Sayville, Long Island, New York.

I befriended a man who had a Piper Tri-Pacer and when he heard that I was a pilot in World War II he allowed me the privilege of co-piloting his aircraft. I thought that it would be interesting to make a comparison between piloting a Pacer vs. my last solo flight with the ME-109. The difference was that the Tri-Pacer had twin yokes and side by side seats instead of a single seat and steering stick and was of course much slower. It also had two rear passenger seats.

After a few more flights with him, I invited my friend Clyde to come along with us. I nearly scared him out of his wits when I banked and sharply dipped the left wing on an angle so I could point out where my house was, directly below us.

That small airport was short-lived because some time after that it was wiped out as the result of a hurricane in the Fall of 1954.

By 1955 I began having trouble with my back. Actually it was an undiscovered complication from the accident that I had earlier in 1949. I was limping and was not aware of it and had developed a side curvature of the spine. My right leg was shorter than my left. As a result, the right hip had lifted and I had to wear a lift in the heel of my right shoe. It was three quarter of an inch in thickness to correct and alleviate the problem of limping.

I often had a painful 'slipped disk' and could not understand why. X-rays taken by my Chiropractor revealed that what had happened (from my fall from the hayloft to the root cellar) was, that in my back (a lower vertebrae) had been broken and it was undetected up to that point. The handicap of an often-recurring slipped disk had become a nasty problem for me, but I knew that I would just have to deal with it for the rest of my life. Had it been detected right after the accident, my disability would have been declared as much more than twenty-five percent. Therefore, the compensation would also have been greater.

In 1957 we made our first trip back to Germany to attend my father's seventieth birthday celebration. At the same time it was a housewarming for the newly built Dulias family home. That of course was done with our financial help. We sent monthly checks home from what we had earned and were able to spare. That lovely house was built in upper Fürstenfeldbruck at the Holz Straße.

Before that first return visit, Hedi often felt homesick and could not quite adjust to her new life here on Long Island. She did not have a license to drive a car so that put limitations on where she wanted to go, and what she wanted to do. She was totally dependent on me for transportation, and we were like strangers in a strange land trying to feel our way forward and become acquainted with both new people and surroundings. But, after returning from our first visit back to Germany, she came to the realization that she no longer belonged there and accepted her new life and felt at home in the United States.

Shortly after we returned, she became pregnant with our first child and also finally decided to learn how to drive a car. She took her driving test one week before the baby was due. The examiner quickly passed her, afraid that she might start delivering while taking the test.

On October 1st in 1958 she started going into labor. It had lasted for three days. The Doctor told her to do some walking. We must have walked together for miles and miles all over the neighborhood until finally, on the fourth day, of October, our first daughter Angela was born. We celebrated and had the baby christened. Afterwards my wife continued working at the Church as a cook and housekeeper. She carried our newborn baby in a bassinette with her every day.

Things were going rather well, when five months later Hedi became pregnant with our second child. Anticipating and hoping for a boy we had bought many blue things of baby clothing. That pregnancy was a slightly different experience than her first. This baby was much more active in the womb.

On December 27th, 1959 our second daughter Elisabeth was born in a most unusual way, feet first. She had a full head of reddish hair, and we were unprepared without pink outfits. We brought her home wearing a blue cap, blue booties and blue blanket.

From then on, my wife could no longer juggle her role of motherhood, (with an infant and a toddler), along with a full time job while trying to maintain our own household. The decision was made that she would stay home.

At the same time I started expanding our house. Clyde and I made a plan that would increase the square footage of our home, tripling it from the original size. That included three extra bedrooms, a dining and living room space, a basement, attic, and garage. An upper floor was created as well as a terraced roof garden by a new flat roof that was situated directly above the living/dining area. Actually, at that time, the neighborhood was still underdeveloped and it was a very nice, quiet and safe place to raise a family.

I still had the job as custodian at St. Francis De Sales Church and School. The School was becoming too small for the population of the growing parish. They were in need of a newer and larger building. The Pastor had an Architect draw up plans that would have attached the new school to the existing Parish Hall.

Once I reviewed the plans I realized that if they used that plan, the building would be blocking the drive-through from the Convent going around the Parish Hall, exiting to Division Street. It would have separated the schoolyard from the backyard of the Parish Hall and the adjoining Convent.

I made a suggestion to the Pastor to build the new school as a separate detached entity, thereby eliminating any blockage and at the same time creating another driveway from the School Yard to Cedar Avenue, behind the school. I drew up a plan of my proposed idea and it was submitted to the architect who then re-designed the new building according to my suggestions. The plan also included a workshop / office for me, as custodian. Now I was able to build more kitchen cabinets for the Parish Hall and also bookshelves for the library in the new school covering all four walls.

As Custodian I routinely had to set up chairs, kneelers and / or tables for the Sunday Masses, Bingo games and special events, in the Parish Hall. After each school day I had to clean and sweep the classrooms, burn the garbage in the incinerator and maintain the two heating boilers in the new school. Charlie, the sexton shared doing those jobs with me. My outside activities included cutting the grass, maintaining the grounds of the Church property, raking leaves in the Fall and shoveling snow during the winter months.

In-between I did a lot of extra work like repairs and alterations in the Rectory and Convent. Painting, wallpapering and even enclosing the front porch of the Rectory creating a recreation room for the priests and an office for the Church secretary, 'Mrs. K.' All this work made me a valuable asset to the parish.

I completely renovated the interior of St. Francis de Sales Church, as I mentioned earlier. In doing that work I guess you could say that I somewhat "felt" the experience of what it was like for one of the great Italian masters, for example; Michelangelo, who painted the ceiling of the Sistine Chapel in Rome as I was lying on my back atop the high scaffold attaching tile for tile to cover the old tin ceiling.

So, I gladly did my duty being employed and serving the Church for fourteen years for just my very modest salary. By doing all those alterations I saved the Parish tens of thousands of dollars in expenses, (compared to giving that work to outside contractors). I was just getting along by receiving the usual cost of living increases to my salary. Since I was eventually the sole income earner, it was not easy to meet all the expenses of our growing household and so I took some extra side-jobs on weekends and evenings to supplement our income.

As I said before with full conviction and belief: I considered that as a payback contribution for the "Love of God" and his help and guidance that kept me alive throughout the war and serving my 3 years time at the Gulags. I was also thankful for having a wonderful healthy and loving family. It was a "Gift from God," and I felt blessed by His loving kindness.

Fourteen months after our second daughter was born, we had yet another daughter, on February 14, 1961, on Valentines Day. That was the easiest delivery for Hedi because the baby was smaller and lighter in weight than the other two babies. The only complication was that we were in a huge surprise blizzard the night before.

In the morning I had to push the front door half way open because a pile of snow was blocking it. I couldn't see our Volkswagen bus parked in the driveway. There were very high drifts of snow that had completely covered the vehicle. After pushing the front storm door all the way open with force against the snowdrift, I quickly shoveled the VW bus free and cleared the driveway and then drove Hedi to Brookhaven Memorial hospital in Patchogue. After waiting less than an hour, our little "Valentine" was born. Two days later we took our little bundle of love home and introduced our new Lucie to Elisabeth and Angela.

That summer, we decided to visit the Kretzing family who were living in Washington, D.C. They were friends of ours that we knew from Germany while I was working at the Air Force Base. We decided to have our youngest daughter Lucie christened while we were there. June and Paul Kretzing were the Godparents. We visited with them for a few days and Paul and June drove us around to show us Washington, the surrounding areas and also the National Zoo where we could see the newborn white tiger cubs. Visiting the various museums was also a great thrill.

Later, while I was still employed as Custodian for the Parish and School I took some time off after introducing a new custodian to the ongoing jobs at the Parish to take on privately contracted jobs. It helped to supplement my income. Then I finally decided to leave my custodial job and work full time as a private contractor earning a more substantial income.

The Harbor House Condominium Complex in Westhampton Beach, Long Island, N.Y. had many two- story apartments that were in need of completion and repairs to their spare rooms and playrooms. It was up to the individual owners to finish the insides of the apartments according to their liking. I worked for various owners to customize their space. The Condo Association was responsible for the external renovations and repairs including the wooden balconies and decks. I tackled those jobs as well, including alterations to their Beach Club on Dune Road and building a boardwalk down over the dune to the ocean beach with end steps at the bottom.

In 1963 on January 8th, my father passed away. Financial burdens prevented me from returning to Germany to attend his funeral. Since I had already taken a trip alone for a visit in the late Fall of 1962 and saw him for the last time; my family was able to understand why I could not be there. We both knew then that it could be the last time to be together and said our sad "Good-byes." My youngest sister rushed from Goldsboro, North Carolina to his side and she held him in her arms, as he peacefully closed his eyes forever.

I remember that it was the same year that President John F. Kennedy was assassinated and the Worlds Fair opened in New York. I continued working at the Harbor House until Clyde recommended me to his boss. He had started working as a salesman for the Bath House Company in Westbury, L.I. They specialized in the renovation of Bathrooms.

I was hired as a production supervisor and inspector of ongoing and completed jobs. My main task was working out cost estimates. That was done by taking on-site measurements, making scaled drawings and figuring out all the supplies, materials and labor that were required for each job. I determined and estimated the actual cost to the company before starting the job. The Salesmen received their commissions based on that outcome and the result of my findings and correct calculations. Later the company expanded and added the renovations of Kitchens. They were then renamed: The Bath House and Kitchen Center.

My parents had planned to come over here together to visit us. That was of course before my dad passed away. Sad as it was, that he was not privileged to see his five grandchildren and make his first trip to America.

It was about one year after my dad's passing, that my mother decided to make the trip alone. After her first visit with us, she returned about every other year, and later on, once a year. We welcomed her visits until her death in 1982 at age 81. She also stayed with my oldest sister's family here on Long Island, enabling her to see and enjoy her other two granddaughters.

I always kept in touch with my friend Gert Nolde. He became a very successful Lawyer in Germany. It was later, around 1965 that he owned his own twin-engine plane, the Aerow 45. Then for one year he owned a Cessna 185, followed by a Piper PA23 Aztec, 1985/87. Gerts father was a Salesman and Inventor. The kitchen stove with the dust free ash-removal that he invented was only one of his numerous inventions. His biggest and most successful one was the coin-operated Telescope, which is still used today, worldwide. You can find it at most lookout points everywhere. He founded the "Graphoskop" Company. They distributed those Telescopes to all locations that featured interesting Panoramas. I was so proud to have Mr. Nolde as my Godfather when I was re-baptized, converting to Catholicism in 1950.

By the mid 1960's our girls were playing with children from around our neighborhood. They often came from a block or two away and were from the Archbold and Brady families. Our backyard had a set of swings, a modest above ground pool, and a little playhouse, as well as a rope-swing with a round four feet wide free swinging platform. I installed a magnifying plastic panel into the rear window facing the yard and that enabled my wife to keep a closer watch of the children playing while she was inside the kitchen.

Things were going rather well in the 1960's and the job I had with the Bath House Company regularly rewarded me with substantial raises. I made a name for myself in the industry, proving to be an accurate Cost-Estimator, earning the Company greater profits. I devised a system whereby I saved travel time. By planning a directional round-trip pattern to visit the diverse jobs I avoided the unnecessary going back and forth to the office.

By creating regional territories I was able to go to the various work sites to take measurements, review contracts with homeowners, and see the customers by appointments that I had originally set up in that pattern. So if I traveled around one day, the next day I worked out of my home on the cost estimates.

There was a time when I trained my daughters how to write out and add up items on Purchase Orders for the various materials and appliances involved in each job. I paid them for each job they completed with written purchase orders and by doing that, my orders were expedited quicker and at the same time I had the advantage of being home about every other day, saved travel expenses, had home cooked meals and enjoyed being home with my family

By 1971 as our daughters were a little older we decided to start to travel by car on our vacations. Our first trip was to Florida to see Disney World in Orlando. I believe that was shortly after its Grand Opening. We did not make any prior reservations hoping to somehow find a motel or bed and breakfast place. So while Hedi and the girls watched the traditional Disney Parade, I went to find out if there were any available accommodations. At the main office I was put on a waiting list for a possible cancellation, since everything at the Disney Park was already booked up solid.

With great luck we were able to stay in a Penthouse Suite in the Main "A" building of the Contemporary Hotel, the one that the Monorail train drove through while making its round trip through the amusement park. From there we had a most spectacular view looking down from that huge balcony that was part of our suite.

The spacious suite consisted of a large living room, two spacious royally furnished bedrooms, a kitchen and an elaborately tiled bathroom featuring a huge Jacuzzi tub.

I particularly remember that there was a huge remote controlled pop-up Television that came up in the middle of the living room in front of a large couch and adjoining easy chairs. We were able to watch a re-play of the same days' Disney Parade on that large TV screen, so I didn't miss seeing it after all. Hedi and the girls even saw themselves on that film, as they stood among the crowd along the curb watching the parade.

We were also served an elaborate dinner we had ordered by room service, and that was quite a "luxury" for us. We felt like an opulent family, enjoying all the unexpected pleasant amenities. In the evening we saw a particularly pleasant panoramic sight from our balcony, enjoying the laser light show and the fireworks over Disney World.

Another surprise was that our rented rooms turned out to be a very welcome bargain, at the expense of who ever made the original reservation and did not show up. We just had to add the small sum of sixty-five dollars to the pre-paid reservation for our two-night stay. It was certainly a great stroke of luck. In later years when we returned two more times to Disney World we were only able to get a room in nearby Motels. I still fondly remember the good fortune of our very first trip there, when we stayed in that royal Penthouse Suite for the mere pittance of sixty-five dollars. How lucky can you get?

In 1973 I was 'bribed' away from the Bath House and Kitchen Center with a better paying offer, to do the same job for Federal Builders Corporation. They were located in Westbury, Long Island on Old Country Road, about two miles West of The Bath House and Kitchen Center Company. After two years there, in 1975 once again I was "bribed" away by TSS (Times Square Stores) Home Improvement. It was located on Sunrise Highway, in Merrick, Long Island. We also did finished basements, some of which were actually separate apartments with newly created bathrooms and kitchens.

My reputation in that Home Improvement industry steadily grew. By 1980, once again, I was given a better offer to work for

Home Products as a Production Supervisor and later also as a factory Representative, with substantial financial gains.

Every New Year's Eve, during the 1970's we visited my youngest sister and her family. They permanently moved to Goldsboro, North Carolina, when my brother in Law was transferred to the adjoining Semore Johnson AFB. My youngest sister's son-in-law, Roy, was employed as an Engineer for the Boeing Company as well as being a Pyrotechnician for the internationally well-known Fireworks Company, Austin Pyrotechnics in Texas. He was in charge of setting up the annual New Year's Eve fireworks display in the large backyard of his parent in-law's home.

While I was visiting there, I participated with the preparations for the show. You would never realize how complex and fascinating that task could be until you experience it, hands on! A complicated network of wiring, connectors and timers had to be accurately prepared and created to produce the intended results. It took almost a week of hard work setting everything up. The half hour of those spectacular fireworks rewarded us with satisfaction of having accomplished something for everyone in town to enjoy. In later years, the increasingly larger shows were moved across the road to an open, broad farmer's field. Half the town attended that successful show, lining the road along that field. Hundreds of cars parked bumper to bumper and crowds sitting atop the car roofs to enjoy the great show.

In 1976 for the Bi-Centennial of our Nation, Roy's company, Austin Fireworks, gave him the job of setting up a huge display of fireworks on the Fourth of July at the Meadowlands Stadium in the State of New Jersey. I was asked to work with him as an "Official Pyrotechnician." The preliminary main set-ups for the fireworks were on the outside of the stadium. The inside secondary ones were to be synchronized with a scheduled program and a spectacular show.

The future President of our United States, George Bush senior, was there for the event and made an inspection of our set-ups. As potential future Vice President he was, of course completely surrounded by security officers of the Secret Service. At that time, he was not yet in office, either as Vice President or otherwise, but he made his presence known as a kind of Official Inspector for the festivities. I remember shaking his hand as he came to meet all of us technicians involved in the project, which was a major historical event for our country, the two-hundredth Anniversary of the Republic.

Those inside special fireworks were synchronized with music, simultaneously, as other fireworks around New York City, were happening. All major fireworks companies were involved in those productions, both from barges on the East River as well as those at Liberty Island, on land, and from the Palisades of New Jersey. We communicated with each other by wearing headphones, equipped with attached microphones, similar to those worn by pilots, while flying their planes.

Roy was certainly a conscious and meticulous expert in his field. Once he was awarded First prize for the U.S.A., representing his company, Austin Fireworks, in an International Competition in Canada. He had a brilliant mind, and always worked with exact precision. Unfortunately, he died young from complications resulting from cancer of the brain. The people of Goldsboro, North Carolina sorely missed him and were very disappointed to no longer have their traditional New Year's Eve Fireworks.

After my mother's death, in 1982, the Dulias' family home in Fürstenfeldbruck had to be sold. No one was left to take proper care of it. I collected from the proceeds what was due to me from my initial investment into it. Then it was my duty as Executor of the Last Will and Testament (jointly made by our parents), to divide equally among my three sisters and myself what we inherited.

With my share from the inheritance I bought into a partnership with the Company: Re-Style Kitchens Inc., becoming its President. It was the same Company from which in previous years the companies I worked for had bought kitchen cabinets and vanities. So, I knew that they were well established. Financially, I again bettered myself. We also started a sub-division for bathroom renovations of which I was very familiar.

I worked very long hours at all my jobs and had less and less time to spend with my family. The children came first in my wife's life and I was so proud that she made it her job, raising our daughters to the utmost, and was a loving expert in doing so. I felt a little deprived of not getting enough attention because the girls came first, but, that was just the way life was and I had to cope with it. Husbands were the providers for the family (also known as a one-income households). Every day they went to work, put in long hours, often did overtime, and didn't complain, while the wives remained at home, and that became their full time job.

Our oldest daughter Angela always had a passion for horses. When she was a toddler she loved pony rides and exclaimed: "Horsey, Horsey, Horsey," whenever she saw what appeared to be a horse. My middle daughter Elisabeth was always shy about petting animals but was a more creative and artistic type. Perhaps she inherited those creative traits from me. Our youngest daughter Lucie was more of a "Tomboy" type and had a love for cars. One time she bought a wreck, restored that 65' Mustang to pristine condition and entered it into a competition. She won First Prize two years in a row at the Auto Show that was held at the Vanderbilt Estate in Long Island, N.Y.

About 1989 I sold the partnership back to the former President of Re-Style Kitchens. I did not want to take any responsibility for the unorthodox business practices of my partners. As president it would have been my responsibility and I had to account for it.

After that I resumed the position as a Cost-Estimator and Production Supervisor at Construct-A-New, Inc., in Port Jefferson. My youngest daughter Lucie was also working for Re-Style Kitchens as the Office Manager. For the same reason as mine she left Re-Style and started working in the same capacity for Construct-A-New, Inc., that specialized in converting selected private homes into group homes for the handicapped and disabled.

From architectural plans and specifications, I had to estimate the cost for materials and labor to convert and modify those homes. Sealed bids were submitted to the Architect. My expertise in cost-estimating those expenditures enabled our Company's bids to win awards for contracts seven out of ten times. At one occasion I remember that we won a bid for a contract of a several hundred thousand dollar job by the narrow margin of twenty-seven dollars! I remained with that company until I officially retired at age 70, but still helping out for a short while afterwards, as part-time, when needed.

Once retired, I took a correspondence course that qualified me as a Certified Locksmith. My previous training in Germany had already prepared me for that type of work. After being certified I began working for a few Real Estate Agencies: (Rustic Realty in Coram, Long Island New York, Belzak and Bodkin in Patchogue and Prudential Realty) and became their official Locksmith. My job duties were to re-key foreclosed properties, install new locks on every exterior door that had to be master-keyed for the various Banking Institutions that foreclosed on those properties. It was an interesting and rewarding job, traveling all over Long Island, often doing several jobs a day. In my basement I set up a locksmith shop and prepared several types of locks master-keyed for the diverse Banks and other institutions, like Fanny Mae, Freddy Mac, etc. Their representatives had to be able to visit those foreclosed homes, having their own master keys to show potential buyers the often bargain-prized properties.

I believe it was in the latter part of the 1980's or early 1990's that I went to the Bayport Aerodrome and wanted to try to fly again. The prevailing asking fee to fly with a pilot and plane was then thirty-five dollars per half hour session. But when they heard that I had been a former Luftwaffe fighter pilot, they let me take the ride for free. I also accepted the offer to become a member of the Bayport Aerodrome Society.

I was never able to afford to buy and maintain my own aircraft. Instead I always was anxious to accept the offer to fly with another member as co-pilot. Later on, I flew often with 'Ace' William Prechtl in his N3N, Navy trainer, an open cockpit bi-plane, very similar to the German trainer FW Stieglitz I learned to fly in at the Berlin Air Academy.

In the 1990's my wife and I became temporary foster grandparents. After receiving the necessary training, we opened our home up for that purpose; mostly on weekends offering 'respite' to families who were permanently taking care of children in the foster care system.

It was called The Circle Program, and was a most rewarding job until we began getting some teenagers for those weekends. They ran up excessive phone bills dialing those "1-900 something numbers" and that put an extra burden on us, even though we were reimbursed for those expenses. It was not easy handling some of those rebellious teenagers, especially the boys. It became too taxing on our patience and after two years we came close to burnout, so we had to quit being part of The Circle Program.

We received a wall-plaque thanking us for the years of dedicated service we gave to the staff, children and families involved with that program. At the time we felt proud to open up our hearts and home to those less fortunate. The plaque still hangs on the wall in my office at home.

1995 AND 1998 RETURN TRIPS TO THE OLD HOMELAND

Königsberg – Now named Kaliningrad, Russia

After the Reunification of Germany, in 1994, the Soviet Union had disbanded. Travel to former German territories was now allowed, before then it was strictly prohibited. I wanted to see what was left of my hometown of Königsberg in East Prussia, now known as Kaliningrad. It had been about sixty years since I left it. So, in 1995 my wife and I decided to make a trip to there bringing our video recording camera along to look for what remained intact and recognizable since I had left. I only had seen a few pictures of the total destruction of the inner town of Königsberg and was wondering if Ponarth, where I lived with my family in the later part of our stay there, was also ruined, or was still as I remembered it.

When we arrived we began our tour by staying at the Hotel Kaliningrad, in the center of town, and made daily sightseeing trips to the surrounding parts of the town and also up to the **Samland** and farther East to Insterburg ,Tilsit, Gumbinnen and other places in that area of the former East Prussia. At the Hotel Kaliningrad we met and hired a Chauffer-Tour Guide. He was a Russian man of German descent and spoke fairly good German.

On Sunday May 28th we visited my former home in Ponarth, it was in the South section of the former city of Königsberg. We found the house that I grew up in, still standing to my pleasant surprise at **Werkstättenstraße** 12. The West wing as well as the center part of it remained intact although it appeared quite aged and neglected. The East wing (left side) had completely burned out and our former entrance at the West wing side was permanently walled shut. An inner connection from the center section joined the two wings together, creating new entrances to the upper and lower apartments of the West wing. The old building was a rather depressing sight with graffiti on the walls and the surrounding area looked run down and neglected.

The glass was cracked or missing and replaced with plywood panels in several of the windows and paint was peeling from the old frames. The trim and doors were also in need of paint and repair.

A crane was standing next to the burnt out East wing, but it appeared to be very rusty and it looked as if the intended process of making renovations and repairs had been long since abandoned.

Continuing my search for things that were recognizable, I located the Pestalozzi School, the one I went to as a little boy. It remained exactly the same as I had remembered it. As we looked around the schoolyard we heard church bells ringing. That tinny clinging sound was coming from the nearby ***Ponarther*** Church, the former Lutheran one, our family had worshipped in. Now it had been converted to a Russian Orthodox place of warship. The bells no longer had the same full reverberating sound as I had remembered hearing them as a child. Now they had a rather tin-like clang to them, perhaps having been replaced by steel bells?

The Hubertus pond where I first learned how to swim was still there but no longer had the public bathing facility I remembered. The rowboats that were always there when I was young were now gone. I even found my ***Kindergarten, we had always called it Spielschule, (playschool)*** and it was still in use as such as we saw small children playing there, singing songs and running about frolicking.

The apartment house where my Uncle Gustav and Aunt Anna used to live at ***Elchdamm*** No. 8 off ***Jägerstrasse,*** was still standing, but also was in a neglected condition and appeared run down.

The ***Ponarther*** Beer Brewery remained standing as it was before, and was in full operation. Only now it has become a bottling plant for mineral water and several other carbonated beverages; so the well known ***Ponarther Märzbier*** was no more, it is now just a memory.

Stalin, the Russian leader had wanted to acquire Königsberg because it was a Port City of the East, on the Baltic Sea. It was in an ice free zone, or better-said, thin ice that enabled to be navigated even by smaller ships during the winter months.

Originally the town was a walled-in and gated medieval city. There are still some preserved remnants remaining today, some sections of the old town walls, towers and also the gates.

Originally there were seven bridges spanning the different channels of the ***Pregel*** River banks. When I was there, I counted only five of them, two were destroyed and only some forlorn pilings remained in the river after the bombings.

There was an old puzzle at pre-war time; to cross all seven bridges in one round trip, but only once each bridge without backtracking and or going twice over one of them. As far as I remember, someone actually did exactly that. I tried it by making a drawing of the locations and layout of the different ***Pregel*** river arms, but was never able to solve that puzzle correctly, no matter how many ways and possibilities I tried. Score: zilch!

The relentless carpet bombings by the American, English and Russian Air Forces did most of the destruction to the inner city and much of it was now completely rebuilt. But not as it was with the former beautiful and impressive buildings I remember. Now there were rows of shabby looking plain building blocks. No longer recognizable as the former beautiful Königsberg I have in my memory.

General Lasch, the former German military commander of the city disobeyed Hitler's orders, which were to: "Defend it until the last drop of blood!" But, in his humane way of thinking, without unnecessarily losing more lives, Gen. Lasch surrendered the town to the Russians after realizing the futility of it all.

Lasch's former command post bunker is now a Museum. It is located between the Hotel Kaliningrad and the newly re-built University of Kaliningrad.

In front of the University stands now a large bronze statue of the famous Philosopher, Immanuel Kant. The Russian people put it there, to honor him, and every day a fresh red rose is placed at its pedestal in his memory, obviously by a caring admirer.

Mr. Kant was born, raised, educated, and then worked in my hometown of Königsberg (Kaliningrad) all his life.

Various old and retired streetcars that had been donated by towns of West Germany to Kaliningrad were rolling throughout the city as their main transportation system on the old still existing tracks, that were set into the cobblestone pavement flat and even. Old Diesel powered buses and trucks were polluting the air with their stinking smoky exhausts.

The Cathedral *(Dom)* of Königsberg stands on an island surrounded by waterways of the *Pregel* River. The *Dom* had burned out from the bombings, but the massive walls remained, without a roof and tower spire. With donations by the present West Germans and also Russians this Historical Building has been and is still in the process of being restored.

While we were there, the installation of the new copper roof of the spire of the massive bell tower was almost completed to its original shape and form. The tower even featured the huge now replicated original clock. The remains of the old clock works are now displayed in a small Museum room off the entrance foyer of the Dom along with other displays, pictures and model replicas.

The Mausoleum with Immanuel Kant's remains is attached as it was at the Northeast corner wall of the Cathedral. It had suffered some damage when the city was bombed, but it was one of the first and most important repair projects the Russians began in post wartime.

Diagonally across from the Cathedral, at the other side of the ***Pregel*** River was the ***Weidendamm,*** at umber three, where our home once stood. We did not find it there. It was also bombed and leveled flat. Instead, a few recognizable remnants of debris from the red brick walls protruded out from the riverbank. That debris was perhaps pushed there by bulldozers.

Going to the North section of the city, we visited the Museum of Amber. It was situated at the ***Wrangel*** Tower Gate, next to the ***Oberteich,*** (upper pond) a former well liked swimming and patronized bathing facility. The Tower was named after a famous German General of olden Prussian times. Passing through the archway one entered the Museum through a courtyard. It featured a vast amount of the utmost rare pieces of amber. They were the ones that contained enclosures of insects and were of various sizes, dating back over twenty million years. We saw spiders, bugs, mosquitoes and flies enclosed in the clear golden ember; also some plant or leaf fragments and small air bubbles. Imagine, all that from millions of years ago, so clearly preserved, that one even could see the fine hair-coverings and feelers of some of the insects. Some beautiful small butterflies were among them with their spread wings. This one of a kind Museum was a very interesting and inspiring viewing event for us; we were able to see God's work and creations of long ago.

We drove to the part of Königsberg, which was formerly called Mühlenhof, looking for the apartment house of my Grandfather Reschke at the former ***Schönfließer Allee #28.*** Before the war my mother inherited it and kept it rented up to the time the war ended.

Now it was no longer standing. I found out that it had withstood the war undamaged but when the city was invaded, Russian flame-throwers burnt it down. The Russians thought that it was owned and occupied by rich Nazis, in that modern building. Now in its place was a drab-looking new Apartment complex. This one was somewhat set back from the old location creating a wider sidewalk.

At the Southwest part of **Ponarth** there was supposed to be a Cemetery. The former *"Friedhof Nasser Garten,"* where my Grandparents Dulias had been buried, but now it was gone. A house and a new school stood at that site. Attached to the house (that the Principal occupied), stood a two-car garage. But I know for sure, at the very same location, the South/East corner of the former cemetery, that under it rest the remains of my Grandparents! I was saddened to find that wrenching situation! The Russians as well as the school children are probably not aware that they are learning and frolicking above sacred grounds!

I looked for another Cemetery, the former *"Invaliden Friedhof,"* where my Grandparents Reschke had been interned. I found out that it also no longer existed. Instead, an Amusement Park had replaced it, with carousels, amusement rides, dance clubs and concert halls. It is quite ironic that a former place of reverence is now used for the entertainment of the population. They are dancing over the graves of thousands of former German people. What a shame, having desecrated sacred grounds in such a way!

It saddened and depressed me after making that discovery! It really is such a shameful disgrace, how could they have done that? Just because they conquered the land; didn't give them any right to ignore what was once there before. Did they think that decades later no one would ever know about it or give it any thought?

The Northwest part of Königsberg showed very little evidence of damage from the war. A Statue of Lenin now stands at the plaza of the North Train Station; (**Nordbahnhof**) Hedi and I found the apartment house where my Uncle Bruno and Aunt Liesbeth used to live. It was still there and well preserved. Also the apartment from Uncle Julius Lappe located in the same building complex. He was the one who owned the confectionery store near the former Imperial Castle.

It was so sad that fifty years later (1945-1995), you could still see and feel the devastation from the destruction and further neglect resulting from that dreadful WW II. The fact is, that had there not been a war at all, what once stood there and had remained, would still be owned by the Dulias' family. Ultimately, I would have inherited all of it. Way back then, when I was still a little boy, my Grandfather had said to me that: "Someday this will all be yours, '**Mein Jungchen'** " (my little boy). Right there I felt like the richest boy in the world as he spoke to me in his loving and proud way.

On another day we took a drive to the Resorts at the Baltic Sea in the area of the **Samland**, where we had vacationed as children. Driving along the countryside we could see stork nests high atop the chimneys of farmhouses and even telephone poles as they were in olden times. I felt so sorry seeing how with time, these birds had changed in appearance and did not have their old familiarity. Instead, due to the vast amount of pollution to the environment, particularly the ponds, (pursuing frogs and other aquatic life), these once black and white feathered birds now had gray feathers instead of the former bright white ones. They appeared so dirty, they couldn't clean themselves from the oily grime that now lingered on the surfaces of many severely polluted ponds and creeks.

When we reached our first destination of **Neuhäuser**, the still existing beautiful resort village and its nearby surroundings, we found that only some areas were accessible; while others were forbidden territory, as "off limits." They now were used and had been converted into military security zones. Only from a distance could we view the **Zipfelberg** of **Grosskuren** where we spent many delightful summer vacations as children.

At this, our new visiting time we went along the shoreline and saw young children searching the beach grounds. In their hands they held found pieces of amber that they offered to us for sale. Their smiling faces were our reward and it not only made them happy that we bought a few pieces from them, but it made us happy as well.

Instead of the public staircase that we used in earlier times to access the beach, the one known as "Heaven's Ladder," there was now an automated enclosed elevator. At the top plateau to the right of the elevator there were now wide concrete steps, replacing the former wooden ones.

I can clearly remember the wooden elevated boardwalk that once stood on stilts and ran across the entire span of the beach. It was now replaced by a modern structure made of steel posts and a concrete "boardwalk". It was colorfully decorated with mosaic-tiled designs of sea life motifs. Various art objects like a decorated clock-sundial and a sculpture of a Nymph, were a pleasant additions to the beach area. Vendors had rows of stands set up along the entire boardwalk railing displaying and offering various beautiful and valuable jewelry items for sale all of which were made of Amber with solid silver artfully arranged trimmings for very reasonable prices. Of course, we couldn't resist and gave in to   temptations to buy some of them; one piece more pleasing and beautiful than the next. Some of those also contained some insects encapsulated in that magnificent golden clear and polished Amber.

On the way back to Kaliningrad we visited an old German Fort at the Northwest end of town, the name of it escaped my memory. It was now a WWI, / WWII Museum of Weaponry. Real disarmed torpedoes, heavy artillery pieces and disarmed munitions, flak cannons, tanks and other war weapons were on display.

Sadly, in 1997 my dear wife of 46 years to the day, passed away.

She was never one to complain, but our daughters and I noticed, that she was unexplainably losing weight. She insisted that she was feeling okay. Evidently she had no pain, but could not eat much anymore and felt full and satisfied after only a few bites of food. She didn't think of seeing our doctor, but we insisted that she should get an examination. The result was, that the doctor didn't find anything of a serious nature, that would indicate any trouble and losing weight was even welcomed by Hedi as she got slimmer. But still, she kept losing more weight and we really got concerned about her health and took her to a gastronomical specialist.

To our shocking and dreadful surprise, the evidence showed that she had cancer of the lower esophagus. After tests and more intense examinations we got the sad news, that an operation was no longer possible. The cancer had spread to the upper stomach and to both of her kidneys. The doctor gave her one half year before the end would come. Hedi still had no pain whatsoever, but progressively could only eat smaller amounts and lost even more weight. She still came along with me on my locksmith jobs of foreclosed houses to help me with the steady increasing number of foreclosures in late 1996.

Late In February 1997 Hedi started to feel pain and then stayed home. We had arranged for hospice service with visiting nurses and doctors and also pain treatments with morphine, so she didn't have to suffer. My three daughters took turns caring for her and often spending a night after we moved her to a downstairs bedroom. She was unable to ascend the stairs to our bedroom. She could hardly eat anymore and even the water she drank did not stay with her. It was a sad pity to see her getting thinner and frail, wasting away and finally she had to stay in bed full time.

On Easter Sunday in 1997, just before the end of March, it was a beautiful warm sunny day, when we brought Hedi out to the front terrace to enjoy the sun. Next to the steps to the side of our front door our daffodils were sprouting and had buds, but they had not quite opened yet to full bloom. Hedi with her frail voice mentioned, that she would have liked to see them in bloom once more. Sadly it was not to be. On the 30th of March she fell into a coma and her organs started to shut down. The doctor from the hospice service told us, that it would be only hours. She developed a high fever and was breathing deeply in long sighs with ever longer intervals, but held out to the thirty first of March, our 46th wedding anniversary. At four ten in the afternoon she stopped breathing and left us, falling asleep, now awaiting her later resurrection. My daughters, their husbands, our granddaughters and I stood around her bed tearful. I was holding Hedi's hand as she passed away; I whispered a final goodbye into her ear and told her, that I loved her.

The funeral Mass was held in St Francis De Sales Church three days later after the open casket display at the funeral home, where hundreds of people, friends and relatives came each day to pay their respects. A bunch of the now blooming daffodils from our garden was laid beside her body along with artful drawings made by her granddaughters Lauren and Danielle.

Angela, my oldest daughter presented a touching eulogy at the funeral mass and my nephews and son in laws, who were the pallbearers, carried the casket out to the waiting hearse. I couldn't help but cry in bitter sadness. My dear Hedi was taken away to the crematorium. It was her wish as mine will be when my time comes, that our ashes should be spread at our favorite place at the beach, where we spent many of our weekends in the summer.

That was later done, after awaiting good weather to fly with five antique planes in the missing man formation along the beach of Smith Point, where my family, friends and relatives were waiting at our favorite sunbathing spot to see our fly over, at low altitude. Ace Prechtl and I in his N3N open cockpit bi-plane sheared up and out of the formation to return once more to drop Hedi's ashes into the rays of the setting sun. The rays turned her ashes into golden dust raining down, while the four other planes kept on flying back to the Bayport aerodrome, where Ace and I landed later too.

After that solemn ceremony we all met at my house for the traditional German ***Totenschmaus*** (celebration in honor of the dead) that was catered and enjoyed by all.

All the numerous flower arrangements and decorative creations that had been delivered to the funeral home, were now decorating all available space in my home.

When the party was over and everyone had left, I felt very forlorn and lonely in my now so quiet 10-room house and it took me a long time of mourning to get used to the new state of being a widower. But for the Grace of the Good Lord and my surviving instinct and will power I made it through all that as the fighter and optimist that I always have been. I trusted Jesus and our dear God, that He would turn all to the best for me, the survivor.

In 1998 my youngest sister and I decided to take a trip back to Osterode, in the former East Prussia.

Osterode – Now named Ostroda, Poland

We selected a Hotel that was in the former town of ***Allenstein,*** now Olstyn, located about 20 km East of Osterode. There we met and hired a guide, ***Frau Herrmann,*** who spoke both German and Polish. She drove us in her car to our former hometown and the first stop was to park at the marketplace. From there we made a walking tour. Going alongside Lake ***Drewenz*** and along the former ***Uferstrasse***, (Shore Street). We crossed over the railroad tracks to get to ***Wilhelmstrasse,*** and were then in very familiar territory.

To our pleasant surprise, our former home # 39 was still standing there, exactly the same way as it was before. Only now it had been converted into a sort of Orphanage or Children's Home. Only the windows had been changed to more modern ones as we noticed.

Our guide, ***Mrs. Herrmann*** spoke in Polish with the personnel of that Institution, and got permission for us to enter and take a tour of the inside of our former apartment. The attendants for the care of the children all wore neat white uniforms, and all the children were of preschool age, like in a ***Kindergarten.***

I was curious to see if any changes had been made to the interior of our former residence. The difference I noticed was that my former room and the adjoining room that once belonged to my sisters had been combined into one large ward. Where my parents' bedroom once was, there was now a large food pantry. The living room and parlor room were also combined and converted into a main dining room. The large kitchen was still in the same place only the former pantries were now part of it and as such enlarged the main working area. The entire interior of the building appeared to be very somber and sterile, nothing like what it once was used for, as our peaceful home.

The long angle corridor was still the same, only at the former end next to my room, the end wall was removed and provided now access to the front hallway and main entrance of the building including the stairway to the upper front apartment for the former ***Werkdirector*** of the still existing and active repair work-plant for the railroad.

The Castle where I once attended meetings as a member of the Hitler Youth was now a big Town Museum. Its courtyard had become an open-air theatre for concerts and shows. The Kaiser Wilhelm Gymnasium, my High School was also still standing the way it was and is still in use as a High School.

Walking around my old neighborhood I had a flash back as I passed the front stoop of the very house where I had once found the cigar box. I reflected back to that time when I had found it with the bundles of money inside of it. It had contained nearly three thousand Marks and I did return it to the traveling students.

After returning to our car at the market place, we drove to the North side of Lake ***Drewenz.*** We visited the ***Bismark*** Tower, it remained to be a favorite recreational site. We had a most elaborate lunch at a new restaurant near the tower and then continued with our tour back towards the center of Osterode.

We drove back to visit the Lutheran Church, the one where our family used to worship. The friendly pastor welcomed us, speaking in perfect English. He had been to America on numerous extended visits and learned to speak English with hardly any accent.

He showed us the familiar inside of the Church. It remained the same as well as the bell tower and through the look out from the top of the West twin tower, you could view the vast surrounding area and the panoramic Lake *Drewence.*

Afterwards we walked over to the nearby Catholic Church. When I was a young boy, it was strictly forbidden for me to ever enter into it. Now, for the first time my sister and I visited it, on our own free will and intent. As we continued exploring the Church, we became acquainted with two nuns, better known as sisters, and they spoke in German with us. They were dressed in their traditional black habits with wide hoods that were accented with white inner linings.

They both held jobs as cooks and housekeepers for the residing Priests at the Rectory. We continued our conversation with them. I mentioned that in earlier times, when we moved to the U.S.A., my deceased wife held the same jobs that they did and that she had also considered becoming a nun, had she not met and married me.

They said that they would like to say prayers for her, in her memory. That gave me the idea to give a donation for a series of Masses that would be said as a dedication to Hedi. While there I lit some votive candles. How I wished that my dear wife could have been with me back at that moment in time. I still keep the paper receipt for the prayer requests dedicated in the name of "Jadwiga" (Hedwig).

The next day back at Osterode, we took a boat ride to Elbing at the Baltic sea by way of the *Oberland* Canal. As a young boy I knew of it and had seen pictures, but never had made the trip before. It is the only place in the world where ships climb and descend mountainous plateaus being pulled over five tapered high hills along the waterway. By using a marvelous German engineering invention, with the use of the gravity of waterpower, the boat goes through a series of water landings and locks. Rising from the lower levels by Osterode and escalating to the higher levels of the **Oberland,** the boat climbed and then descended further down to ever deeper plates by way of cradle cars on rails rolling over five plateaus, down toward Elbing. It was a slow process of a push and pull motion through the water / rail system. The trip took eleven hours one way. We returned to our Hotel in Allenstein much quicker by train that same evening, after enjoying an elaborate dinner in a friendly Polish Restaurant for a surprisingly low price.

One day we visited Nikolaiken in the eastern region of East Prussia by rental car. The place near where I spent time in Lubjewen when we were in the process of waiting to move to Fürstenfeldbruck. The crowned **Stinthengst** Fish was still chained to the pillar of the bridge. Alongside the bridge was a modern sculptured statue of the Fish King with a plaque written in Polish telling its legendary story. So, the Polish people carried that old tradition and legend about the king of the lake fish further on.

While back in the village of Nikolaiken we visited several stores that sold Amber jewelry as well as loose Amber gem pieces. We bought quite a few pieces because the prices were very reasonable and easy affordable for us. We couldn't resist buying piece after piece from the huge selections offered at these gift stores. Than we had a relaxing lunch at the market place restaurant and got ready for our return to Allenstein.

We took a different route on our way back so we could visit the town of Rastenburg. There we passed the institution where my brother Ulli spent the last years of his life and was probably buried there.

Nearby was Hitler's largest former command post called the **Wolfsschanze**. That was where he was stationed for the final months, directing the latter part of the war, before the Russians forced him and his staff to retreat to Berlin. It was almost a complete city by itself, consisting of huge and massive bunkers and underground facilities. It was an interesting as well as historical place to visit.

Those thick-walled bunkers withstood numerous attempts of demolition using dynamite by the retreating Germans. Only the insides of them were damaged, while most of those thick and massive concrete walls showed only a few cracks. That was certainly a sign of the well-known German workmanship that was always acknowledged throughout the world, and still is today.

The Wolfschanze was the same place where the Aces of the *Luftwaffe* had to appear on command to receive their various medals and honors of: The Knights (Iron) Cross, the Oak Leaves, the Crossed Swords and finally the Diamonds, that were for the highest achieved honors that Germany had to offer to those deserving heroes.

It was getting late and we returned to our Hotel in Olstyn after a long day of searching for the old familiar places of long ago.

On another day we drove this time to Elbing and visited the nearby town of Frauenburg, where in its Cathedral the Astronomer Nikolaus Kopernikus (Copernicus) taught his theory. That was that: "The Earth was circling the Sun," instead of the Universe moving around the Earth as was then taught by the Catholic Church.

For some time, Kopernikus was living and teaching in the Castle of Olstyn. He was excommunicated by the Catholic Church for his revolutionary and then unorthodox teachings and was also banned from his teaching posts. His last words while on his deathbed were: *"Und sie bewegt sich doch!"* Meaning: "The Earth is turning yet after all!" Well, how right he was!

On the way back to Olstyn we were able to visit the town of Danzig, now called Gdansk. It was our first visit to this former German Baltic Port City. We stopped at a Restaurant for lunch and there we met a former German man who became a Polish citizen after the War. He joined us as our guide and walked us around the town showing us the points of interest, including the famous *Krahntor* (Crane-gate). The well-known landmark was in working order, functioning as a crane, loading and unloading ships at the river quay.

Once again, we found more vendors selling Amber jewelry and art objects. One piece was more beautiful then the next and we simply could not resist buying more of those artful pieces. Everywhere we went we found and kept adding more and more of it to our collection. They were of excellent quality and value and we never regretted our "splurges."

Upon returning to our hotel we hid the golden treasures that we had acquired from Gdansk as well as those from Nikolaiken. We wrapped them in our underwear and socks to carry them home safely tucked away deep in our luggage. We were successful in our efforts without being found out and once gotten home had wonderful presents to give to our friends and relatives. They were pleasantly surprised when they opened their valuable souvenir-gifts. Then again, we were not aware if there were any restrictions for the transporting of Amber out of the country, but to be fairly safe, we took the trouble of hiding our treasures very carefully, the best we could. Luckily, our luggage was not searched and we were able to bring all safely home. For a long time we always had ready and welcome presents for friends and relatives on special occasions.

Returning to Germany after leaving Poland we visited old friends and relatives and also attended the Bi-Annual Dulias Family Reunion. It was again held in Bad Karlshafen, a (Cure-Spa resort town). It was interesting for us to learn more about our Huguenot ancestors. Many of who had settled around that same local area, after having been driven away from their land and ancestral homes in France just for their Protestant beliefs.

We visited the Huguenot Museum there and so acquired a better understanding of their real loss and suffering, as they were welcomed in that area and at the invitation of the King of Prussia to come to East Prussia. They were offered free land to re-populate East Prussia that had lost two thirds of its original population due to the Bubonic Plague, which had ravaged that entire area. The new citizens were welcomed there with open arms, they brought new life into the area and also brought many of their crafts and traditions along, which then formed and developed the new and then prevailing East Prussian trend.

Returning to our new homeland, the good ole U.S.A., after the double trips, we had an abundance of videotapes that we were able to show everyone of what we had seen and encountered while visiting our old homeland cities of Köningsberg and Osterode, the old stomping grounds of our youth. As the saying goes: 'There is no place like home', we were glad to be home again and to our friends and relatives we had much to tell and show about our long and pleasant trip and especially our vast Amber treasures that we were able to bring home.

The "oh's and ah's about those beautiful and artful pieces never ended.

I guess it was around 1999 that my youngest daughter told me I needed a computer and she gave me one that she had built herself from scratch. I said: "What do I need that for?" She said: "Pop, I'll show you how to use it!" The first thing I became familiar with was the operating system, and how to get it started. The next thing I learned about was "E-mail" I said: "What's that?" After that she walked me through the procedures, step by step, and helped me create an email account with AOL. I learned how to make a connection, to go on and off line, and create a password. Little by little I caught on to it, and began to like this new invention. Nowadays, I would not know how to do without it.

It practically developed into my new lifeline. Without my computer I never would have been able to write this book in the first place; and also presently this, my 2009 revised and expanded edition; all stored in a single memory stick.

In 2001 I once again attended a Dulias family Reunion in Germany. On September 11ᵗʰ I was in a medieval town called Bernkastel-Kues, which is located along and both sides of the Mosel River, (where there are many vineyards which are grown and used for wine making as well as fresh grapes at super markets. While there in town, I went into a store to buy some colorful picture postcards. I wanted to purchase some so I could then write them out and send them back home, to the States.

While in the store, the salespeople were watching their store television. I also looked up at it and saw some scenes of what I thought were a Sci-Fi movie. I said: "That's a very realistic looking movie showing scenes of New York with the Twin Towers burning." I then found out about what had really happened. I was shocked and saddened to find out what was happening in New York while I was away. After that I was unable return to New York on my booked and scheduled flight. Suddenly there were restrictions and delays. Instead, I returned several days later after spending a few more days with family and friends while remaining in Germany.

A COMPLETE SURPRISE

I started writing my autobiography November 13, 2003. It was shortly after that when things started to fall nicely into place. The task of writing my story was not as difficult as when I first started it. Suddenly the words and memories just came before me and fell into place.

One Saturday morning I received a phone call from my Chiropractor, Dr. Ron and he told me that he had a surprise for me. For quite a while he mentioned something of a sort, but I could not imagine what it could be.

Over the past few years I did share with my Chiropractor different aspects of my personal life that went deeper than just the pain in my back. I let him know about the pain and suffering that I had experienced in my lifetime, as a prisoner of war in World War II and that I was about to write my life story into a book. Dr. Ron was yet another person who encouraged me urgently to do so.

We set up an appointment to meet at 11:30 on Saturday, November 29, 2003 at the Bluepoint Diner in Long Island. However, I became confused as to where the meeting place really was, as I had not written it down. At first I went to the Sayville Diner, and was there on time, but my Doctor did not show. I saw before me a group of Civil War Re-enactors who were dining there and at the same time realized that I must have driven to the wrong diner. I had a brief conversation with those re-enactors, mentioning my own involvement in re-enacting. I did not know which event they came from or were going to. I told them, that I too was a re-enactor with LARA and that we performed at various events in Pennsylvania, New Jersey and other states as Luftwaffe representatives. As I was in a hurry to leave, and started to exit, they gave me a salute that I proudly returned.

So, I finally met Dr. Ron at the right place, the Bluepoint diner. We sat and talked over a cup of coffee and then he said he wanted to show me something. Ok, I was game for anything. Not knowing what to expect, I went along with him in his SUV and we arrived at a nearby residence. We walked into the private house of a person I had never seen in my life. It seems that this man was the father of one of the Dr.'s patients. We were welcomed by that man and then he lead us down into his basement.

As much as I would want to, I cannot find the right words to describe exactly what I saw right before my very own eyes! I can only tell you that in all the years of my life in America I never saw such a treasure, as the one 'buried' in that basement! A treasure that is so priceless and especially to me, I saw things I never imagined I would ever again see in my lifetime. This was a most "awesome" and very wonderful and surprising experience. I found a private collection of an entire lifetime, better and uniquely complete than in any Museum that I had ever been to. This man had each and every authentic and original German World War II memorabilia and paraphernalia that one could imagine. When I saw this vast collection, I felt like a child in a candy store! Wow, after all these years, to find all the things that were once part of my life and were now here on display no more than a fifteen minute drive from my home.

It was just so amazing to be able to see again the real and original uniforms, hats, helmets' side arms, daggers, decoration medals, including the Pour Le Merite, Ritterkreuz with all stages of the various grades, Iron crosses of all classes, emblems, a vast variation of swords and daggers and any and all paraphernalia connected with all and every branch and sub-division of the entire **Wehrmacht** (Armed Forces), including weapons, ammunitions, bayonets, guns and rifles. There were even personal items that once belonged to Hitler, such as his eating cutlery and monogrammed handkerchiefs! There was also a vast array of original toys, depicting all other military equipment in finest detail and originality, like tanks, trucks, motorcycles, field-kitchens and-bakeries, trucks with pontoons that were used by the pioneers branch to build bridges, models of various planes etc., etc. --------Everything one could think of and or never even heard of, were there displayed in museum style fashion, that even the Smithsonian Institute in Washington does not possess !!!!!

So un-believable as this is, without having seen it in person, no one could ever imagine, what had awaited me here as the greatest surprise ever in my entire life here in the Good Old USA !!!------ Awesome !!!--------Overwhelming--------the greatest surprise------what a treasure trove !!!! Unbelievable !!!! One has to see it to believe it !!!

This unexpected event brought forgotten memories up and also it happened at just the right time in my life. I was able to compile all the lost as well as found information which helped me write my true life's story.

CHRISTMAS **2003**

Christmas Eve 2003 was spent at my daughter Angela's house. For many years now, and especially since my wife's passing, she has invited our remaining family over to her house located at the North Shore of Long Island, New York. Now the Holiday is celebrated in a more traditional, American way (perhaps with even a hint of Martha Stewart). However, there was also a slight tinge of keeping up with some of the German customs.

As we arrived at her house in the evening, we assembled and greeted one another in the living room. There we casually sat on sofas and easy chairs around a large cocktail table loaded with culinary delicacies and began the festivities with a great variety of hors d'oeuvres along with a beverage of our choice. It was a very casual and relaxed atmosphere with Christmas music in the background.

There was no formality as to how we should dress but I usually like to wear a long sleeve shirt with a colorful necktie, accented with a tie tack that is an angel pin. My completed attire was a nice pair of trousers and a sport jacket. As a contrast, many times my younger granddaughter Danielle would arrive at family gatherings wearing her hip hugging ripped up blue jeans, because that's the style right now, her short cropped top so she can show off her pierced belly button, her sneakers and if she found a little time, she would have put on some makeup too. In contrast, her older sister was always dressed in more conservative fashion. But because it was Christmas, for a change they both wore their brand new dresses.

Traditional English as well as German Christmas songs could be heard in the background of our conversations. The music came from the new electronic entertainment unit.

There stood a tall, large natural pine Christmas tree positioned near the gabled window wall. It was brightly decorated with colorful hangings and strings of electric lights, some of them blinking. The base of the tree was surrounded by a vast stack of colorfully wrapped packages with ribbons and bows with identifying nametags for each intended receiver.

When it was time for dinner I was seated at one end of the long glass-top table, and my son in law Bruce, Angela's husband at the opposite end. Everyone else surrounded us at both sides of the table.

It was set in a coordinating Christmas motif and pattern. There was a colorful decorated tablecloth, napkins in ring holders and lit candles on single holders.

Our dinner was as always, an ample feast with most items homemade. Angela has culinary talents that I believe she inherited or learned from her mother. It seems she took it upon herself to follow in her mother's footsteps and has always tried to keep the family together for the holiday meals. She not only knows how to cook but also knows how to serve a large group of guests.

Here goose is never served for Christmas Eve, as is customary in Germany. Actually, here it is ever so rare for anyone to make it for a holiday meal. Instead, it has been a more common practice to serve a choice of turkey and or ham. To go with the meats there were an assortment of hot and cold dishes to choose from. Among them stuffing, mashed potatoes, red cabbage, gravy, green vegetables and some accompanying condiments.

Settling our stomachs after a little break, we continued our dining together a little later on. Out came a rich selection of different cakes and cookies made from both American and German recipes served with coffee or tea. This was followed by our exchanging and opening gifts.

Upon leaving after the festivity each of us got a *"Bunten Teller"* (colorful plate) with a great variety of delicious home-baked cookies, tarts and miniature cake-loaves to take home.

So now, after being in America for a little over fifty years, I have adapted to the American tradition of how I spend my Christmas Holiday. Actually, what is tradition? For me it is learning how to adapt to the prevailing situations. That is how I see it. The Christmas experience, when I first came to America with my wife was quite different for us as we were settling down and making a new life of our own. Our Christmas was quite delightful at the times when my own children were growing up. In German tradition our decorative **Weihnachtsbaum** (Christmas tree) always featured live-lit candles and the pleasant aroma of them together with the scent of the tree itself permeated our living room. Of course, careful setting of those candles had to be observed and the candleholders securely clipped to the branches of the tree, so only empty spaces were above each candle to prevent a fire. Never did we use any of the strings of colored electric lights, as is the custom here.

The Christmases I spent in Germany as a young boy have left an indelible impression with me. Those Christmas Eve celebrations of "Grand Performances" are now just fond memories and are reminders of just how special Christmas had been; and always will be to me. I also reflect back to the times when due to dreadful circumstances my Christmases were lost for a time but were not forgotten because I was away from home in places that I would rather not experience and be there ever again as POW.

I always had a fondness for watching the wonderful Christmas programs and specials on television. Very often there are musicals, concerts, and traditional choirs. I cannot recall from which program it was that I heard for the first time, here in this country, the beautiful and touching song: "Amazing Grace."

It was such a moving song, sung as a Hymn. I later heard it repeated again as gospel and realized that the song is very much part of the American culture, often sung at special events. I reflect back to the time when I heard the Prison Chorus perform their newly composed songs. It seemed to me that there was a similar melody to one of their songs, yet it never made it to the outside world and sadly is lost forever.

Renovating, Adding on to "Our Dollhouse"
1959

With Our Girls in the 1960's

From Left: Oldest, Middle, Youngest

Our Two Grandaughters

Our Last Christmas Together

Vacation Time

Eleven

And...
This Is Not
The Final Chapter

After having reached the Anniversary of being in the United States for fifty years, in 2003, the one main regret I have is, that I did not have my wife Hedwig with me these past few years. I guess I'm from the "old school" where a man just took one wife, and that she would be his lifetime partner. Hedi was my everything, the love of my life, and for the longest time after her passing I was at a total loss.

When I reflect back to her passing away, as I often do in memory of my dear Hedi, I still get into a state of sadness, even if only momentarily. Nevertheless I am trying and getting used to coping with living alone as a widower.

Each day I wear her funeral card in my left shirt pocket, so I have her close to my heart as a steady reminder of the blessed forty-six years we were privileged to live as a married couple. Every morning when I get up and every evening before I go to sleep, I look at it, I greet her and tell her that I love her and that we will meet again at the new system of things. I strongly believe with conviction that Jehovah God will grant us that privilege.

So here follows a more detailed version that I should have placed into the beginning of chapter nine to be set in chronological order.

Now in 2009 while revising my book and came to that missing sequence of the heading for chapter nine that stated, that my dear wife Hedi had passed away in 1997, I found to my embarrassment, that in 2004 I had failed to follow up with that happening when I wrote chapter nine. So now I composed a curtailed description of Hedi's passing and her funeral where it should have been set in place.

HERE IS THE ORIGINAL:

My dear wife Hedwig passed away on March 31, 1997. Her date of death was to the exact day we were married, on our forty-sixth wedding anniversary. Unfortunately and almost ironically she had developed cancer of the stomach and esophagus. I say ironically because by trade she was a professional cook. Who would ever have thought that she would become afflicted with that type of illness, and in that location of her body? I still today regret that we were not able to be together and celebrate our golden wedding anniversary. That was just not meant to be.

Well, as I already mentioned, I must move on. So, after her passing, my wife was cremated, in accordance with her wishes. I came to the final closure about her death by flying in the "Missing Man Formation" along the shore of the beach at Smith Point in Brookhaven, Long Island. The funeral and mass in our local Catholic Church were held a couple of weeks earlier. That was to allow time to arrange, coordinate and schedule the fly-over when it could be done in suitable weather.

I flew as a passenger in the N3N open cockpit biplane with my friend and the owner of the aircraft, 'Ace' Prechtl. I carried Hedi's ashes, they were contained in a brown paper bag. The bag was attached to a ten-foot long twine wound around it with a looped end attached to my wrist.

When I was ready to toss it overboard, it would unwind itself by gravity, and at the end the bag would burst open, releasing the ashes, as I held the other end of the twine at my wrist. This ingenious "technique" was thought up by Ace and it worked perfectly as it proved to be on other such occasions.

To form the Missing Man Formation, four other friends flying their planes accompanied us. My family and many friends were assembled at the sandy shore at the spot where the ashes would be scattered. That spot was where Hedi and I spent most sunny weekends during the summer months and some weekdays too when ever time allowed. Our special place was located about two miles west of the Smith Point Beach Pavilion at a section of the National Seashore, far away from 'prying eyes'. That's where the "clothing optional" area begins, stretching for a mile further West.

Prior arrangements were made for everyone to meet at the same part of the beach, close to sundown. The 'ground-funeral party' awaited our flight-formation as we flew coming from the West over and passed them. At the pavilion we made a 180-degree turn and flew very low (50 feet) back along the shore. As we passed them, Ace and I, in the N3N, pulled up in a sharp left turn back towards the pavilion. At the same time the other four planes kept going straight, to the West, disappearing into the far the horizon.

That flight procedure is in aviation terms called: The Missing Man Formation Fly-Over.

At the pavilion, once again we turned back and flew even lower towards our target place. We were directly above the waiting crowd, but still over the water, when I dropped the "package" and as planned, the bursting bag scattered the ashes. The bright amber rays of the sundown turned the ashes into sprinkled gold dust; my youngest daughter Lucie caught that beautiful sight on tape with our video camera from below.

The pilots and all funeral guests met at my house that evening to continue with our memorial party. I would like to consider it more of a celebration of Hedi's life, rather than her death. My daughters and I had the party catered, it featured numerous culinary delicacies welcomed by all guests.

It is customary in Germany to hold a "***Totenschmaus***" (Deathfeast) when someone passes away. That is what we did, keeping up with our old tradition.

My house was still decorated with many of the well preserved flower arrangements and wreaths that had been delivered to the funeral home for the three day wake earlier and then brought home. In concluding our feast of memory, I thanked my fellow pilots for their perfect performance and all our guests for coming and participating in this memorial in Hedi's honor.

I later placed a stake at the location of where Hedi's ashes were scattered. The stick had artificial flowers attached to it and also the laminated funeral card with her picture on it. I still visit the site replacing the flowers and card on special memory anniversaries. Unfortunately often storms and seashore erosion keep washing it away. So, from time to time I replaced that flowered stick and card higher up at the dune.

I always like to wear a shirt with a pocket at my left chest. There, each and every day I keep a funeral card with Hedi's picture on it, so she is still always with me, well at least in spirit and that keeps me going on.

The touching poem on her funeral card reads as follows:

I AM FREE
Don't grieve for me, for I'm free
I'm following the path God laid for me
I took His hand when I heard Him call
I turned my back and left it all.
I could not stay another day
To laugh, to love, to work or play,
I found that place at the close of the day.
If my parting has left a void,
Then fill it with remembered joy.
A friendship shared, a laugh, a kiss
Ah yes, these things, I too will miss.
Be not burdened with times of sorrow,
I wish you the sunshine of tomorrow.
My life's been full, I savored much,
Good friends, good times, a loved one's touch.
Perhaps my time seemed all too brief:
Don't lengthen it with undue grief.
Lift up your heart and share with me,
God wanted me now, He set me free.
Author Unknown

A year later, after this unusual funeral, my daughters and granddaughters accompanied me on a trip to Germany. That trip was not only to bring some of my dear Hedwig's ashes to her former home, but it was also the first time that they had ever been to Germany. The trip was to show them where their mother (and grandmother) grew up as a child and also to show them the place where my dear Hedi and I first met; the house and garden of Doctor and Mrs. Christ. Since then I have returned to Germany several times.

So, after losing a spouse there is a period of adjustment to be made. I remember there were many days I sat alone in my empty house thinking about the good times Hedi and I had together.

I played in our entertainment unit some of my wife's favorite melodies, especially a composition by the new age artist Yanni. It was titled: "Before I Go." This tear jerking rendition of a heart warming and touching rendition of such beautiful soothing and peaceful music made me cry uncontrollably in my grief. Even today, whenever I play it again, the tears come rolling down my cheeks as I think back to the forty-six years to the day of her death that we had together.

Also the fact remained, that where did all those years go? Time passed now so quickly. What was I going to do? Everywhere I looked there was something to remind me of my dear wife. Especially working in her kitchen. Now I had to tackle the task of preparing and cooking my own meals.

Having been with Hedi side by side in the kitchen for so many years I had made a mental note of how she prepared meals. I guess it was more of a mystery to me. A little pinch of this and a little pinch of that mixed together with her loving kindness, is what always made a delicious dinner. "Voila" a dish was put before us on the table. I could never understand how she did it. Now I have a greater appreciation for anyone that can cook.

Now it was my turn. Let's not only call it a period of adjustment after my wife's death but at first, it became a period of experimentation.

To this day, I can say that I can cook some real good and delicious pots full of soup, and that includes Kapusta. I bake cookies and cakes and once in a while may even surprise myself turning out something "spectacular." Well, that's just another form of survival. One has to eat to live. I leave the more formal dinners and Holiday meals to my daughters and friends, at which time I just enjoy the treat at their homes.

FINDING A NEW SWEETHEART, MY ME-109

Well, while other widowers choose to go out and try to find a companion because they need someone to cook for them, I did not have that desire. Instead, I turned to my second love, airplanes.

I became more actively involved in The Antique Airplane Club of Long Island. I am presently serving my third term as vice president with them. The Bayport Aerodrome Society and The Early Flyers Club are other organizations that I am proud to be a member of, as well as being an honorary member of no less than three model airplane clubs.

I attend their local meetings as well as sometimes participating at their fly-ins and other events on weekends, either in upstate New York, New Jersey, Pennsylvania and Delaware. That became my support system to help get me through it all and keep my mind occupied.

It kept me from dwelling in grievance over the loss of my wife's love and partnership and gave me comforting consolation and change of venue. Being an active member in these clubs and organizations is what kept me from sad memories.

One day I decided to go alone to the Long Island balloon festival and air show held at the Calabro Airport in Brookhaven, Suffolk County, Long Island, New York. I believe that it was held on the weekend of August 23rd and 24th, 1997.

Because of insufficient publicity for the event there appeared to be only a small crowd. Some twenty antique aircraft were on display. But the real stars of the show were the latest aerobatic aircraft, the YAK 55, the Sukhoi 29 and German Extra 300, professionally flown by some of the country's leading aerobatic pilots. Also flying were a number of excellent homebuilt aircraft, sailplanes and also large-scale radio controlled model airplanes. About eleven hot air balloons performed, operating early morning and late evening when the wind was calm.

While walking the grounds I was startled and stood amazed as to what I had found. There was my beloved Messerschmitt 109. It was like finding my old sweetheart again. Of course it was an exact replica of the ME-109, not the actual plane and it was not yet ready to fly. I stood there silently and in awe. I was so mesmerized by the site of seeing my plane now decades later. It was the very aircraft that I flew as a WW II Luftwaffe fighter pilot. Many people wanted to take pictures of this colorful fighter plane and or pose in front of it. The occasional firing of the oxygen / propane 'guns' proved to be a real attention getter.

S.O.A.R.

It was there that I had the pleasure of meeting Al Rubenbauer. Al started S.O.A.R. (The Society Of Aircraft Restoration) about ten years ago. I told Al that I had flown the 109 during World War II as a young, nineteen year old pilot. I thanked Mr. Rubenbauer for showing my plane. It was not just the fact that it was the plane I piloted, but also the fact that history was being restored here. To find it practically in my own neighborhood was astonishing. Keeping the ME-109 at the hangar at Calabro Airport certainly has been the best-kept secret. Once I asked Al (Alois) why he built the ME-109, why not create some other plane? His reply was: "I wanted to do something that no one else has done!"

Mission Statement

The purpose of S.O.A.R. is to establish an organization dedicated to restore into flying condition, combat aircraft of all nations, to exhibit such aircraft in air shows and meets, to maintain these aircraft as a tribute to our aviation heritage.

A Member of:
EAA Warbirds
Warbirds Worldwide
Replica Fighters Association
Deutscher Jagdflieger (German Fighter Association)
L.A.R.A. (Luftwaffe Aircrew Re-enactors Association)

World War II Aircraft are often referred to as "Warbirds." Whether dynamically demonstrated in numerous air shows or in television programs such as 'Wings,' or on Public Broadcasting stations, Warbirds are proving to be of great interest to the public at large.

Unfortunately, the numbers of flyable examples of them are very few, and becoming fewer due to accidents or by becoming 'worn out,' and then retired. While flying examples of U.S. military aircraft are limited, those of their adversaries, the Axis Powers, are virtually non-existent. For example, from the over thirty six thousand ME-109 aircraft that were built in Germany, only one true flying example of the aircraft is known to exist at this time. That aircraft is believed to be located in England.

This was the reason for S.O.A.R.'s decision to construct a full scale and flying replica of this famous aircraft. While it was the initial intent to restore an actual aircraft, it soon became evident that no such rare aircraft could be found nor were suitable components available.

Visitors to the ME-109 construction site often question us: "Why not build a replica US Warbird?" While that is probably a patriotic reaction, and well understood, S.O.A.R.'s motivation was the desire to produce a truly unique aircraft, known to many because of its reputation, but actually seen by few in modern times.

As such, we expect that our replica, finished in the colors and markings of Erich Hartmann, the world's most successful ace pilot, with his three hundred fifty two confirmed combat air victories, will certainly prove to be a real "attention getter."

While some viewers of the aircraft have questioned the appearance of a swastika on the tail, that symbol was common to all Luftwaffe aircraft, as were the black and white beam crosses on the fuselage and wings.

Liking the markings on the plane or not, they are historically accurate. The exclusion of them might be considered politically correct, and embraced by others, but by being historically inaccurate, would be dishonest, and we would not want to patronize that.

The original S.O.A.R team members that were involved with it since its inception approximately ten years ago, have been as follows:

Project Director: Alois Rubenbauer
Project Engineer: Dr. Robert LeCat
Public Relations: Ronald Spencer
Asst. Directors: Phil De Luca, Vincent Stano,
Sid Weils, Emil Cassanello
Designer: Marcel Jurca
Legal: Raymond Clancy
Accountant: Carol Hernandez
Electroplating: George Sumereau
Video: Michael Esposito
Chief Mechanics: Joseph Loccisano, Michael Dukich
Electrical: Frank Sanzone
Newsletter Editor: Mary Ann Esposito
Photo Layouts: Bob Coiro
Web Designer: Charles Geier
European Rep.: Hans-Josepf Dinkle, Spieglplatzstrasse14, 8714 Wiesentheid, Fererbach, Germany

Building The ME-109 G-6 Replica

What started as a homebuilt aircraft, literally being built in a garage, is now approaching completion. Although the replica has the same dimensions as the original, as well as most of its instruments, it is constructed mainly of wood and aluminum. It's designer, Marcel Jurca of France drew up the plans for the plane.

While it is the only aircraft of its type being built here in the United States, two more are under construction in France, as well as one in Germany.

Retired Grumman employees have been building the ME-109, with work divided among specialists in mechanics, hydraulics, armaments, and part fabrication. Whenever possible, parts are copied from the originals.

Ranger Aircraft Engines, a division of the Fairchild Engine and Airplane Company of Farmingdale, L.I., NY, had manufactured this new built ME-109's engine in 1946. The engine came from surplus, new when installed, has never been previously in operation.

This inverted V-12 Ranger engine packed 770 H.P., was used in the Navy's Curtiss SO3C-1 observation aircraft during World War II, (some eight hundred of them were constructed).

Despite having been crated and preserved, stored for fifty years, the engine started readily and runs extremely well, idling and accelerating smoothly while being test-run; securely mounted to the fuselage, but not yet covered with cowling at first.

Over the past few years, several fast ground taxi tests have been made, while a chase fire truck supplied and operated by Brookhaven Airport stood by. Each test run video is made to try to establish the best way to handle this prototype aircraft.

For Information about our project, the ME-109 and to read progress reports by S.O.A.R., you may go to: <u>www.Luftwaffereenactors.</u> <u>org/soar.htm</u>

As one chapter in your life closes, another opens. Finding the ME-109 practically in my own back yard and making the acquaintance of Alois Rubenbauer led me onto a new path for my future and my destiny. I believe that my being at the Balloon Festival and Air Show gave me a new direction to follow. One thing leads to the next, and by having attended that event had paved my path for what was yet to come.

It was on December 29, 1997 when I had the pleasure of meeting for the first time a few of the team members as well as guests of the S.O.A.R. project, ME-109. The get-together was held at Hanger 21, at Brookhaven, Calabro Airport. We all came together to inspect the replica, "My Sweetheart," and exchange our stories about our WW II experiences. Some of our group included Col. Francis (Gabby) Gabreski, the leading WWII American "Ace," Rudy Opitz, a Luftwaffe test pilot for the ME-163, Komet, the rocket powered aircraft, and Alois Rubenbauer, project director of S.O.A.R.

THE BUILDING OF AN AIRCRAFT FROM A WOMAN'S POINT OF VIEW

By: Mary Ann Esposito, than fiancé of Alois Rubenbauer,and as active team member in the S.O.A.R project, ME-109.

Quite a few years ago I became exposed to the joy and excitement of flight in a single engine, private aircraft. Since that time I have learned a lot about flying, navigation, preparation and the care that is involved in flying in such an aircraft. It has opened up a new world to me that can sometimes be exhilarating and at other times frustrating or nerve wracking. It has made me respect the elements and the quickness with which they can change.

Since I have become involved with a man who loves flying and whose current project is building a full-scale replica of a WWII fighter, I have had to learn how to deal with that "other woman" in his life. She may only be made of metal or wood but she can occupy much of his time, thoughts and concerns, sometimes to the point of complete distraction. Sometimes I think that even his sleeping hours are filled with dreams and thoughts of "her."

I quickly came to the realization that if I wanted to be with him more than one hour a day at dinnertime, which even that has to be held up until, he is finished with "her," then I would have to become involved with her construction. That was one of the best decisions I have ever made. Not only has it opened up another new world for me but now I can also experience the thrill and excitement when the pieces start falling into place and the project starts to take shape and form. I also find that I have become even more important in his life because he looks for and respects my input and suggestions, asks for my criticism and has the need to use me as a sounding board for his ideas. Also, by my doing so much of the time-consuming tasks such as letter writing, searching for people or things that we need, telephone brigade, typing the progress reports and running errands, I can give him more time for the mechanics of the project.

By sharing this project it also gives us extra time to do some of the other things that we like to do together, which is necessary for both of us. It has made this "other woman" into a friend instead of an enemy.

L.A.R.A.

It is now about three years since I first discovered and joined the newly formed organization called: L.A.R.A. (Luftwaffe Aircrew Re-enactment Association). It is the only one of its kind from the existing and newly evolving groups of enthusiastic Americans forming German Re-Enactment groups.

There are many eager participants who volunteer and are showing up at various events. We count our membership in the hundreds by now, taking into consideration the various divisions existing throughout the U.S.A. and abroad.

We also have a website, where interested individuals can bring up a vast amount of information about us and also other affiliated groups of re-enactors.

This is its website: www.Luftwaffereenactors.org

The founder, Larry Mihlon always had a fascination with the **Luftwaffe.** Here is what he has to say about how his group came into being:

"I had been a re-enactor since my college days, and a combat aviation buff since early childhood. Having no idea if anyone else had the same interest in Luftwaffe Aircrew, I assembled a Luftwaffe Pilot's impression in the early 1980's. When I realized that there were pockets of individuals out there who had the same interest, I decided to form L.A.R.A. The initial support in forming the Association was tremendous and I had much talented help in every area of the organizational design of the now famous LARA shield logo. The highest honor we could have received was that of Gottfried Dulias' support and affiliation."

"A quick word about that logo… the obvious absence of the swastika in the talons was intentional. While historically correct, the swastika contradicts the true purpose of the German combat aviator and the LARA contemporarily. In a small way, omitting the swastika from the shield was our way of saying , that's not what we're about and that's not what "They," (the pilots) were about either. We can't do anything about it on our uniforms or equipment… without compromising our accuracy and authenticity to the point of misrepresentation."

"Some of my earliest memories included reading books, watching movies or building models of and about war planes. I knew who Von Richthofen was before I knew how to pronounce his name. My father was an international traveler (for business and had professional acquaintances at high levels of government… especially in (then), West Germany. He and I shared an interest in German aviators and all other aviators from the Second World War. I remember going to see the premiere of the movie: 'The Battle Of Britain,' in New York, in 1969. We attended it with the British Hurricane Pilot, "Bulldog" Drummond and, coincidentally, had dinner with one of the stars of the movie, years later, -Trevor Howard."

"My last name is German and my father taught me some German during my early years. While no direct relative can be identified as a WW II Veteran, I grew up with the son of a Junkers 88 pilot. He was a meticulous model builder and made museum quality replicas of every aircraft the Luftwaffe had during the war. I remember a humorous discussion with him about the war...

I asked him (the JU 88 Pilot): What kind of Allied aircraft the Luftwaffe had feared during the war. I thought that I had seen an Allied plane. When I did, I exclaimed: "I need to get out of here, not, Oh!!! Was that a P-51?""

Larry researches the prevailing history and then instructs the re-enactors by a briefing as to how to present the information to the public. I remember that at the World War II re-enactment two years ago in the hot month of August, in Frederick, Maryland, we were listed on the program schedule to show a skit along with the American re-enactors. Going back exactly fifty years in time, the scene took place on August 17, 1943. It portrayed the Schweinfurt-Regensburg mission of air raids by the 8th Army Air Force Division, with their B-17 Bomber groups vs. the Luftwaffe ME-109's, FW 190's, and ME 110's.

Mission Statement

The Luftwaffe Aircrew Reenactors Association is an international network of living historians and re-enactors who bring life to the study and recreation of the German combat aviator of WW II. The mission of the LARA is the representation of Luftwaffe Aircrew at historical displays, battle reenactments and air shows. As such, members have the opportunity to work around many interesting and rare aircraft.

...The German Combat Aviator
Is An Icon To Aviation.

No German Re-Enactor or living historian supports the political views of the Nazi Party. The LARA is no exception.

Here is a recent list of some of the active members of L.A.R.A. and their Aircrew Rank (listed in no particular order):

1. ***Oberstleutnant Lothar Mihlon Now General Major***
2. Larry Mihlon, LARA Founder and Director
3. ***Leutnant Gottfried Dulias now Hauptmann***
4. LARA Association Advisor, Luftwaffe Pilot Veteran
5. ***Hauptmann Alois Rubenbauer***
6. Al Rubenbauer, LARA Period Aircraft Coordinator
7. ***Major Heinrich Krist***
8. Tim Krist, LARA Central (US) District Commander
9. ***Hauptmann Erich Kohl***
10. Dan Jackson, LARA Texas District Coordinator
11. ***Hauptfeldwebel Michael Graf von Heinen***
12. Mike Heenan, LARA Northeast District Commander
13. ***Stabshelferin Dawn Dupre***
14. Dawn Dupre, LARA Helferin Coordinator, NE District
15. ***Hauptmann Paul Haberman***
16. LARA Recon/Liason Pilot
17. ***Leutnant Allen Hiserodt***
18. LARA Fighter Pilot Re-enactor
19. ***Oberleutnant Chris Curran***
20. LARA Fighter Pilot Re-enactor
21. ***Kanonier Franz Hever***
22. Neil Hever, LARA Ground crew and Flak Coordinator, NE District
23. ***Flakhelferin Elizabeth von Mannteufel***
24. Rachel Putnam, LARA Helferin Coordinator, Central US
25. ***Leutnant Manfred Richter***
26. Kevin Richter, LARA Fighter Pilot Re-enactor
27. ***Oberleutnant Todd Eaves***
28. LARA Fighter Pilot Re-enactor
29. ***Oberfeldwebel Pete Johnston***
30. LARA Bomber Crewman Re-enactor

31. ***Flieger Hans Meidel*** Todd Price, LARA Central District Ground crew Coordinator
32. ***Hauptmann Erich Bar***
33. Scott Thompson, LARA Fighter Pilot Re-enactor
34. ***Leutnant Ulrich Brenner***
35. Brian Calabrese, LARA Fighter Pilot Re-enactor
36. ***Feldwebel Hans Fischer***
37. John Fischer, LARA Fighter Pilot Re-enactor
38. ***Flieger Phil Keller***
39. ***Phil Keller, LARA Ground crew Re-enactor***
40. ***Oberleutnant Walter Spengler***
41. Bill Bennett, LARA Signals Coordinator
42. ***Reichsmarshall Hermann Göring***
43. Laen August (Specific Character Impression of Göring)

New members are arriving frequently and with enthusiasm to join our Association and become Re-enactors. Both men and women are always welcome.

Today, German WW II Re-enactment groups in the United States are respected with the highest regard. However, citizens in today's Germany do not value our Re-enactment groups in this country. On a recent trip to Europe, as I talked about this and showed pictures of us in uniform, that fact was expressed to me. The Germans do not see our Re-enactment as a restoration of history. They feel it should be left alone; perhaps they are ashamed, as it may be taken for Nazi propaganda, a thing of the past.

In contrast, here in the USA, the interest for Re-enactment and their diverse groups is growing. That is not just for those aspects depicting American History, but also those representing other nations that were involved in the various Wars. The soldiers and other military personnel try to Re-enact authentically capturing the history in the way it had happened then. More and more groups are evolving and memberships are growing.

GROSS DEUTSCHLAND

There is also a large group of Re-Enactors portraying the 7th *Kompanie* of the well-known elite group *Panzer Grenadier Regiment "Grossdeutschland,"* circa 1943. This particular group is one of the oldest Living History German units here in the United States, having celebrated their twenty-fifth Anniversary two years ago, at The Mid Atlantic Air Museum's WW II Weekend in Reading, Pennsylvania. They are a dedicated group of military historians who recreate the time period between 1935 and 1945. They have an inner organization group called the "World War II Historical Preservation Group, Inc.," and have obtained status as a not-for-profit charitable organization that is seeking supporters for their efforts. They like to call themselves: *"Lebende Geschichte Gruppe,"* meaning: "Living History Group."

This Is Their Website: www.Grossdeutschland.com

Three years ago, at the WW II Weekend at Reading, Pennsylvania, I saw one of them acting as: *"Fahrradsoldat."* (Bicycle-soldier). As I saw him for the first time he was a soldier in uniform, carrying a rifle and riding a period-styled bicycle. I asked him, "Where did he come from?" He then pointed over to a tent display and campsite. I visited that site, and was totally amazed as to what I found. There were all original weaponry such as: hand grenades, machine guns, vehicles such as: an original Volkswagen Jeep, BMW motorcycles with side cars, field telephone stations, a field *Lazarett* (Hospital), and even the old familiar German field kitchen, the *"Goulasch Kanone."* All the things that I saw in my past life were right before my very eyes!

I became acquainted with the many members who belonged to that group, including their Founder and Leader, *"Hauptmann"* Bob Lawrence. We then made arrangements for his group to come to our L.I. Calabro Airport to meet "My Sweetheart," the Messerschmitt 109.

That event drew a fairly sizeable crowd. Among the group was Gabby Gabreski as well as some of the Tuskegee Airmen. Photos were taken that day, but they could have very well been taken as originals from World War II.

At many events both L.A.R.A. and Grossdeutschland join together and support one another.

Evidence of this growing membership in re-enacting is portrayed by my own participation. Today's Air Shows, for example; in Frederick, Maryland, or in Reading, Pennsylvania, are crowd-pleasing events. You would not only find there an extremely strong interest in anything related to WWII but would also see that the population of active and very interested younger participants is growing. Younger and younger people are getting involved in capturing a little part of history. It amazes me, that in reality I could be their great-grandfather yet we experience a comradely bonding. More recently, one new recruit into our L.A.R.A. group was only sixteen years of age. He wanted to be part of the total experience.

I myself represent "Living History," as do so many other veterans from various wars. Numerous times, when participating at these re-enactment festivities, spectators approached me with such an uncanny curiosity about all aspects of my life; especially my service in the Luftwaffe.

They wanted me to share with them as much as possible from my life's experiences. Now, when I attend these gatherings I come prepared with a free handout, a (two page) synopsis of my autobiography.

As I handed my story out over the past few years, interested individuals have enthusiastically encouraged me to get my life story written into a book. "You have a great and fascinating story to tell, you are a living history." I guess you could say that I'm somewhat of a legend by now and already have a Fan Club. Almost daily I receive sometime long letters with the request to sign cards and pictures of me as a cadet, of my plane and more recent pictures of me at various events, that they may have gotten from vendors at E-bay, and sent along with stamped return-envelopes, to save those expenses for me.

Continuing to be actively involved portraying a Luftwaffe fighter pilot; I have also become an Advisor as to the authenticity of the uniforms, props, weaponry, etc. In re-enactment we are also careful about the use of any symbols.

For us it is the concept of the authenticity and representation of depicting everything to the smallest detail. Even down to the books, stationary and the hand stamps that were used during that period of time by the military. For example: The ***Soldbücher*** (the Payment record books), which were issued to each soldier.

Now how, in the world, can the symbol of the Swastika be eliminated and still depict history correctly? That is bizarre and doesn't make sense! The "law" in Germany forbidding the display of this, and other such supposedly "Nazi" symbols as well as other legal rules and regulations gave me the impression, that Germany is still pretty much a "Police run state," as it was in the past.

It is a fact that the Swastika was and has been a distinct symbol of ancient Germanic tribes. It represents the sun. For at least eight thousand years it has been the mark of the Hindu people, implying prayer for success, accomplishments and perfectionism in every walk of life, and can be seen in a temple in Delhi, India. All Aryan scripts (Roman, Greek, Latin, Siamese, Japanese, Sanscrit, Tibetan, etc.) are believed to have originated from this symbol. So how dare the German government forbid the display of that as a Nazi symbol? It merely was used as an old Germanic one by Hitler, but in reality should not be perceived as an outright Nazi symbol; that is certainly not the case here.

The original uniform for the Luftwaffe was made of wool. Synthetic materials were not in existence before wartime. To use a fabric other than wool would not be authentic. Most times we do our Re-enactments in the heat of the summer. It's very tough wearing wool when it's about ninety or more degrees standing in the hot sun with perspiration dripping down ones face while feeling the sweaty shirt and underwear cling to your skin.

You crave a little breeze of cooler air to get relief. The unbearable heat doesn't make our task of re-enacting too great a pleasure, especially, when you see the public dressed in light and airy garb. That makes one envious of their apparently comfortable situations. What a sacrifice we have to make in doing our 'job' of trying to share with everyone a small portion of history!

More recently I have made the acquaintance of Mr. William Tucci. He is a very successful young man; he has a great respect for my life story and me. We frequently greet one another at meetings of The Antique Flyers Club.

He is a well-established cartoonist of the Crusade Comics:
www.CrusadeFineArts.com

He has been successful with of the publication of: "Shi, The Way of the Warrior," in both North America and Europe.

Now he has other interests, including Filmmaking. It was in the year 2002 that he asked me to participate as a stand-in character in his first short film. It was called: "Some Trouble Of A Ser-r-ious Nature," a comedy. I did not have a speaking part but I pretended to be a farmer in that film. He did win an award for it as a "Best Short Film."

In January 2004, some members from L.A.R.A. decided to come to Calabro Airport to produce their own short film; the name of it has escaped my memory. They were using the ME-109 for action by a green background and for creating re-enactment scenes, were using a script to portray a war story. Once again, I was their technical advisor even to the point of coaching the German dialogue.

That's Just Another Day Of Re-Enacting, Reminiscing,
And Advising, But There's More to Life Than That!

Dianna, "The Lady In Red"

When I returned home from my trip to Germany, in September 2001, I felt the need to find female companionship. I didn't miss it before, but my youngest daughter Lucie, the one who gave me my computer, thought that it might be a good idea for me to search online.

She helped me prepare an introduction as to whom I was, and what I was looking for, and the rest would be up to me. One day I received an email from DreamMates, and decided to see what it was all about. In response, several ladies found me and started correspondence, but the problem was that they were out of town, and state, being "geographically, undesirable," and even perhaps not to my liking. I needed to meet someone in person who was attractive, as well as being "geographically desirable," and intelligent. I also wanted a woman I could share some common interests with. I was drawn to "Colorful," and I was "ME-109."

I liked reading her profile, she stated that she had an 'up-beat', but sometimes 'offbeat' personality, and that every day is a new adventure. Included with it was a quotation by D'Souza: "Dance as though no one is watching you, sing as though no one can hear you, love as though you were never hurt before, live as though Heaven is on Earth."

She didn't have a clue as to what ME-109 really meant. Yet, she continued emails with me, as I did with her and we exchanged more pertinent information with each other. That seemed to be her 'screening process.' She later admitted that she perceived me as "non threatening," that I seemed quite respectable, and that the contents of my emails were interesting.

Finally, after we both felt positive "vibes," she phoned me. During our first conversation she said: "I detect an accent, may I ask, where are you from?" She then found out that I was born in Germany and was now an American citizen. For her, that presented a feeling of familiarity. Her own father was an immigrant in 1923, from Schweinfurt, (a large town in Bavaria), Germany, and had arrived in New York, by ship, entering via Ellis Island.

We first met at a local Diner for breakfast and I presented her with a bouquet of yellow roses. I said: "That was for "Friendship." She told me later, that I turned out to be a most pleasant "surprise" because she had anticipated meeting a 'crotchety' old man, wearing a plaid flannel shirt, and was prepared to leave, if necessary. Seeing her I detected some sadness in her eyes, which her smiling face could not betray. I am good at judging people, and had a 'knack' for it, after getting experienced and had learned from such situations as POW in Russia.

I came dressed with my sport jacket, shirt and tie, and she later told me that she was impressed because that was the way a man should meet a lady for the first time, rather than the usual customary T-shirt and blue jeans.

Many times I called and asked her if she would like to go over to the Planting Fields, Arboretum, to look at the plants, flowers and trees in Fall colors; but she was always too busy, and I didn't want to act 'pushy.'

Finally, we arranged to meet at a later date once again meeting for breakfast in the same diner as before. She brought pictures along that she took with her digital camera. I in turn, presented o her a stack of printouts of our emails and chats up to that time and point.

Yes, she favored wearing something with the color "red," like what she wore in her photo with her description, and she was a 'bubbly' redhead as well. We continued our conversations about all different things, but more often reminisced about Germany.

She suffered a mishap on one day in the morning that we were supposed to meet for lunch. She wore a new pair of high-heeled shoes while shopping at the supermarket and suddenly she slid forward, groceries and all, and cut her lip, and also chipped one of her front teeth. She said that in the shopping bags were a number of cat food cans and she thought that they broke her fall and prevented her from further injury.

In a joking way, she said: "It spared her life." I received a phone message stating: "Sorry, I will be meeting you much later, because I was just admitted to the hospital, I think I'll need a few stitches, so I'll see you later." Yes, in remaining "upbeat" about the bad situation we met later that afternoon, and had a late lunch.

Dianna was and is a "cheery soul," but yet couldn't help seeing sadness reflected from her eyes; an I told her so. She revealed to me that her mother of eighty-nine years had passed away that August at home, as a result of complications from Alzheimer's disease. Yet, when meeting with me, she tried to remain "cheerful," and did not dwell on her sadness and was trying to hide it. She had taken care of her mother for several years and was under stress. She wondered as to how I knew about or detected her secret; so I told her about my experiences as a POW in Russian Gulags and clearly could read it in her face, especially her eyes.

Shaking her head she said: "That's amazing!"

I liked that "positive thinking," of hers and I continued to stick with our friendship, despite the difference in age of about twenty something years. She decided that it was best to meet on Tuesdays because she wanted to get back into her weekly routine on Mondays, and for the other days she had already set   plans.(booked up, so to speak.)

Meanwhile, I became more and more involved with my newly found groups as S.O.A.R. and L.A.R.A. Dianna did not yet become involved, and kept to herself. She had her life, and I had mine.

Actually, she did not even have a clue as to what I was involved with, yet I reported back to her about the various "happenings." She became more and more interested and admitted to me that she knew very little about World War II, only what she learned in public school.

One day I drove her to the Calabro Airport to meet Alois Rubenbauer and see "My Sweetheart," the Messerschmitt 109. She brought her digital camera along and took some pictures of it. That was the first time ever that she saw or even heard of such an aircraft. Then she finally came to realize the meaning of my screen name.

In the Summer of 2002, Dianna and her daughter accompanied me, along with Mr. Rubenbauer and his fiancé' to see what the World War II Weekend at Frederick, Maryland was all about. That was a "first" for both of them. It turned out to be most impressive, despite the prevailing heat.

The Chiccolini mother-and-daughters were also present. They were always a "warm welcome" at the re-enactment weekends. The mother dressed as a **Haus Frau** (Housewife), carrying a basket of freshly baked bread **(brot)** wrapped in a gingham cloth. One daughter wore a **Dirndl** (traditional German) dress, with a lace- trimmed apron, while the other one wore the uniform of the WW II **Rote Kreuz** (Red Cross) nurse. Their brother was a re-enactor with the Military Group **Grossdeutschland**, and most, if not all of the soldiers from that group were camping overnight on the field for the duration of that weekend.

It was after that weekend that Dianna decided that she too wanted a **Dirndl dress** of her own. She surfed the net and made her selection from the Company of Ernst Licht. The dress was a Kelly green one, embroidered with Alpine flowers, accompanied by a contrasting white lace trimmed embroidered blouse and apron. She later wore that outfit to all the various Christmas parties. At the same time, Dianna along with her daughter became better acquainted with some of the re-enactors and also became interested in their activities.

Dianna's daughter was adopted, and because of it she took a special interest in a volunteer job with "C.A.S.A." (That is the equivalent to: "Guardian Ad-Lightem," which is a volunteer program that is also offered in other States). As a volunteer you receive some preliminary training at a court of Law, which familiarizes you with family law as well as the different agencies offering their services within that system. After completion of the training, the volunteers are then 'court-appointed' to a specific family, by the presiding Judge. The job of the volunteer is to periodically visit and then prepare a written progress report about that family.

A report about the findings is then sent to C.A.S.A., and includes all information of the observations and possible recommendations about everything that is in the "best interest" for the children of that family.

It was in the Fall of 2003 when a terrible story was published about children living in New Jersey who had been adopted and were found severely malnourished, they were starving. Dianna read her daily newspapers, watched some TV programs and continued to follow up on that headline story. In particular, she watched and carefully listened to one talk show about it, and then went to sleep that evening, but she did not give it any further thought before going to sleep.

The next morning, November 13th, she awoke at three o'clock AM with a "brainstorm of an idea." Seeing the analogy between my prisoner of war story, and the story of the starving children living in the State of New Jersey, she sprung from her bed and immediately started writing.

She could almost feel the experience of what real starvation was about. By seeing the images of those pitiful children, and hearing that they picked food from a garbage can, out of the blue, the title came to her mind "Another Bowl of Kapusta." It was because she repeatedly heard my story over and over again about my own experience with starvation, how I existed with very little nourishment, but mostly had Kapusta, the main 'diet' of POW's in Russia.

Later that morning she phoned me and said: "I woke up at three in the morning and started writing your story, I'm still doing it now, and I gave it a title, I'll be right over to bring you the copies of what I started." I just said, "OK!"

Dianna came over and handed me the copies, and said: "Now, here, it's up to you to continue because it was your life, and you have to tell your story." Well, I guess the idea did not "sink" in, as I remained calm, perhaps even startled by it.

I never said to her: "Please help me write my story!" Yet, she's a good listener, and for the short period of time that I knew her she was absorbing and retaining all of my shared information. This information, that I never ever had revealed to anyone, not even to my dear Hedi in all those years we were together; for fear of suffering more nightmares.

After that, everything and anything that she wrote she then gave to me to look it over, proofread and edit. As I read her copy, it felt almost as if she had crawled into my mind, because all my innermost thoughts were expressed through her. In other words, her heart and soul was put into it, and she was like my appointed messenger.

I invited her to accompany me to a Christmas party with the Early Flyers Club that was held at the Bavarian Inn, located in Ronkonkoma, L.I., New York.

Christmas parties always lift my spirits. They are a once in a year opportunity to be together with familiar faces as well as being able to make new acquaintances. However, this time I was even more enthusiastic attending these events than I was in former years attending alone. I was excited because this would be the first opportunity to tell my friends, acquaintances and fellow comrades-in-arms that now I was indeed finally writing the book that they had been encouraging me to write for so long.

The morning of the party, December 15th snow started coming down and rapidly accumulated. We wondered and feared that the party would be cancelled, but thankfully was not. We ventured out, allowing plenty of time to travel to the place. Cars were skidding to the right and left, and emergency vehicles were zooming by with flashing lights and sirens blazing. We safely arrived there after navigating through a heavy fog as we approached and drove along the shore of the lake area in Ronkonkoma.

At the Bavarian Inn at one o'clock in the afternoon I estimated that only about half of the expected members had shown up. Still some of them made it there traveling from as Far East as Riverhead and Southold, Long Island. I guess when they finally reached their destination, they considered it a "victory." Many members are veterans from both World War II and the Korean War. So we all rallied around, and the party began!

We were served a very nice full course hot lunch. Two elderly gentlemen were the DJ's by the name of "The Frankie B's". They played some of the golden oldies tunes, with many songs that I recognized. They expected a Lady singer, but due to the inclement weather, she had cancelled.

There were also some nice raffle prizes, so Dianna and I took quite a few chances because with fewer people in attendance we had a better chance of winning, and she is often very lucky that way.

People were having a good time as we listened to the music and many got up to dance. I asked Dianna to dance with me. Because I wear a hearing aid, many times the music just sounds like a lot of noise and static. So only when the slow tunes were played, did I ask her to dance.

She asked me where I learn to dance. I told her that my sisters taught me after I returned home from Russia. She then said that in Europe when someone asks you to dance, it is usually polite to accept the set of three dances. So, after the first dance we were the only couple that remained on the dance floor for the next song.

Dianna wore a very stylish red dress that day. It was in a full flowing draped design and the length was just below her knees. When she danced, it swirled around. It was the first time that I ever saw that dress on her. She told me that was the dress that she wore earlier in the year, to two weddings she had attended, one of them was in Colorado and the other took place in Connecticut. I paid her my compliments on her good looks in that magnificent attire.

It seemed that Dianna was the only lady dressed all in red, even with a matching neck choker, high heeled open toed shoes, handbag and red nail polish. One man kept admiring her dress because he used to work in the Garment Industry. The style of dress today is much more casual and many ladies prefer just wearing that "little black dress."

So as we continued dancing at the second song, it turned out to be "The Lady In Red." The words went on... "The Lady in Red, Dancing

With Me"… (Originally composed by Chris De Burgh). Well, needless to say, that was a real "attention getter," with many smiling faces all around.

Then, as was predicted, the snow turned to rain. So, as fast as it came down, just as fast it washed away.

As the party was coming to a close, it was time for the raffle prizes. There were a nice variety of prizes including; bottles of wine, wrapped coins, poinsettia plants and books titled: Pioneers of Aviation. Because they forgot the roll of real raffle coupon tickets, we were requested to write our names or initials down on folded small pieces of paper.

Ours were G.D. and Dianna P. So, at the first drawing wouldn't you guess it? Dianna won! She went to the table to make her selection and was asked to pick the next winning ticket. This went on for a few minutes until I was called and I selected the book as my prize. Then alternately, Dianna was picked for a second time, and they called out: "The Lady In Red." Then I was picked for my second prize, and a few minutes later we again heard "The Lady In Red."

So that really turned out to be quite a party, quite a dance, and quite a happy ending for an otherwise dreary day. A great time was had by all of us few attending that pleasant party.

Up In The Clouds We Are All Equal

March 10th, 2004 turned out to be a most inspiring evening for all those who had the privilege of attending a program that was given at the Brookhaven Campus of Dowling College, School of Aeronautics. Two former WW II Tuskegee Airmen and good friends of mine, Bill Wheeler and Victor Torreon had invited me there. I was to give a speech along with them and another guest, Ruby Basic, a Lady Civil Air Patrol Pilot that evening.

Earlier at that evening, a delightful dinner was served by Michelangelo Caterers. At my table Alois Rubenbauer joined me along with his fiancé Mary Ann, my co-author, Dianna Popp and Dr. Robert

LeCat. Monsieur LeCat was originally from France and served as a WW II fighter pilot. Later he had a career working at Grumman's. He has been the project engineer for S.O.A.R. and the building of the ME-109. He supervised the construction of it, with the hope that eventually it would be able to fly.

Ironically, the men who were once enemies flying way up in the clouds doing their sworn duties as fighters, have now become friends as former comrades-in-arms that they really were.

Ruby set a wonderful example of how an African-American woman, at forty years of age, became a pilot. She had her dream and was determined to make it happen, and she really did!

The faculty of the Dowling College flight school gave a tour of the building,

(it was formerly an active airplane hangar). What was fascinating and also most impressive, was seeing the modern, even futuristic classrooms set up with "state-of-the-art" flight simulators and a reality type laboratory, which featured an Air Control Tower.

Parked out on the Airfield was a new twin engine Piper that one of the guests had just flown there, arriving in only thirty-eight minutes from Delaware. Along with the Piper, out on the field, stood Al Rubenbauer's plane he had towed over and proudly displayed "my sweetheart," the replica ME-109. It was parked out on the tarmac next to the school building for all to see and inspect.

An eleven-minute long film that was made in the 1940's and narrated by our former President, Ronald Reagan was shown to inform us about what Tuskegee and their Airmen were all about.

After all our speeches were given, questions were asked, and answered by the panel. A book signing by the Tuskegee Airmen followed and a Presentation Plaque commemorating that evening was presented to each one of us by the faculty president.

That particular evening at the College was the first ever of its kind whereby guest speakers were invited to speak before an audience of both the students and the general public. As is in this case, to hear and meet former WW II veteran pilots and one female pilot of post wartime. Perhaps they will consider doing it again in the future by inviting other war veterans, because it certainly turned out to be most successful and well attended.

It has been many years now since my three daughters left the nest and went off, got married and made lives of their own preference. Each one of them is unique and successful in their own way. We never had any disciplinary problems with our girls and they never had to experience any of the childhood abuse as I did while growing up. But I do confess that at some occasions I was harsh with them. Since then, I have mellowed with age. Perhaps like a fine wine, the older, the better!

The one regret I have today is that we did not speak the German language in our household so our daughters could have learned it in early age. Today it is common for families to be bi-lingual. But back then, when our girls were growing up it was not recommended that they learn a second language. Our Pastor advised me that it might confuse them by mixing up those languages and that they would encounter trouble in school.

To counter that ill-conceived view, an Italian friend of mine, who had a German born wife, taught their three children to speak and understand Italian as well as German. The children were quick to learn the languages and were never confused or mixed up knowing them each as separate ones. So later, Hedi and I did regret having not taught our girls the German language while they were still young.

However, later on, our eldest daughter Angela took it upon herself to learn to speak, read and write in German. She had made the acquaintance of a non-German born person who took it upon himself to learn the language. She decided that if "he could do it, so could she."

Perhaps we were one of the few foreign born people who decided to make a new life in our middle class neighborhood of Patchogue, Long Island, New York. Most foreign-born people stayed closer to a big city, New York.

I guess it was better and more convenient for employment purposes.

For that reason and in many ways, we were somewhat detached from the German culture. It has only been now that my whole world has turned around and I have been re-connected to my roots, the existence of my being and perhaps my mortality.

I still live modestly in the house that Hedi and I bought together in 1954. Of course now it looks totally different. It had expanded over the years, when we added rooms to my real "Doll House," as our family grew. It is now triple the original size and has two stories. Looking back, I must have been crazy to do all that work. Today people buy and sell homes as the family grows without giving it much thought. But I like my own solidly built space and living in one home for fifty years shows stability. It is also another type of living history.

Well, it's been a long and winding road of travel and life long experiences to get me to where I am today. I also love driving cars and continue to keep a valid driving license. I always liked the 1995 Chevrolet Astro Van and have a turquoise colored one, which runs smooth and gives me good mileage to the ever-changing prices of gasoline. It was only on rare occasions in my entire life of driving that I ever purchased a brand new car. The last one of them in late 2004 when I traded it in for a brand new long type 2005 Astro Van featuring numerous new conveniences. As power locks, automatic transmission, power steering and brakes, side sliding door, rear wind shield wiper mounted on the flip-up upper window panel, two opposing lower back doors, power drivers seat, both front seats with reclining backrests and an eight speaker radio and sound system both with tape playing and CD disks, roof rack and more.

Sometimes a passenger in my van would make a comment that I may be driving too fast or that I make quick, sharp turns. I remind them that I was once a Fighter Pilot, and that you had to make split second, quick decisions in any situation; and I still had that in me. One reply was: "But you're not one now, that was then, so please, take it easy, you're not a Fighter Pilot anymore!"

I continue driving to the Smith Point Beach to visit the memorial site where I scattered Hedi's ashes. By the way, now at the opposite end of the same Smith Point Beach stands the completed memorial for the downing of TWA Flight 800. Anyway, one day, maybe slightly more than two years ago, I became annoyed because I could not park close enough to get out of my van and walk to the site where Hedi's ashes were scattered. The parking spaces closest to the wooden walkway were designated for the "Handicap Blue Parking Zone."

One day a friend took the ride, accompanying me there and said: "Why don't you go to the Department of Motor Vehicles and get the handicap form. Have your Doctor fill it out and that's all you have to do to get the blue sign to hang onto your rear-view mirror. Then you'll have that space! Why not make your life easier? After all, you earned it! You have a pacemaker; you are an older person with back problems. So go and get it, and you deserve it as well!

I took that advice and I got that handicap parking sign for my car that is now valid for at least five years and is such a convenience! I look at it this way: I am just like everyone else! I never expected any privileges. No fame, no fortune, nor glory. But, as the friend did point out, I already paid my dues in the game and school of life! So I deserve the privileges of being able to now park in the blue marked zones.

Luftwaffe Fans

November of 2003 I received a request by a twenty three year old young man from England, a person I never met or heard from before. He asked me if I could please send him my autograph. He was so impressed and interested in the valiant battles the mostly outnumbered German Fighter Pilots had to fight in a war, which had occurred long before he entered this world.

Not only did I send him a copy of my signed picture as cadet in the Berlin-Gatow LKS(**Luft Kriegs Schule**), the Air War Academy, but also the two page synopsis of my autobiography. Other pictures of me from that time and the present, as well as a copy of Francis (Gabby) Gabresky's autograph with a personal dedication to me, as his friend were also included in that mailing. I believe, that his fan letter to me is worthy of recognition. It may be of interest to some of my other fans as well as anyone else reading this. So I will now share it with you: An exact word for word copy of his writing:

Monday, 17ᵗʰ November 2003

Dear Mr. Dulias,

I would like to take this opportunity to thank you for your wonderful gesture in sending me your autograph. I was pleasantly surprised as I never expected to receive something so special and I would just like to say I would treasure it always. I got your address via the American phonebook in my local library. I read your story through a friend, who had seen a write up about you on the Internet and he printed the story off for me, as I don't have access to a computer. I correspond by "Snail Mail!" I would just like to say, that it means a great deal to me to be able to correspond with such an honorable man as your Good- Self.

I do hope we can keep in touch from time to time. Just to tell you a bit about myself, I work for British Telecom as an Engineer and live in a small village in the North West of England with my girlfriend " Susan." We don't have any children yet!! She sends her best wishes to you.

I have a sister, Margaret; she recently got married and my father "Arthur," who is a retired machine fitter at a local Glass Bottle Company. I never knew my mother, as she died when I was eighteen months old from a brain tumor.

My chemotherapy is well in remission now thankfully. The only setback is that before the treatment I had blond hairs, now I'm dark!

Take care,

John

Es grüsset Sie herzlich, Ihr unbekannter Fliegerfreund, John

Translation of the above greeting:

"Greeting you heartily, your un-known flyer friend, John."

Well, this letter of his, is just one example from numerous others that I continue to receive almost daily. But this particular one impressed me as especially touching. Here is a young man in Europe, whom I had never met, afflicted with cancer (thankfully in remission), and living with the fact that he lost his mother when he was practically a baby. He took it upon himself to get in touch with me, a stranger to him, just because he heard of me. It was for the mere purpose of satisfying his interest in Aviation and particularly his admiration for the valiant German fighter pilots.

The Thank you card and his inserted letter were written in German in the same neat handwriting, all in capital letters.

Now, wasn't that nice of him? I too, will treasure his letters as an example of the fact, that there are young people out there, who show a genuine interest in learning more about history and particularly WWII. Very commendable!!

Here are a few excerpts from other fan letters that I continue to receive:

From another man whom I have never met, also living in England, John Ashley: Again in his exact words!

"I often wonder about the Re-enactment movement… of which I myself am a small part of. Despite the horrors of reality and terrible memories, we all try to bring it, or at least part of it back to life.

What we do is sanitized and no one gets hurt… I can't help but admit to a certain amount of reveling in the uniforms, the bands and so on. Are we perhaps doing a disservice not only to our children but also to those folks such as yourself who must see many a dark and vile shadow lurking amongst the otherwise bright and brave show being portrayed? Is there any danger, perhaps it is the very fact that the true horror of war cannot be depicted effectively.

I can't wait to be able to read your book as it will all seem that much more real, for the privilege and honor of being able to number you amongst my friends albeit by email and telephone"…

From Bill Wheeler, Tuskegee Airmen:

"Just found your "Final Afterthought." You wrote the page; however, the universality of your profound thought and warning will affect all who read it. It is a fitting commentary that should be emblazoned in the mind of every human being.

You leave those who vicariously shared your terrible trials and challenges with a deep gratitude for the positive philosophy you developed after being treated in such a vile, hateful-all but fatal-manner.

You are to be commended and revered for ending your shocking story with words of platitude that will remain seared forever in my mind and, hopefully in the memories of all who shared your nightmarish experiences. I believe that God, in his infinite wisdom, spared your life so that you could bring to the rest of the world the indescribable horrors and final conclusions you have reached to give us hope for our survival, as we traverse this treacherous world. I am so happy that you are a "Known Soldier," with a voice and a gift for sharing your exceptional life –hopefully to help mankind avoid the necessity for future wars and "Unknown Soldiers."

May God Bless You … Congratulations with the excellent progress you are making as you enter the "final stages" of completing your book.".…

From someone who listened to one of my speeches:

"I was particularly taken with your account of life in a Soviet Russian Gulag, and I was very pleased to hear that you are engaged in writing a memoir of those days. I believe as you do, that it is a very important project, and that your desire to bear historical witness for those who cannot speak for themselves ranks among the loftiest goals of literature.

Thankfully, I can never hope, nor would I wish, to truly understand the horrors that you experienced in Russian captivity, but it is my belief that reading or hearing about such experiences opens a door in the mind which, once open, is not easily shut again. For you the door is always open, and God grant you strength as you gaze in.".…

From a man in Reading, Pennsylvania:

"This history must be told and your contribution to the documentation of that era is invaluable. I was in Saarbrücken, Germany last July with an old friend. I asked her the same question that I had asked another old friend from Berlin. Why are there no memorials to the German dead from World War Two? They said it is still too sore a subject to memorialize them. But, my point is that they were young men taken away from their homes, their factories, their farms, etc. and they died. They were not great planners of world destruction; many of them were just "boys."…

One more letter from a female Fan:

"Your story is so powerful! I heard you speak last rainy Saturday in Reading. All of us in the tent were spellbound, and you could have heard a pin drop in spite of the airplane noise outside. Since I came home, I told many friends and family of your experience, as I could not imagine such torment-so many emotions going through your head and each day trying to stay alive. It truly makes one appreciate the freedom we have here."…

COMRADES-IN-ARMS

Gabby Gabresky did indeed become a good friend of mine. That was after having been introduced to him by another good friend, Ronald Spencer. Ron has been a team member of S.O.A.R., and came to know "my sweetheart" before I ever did. With enthusiasm about the project, he used to show and tell all that he knew about it, to various school groups.

Ron stands tall, is slender in stature, and has bright white hair. On a Friday evening, after leaving a school where our model air plane club was flying indoor radio controlled model aircraft and also tossing toy gliders up, we met up at a diner for supper. A stranger at the table next to us made the comment that Ron was striking in appearance, perhaps resembling an actor from an old war movie like Spencer Tracy or Kirk Douglas. He smiled and revealed that "yes," he was indeed an ole' war vet.

In WWII Ron served as navigator in a B 24 bomber of the 8th Air Force Division. He flew missions over Germany. That was at the same time when I was a young novice in JG 53 Pik-As *Geschwader* (Hunt Squadron 53 Ace of Spades). It was very likely that at one time or another we crossed each other's paths in the sky over the homeland that I was sworn to defend.

Former Lieutenant Colonel, Francis S. Gabreski, (as I hope most people know), was the all time top Ace fighter pilot in WWII for the American Air Force. Actually he earned the title: "America's Greatest

Living Ace." With his twenty-eight victories in air battles over Europe, he ultimately became a POW of Germany when he flew too low attacking an airfield on his last mission.

The propeller of his P 47 fighter plane was actually and literally "cutting the grass," as the jargon goes in aviation terms.

He had to make an emergency landing and became a POW in 1945, just like I did under similar circumstances in Hungary. Thus, having so much in common with one another was one of the main reasons we became friends.

Gabby and a few of us old war vets wanted to get together for lunch one day at the nearby restaurant. We set a date, but unfortunately it was the same time that Gabby had a more important date with the Lord. He was taken from us on that same day forever, in January 2002.

The Westhampton Airport located in Westhampton, Long Island, New York was re-named after him in his honor and memory: The Francis S. Gabreski Airport, and so his legacy lives on.

Another good buddy of mine is Emil Cassanello, a team member of the original S.O.A.R group, and also a post-war veteran. We became friends at the same time I met Ron Spencer, and we both shared the love of flying. Often times we would go up together for a spin in his Cessna 172 with me as co-pilot taking over the controls. More recently, due to health problems he was no longer able to renew his pilot's license, and had to give up flying. You must be able to pass a physical to keep a valid license. Looks like we are "both" in the very same situation!

As I am now writing this expanded edition, I must sadly report, that he too was taken from us, succumbing to his illness shortly after I visited him in the hospital.

The special joy in my life right now is having my black kitty cat Petey for a pet. He is of an American longhair breed and has a long bushy tail, like a skunk. He holds it up proudly as he walks by. In Germany, a black cat is good luck and black cats are usually named 'Peter', (and being black), ***"Schwarzer Peter."***

That is also the name of a German white wine and a children's card game. Petey has the life of a king. His feast is always waiting for him on my dining room table. There are two rows of twelve jar caps and re-cycled cat food cans. Each one contains a different variety from the selection of dry foods and treats.

I guess he could serve as a good commercial subject for selling cat food and treats. Those twenty-four varieties of treats, moist and dry foods and specialties are always at his disposal. Whatever he likes, he eats and less desired varieties, he leaves alone after taking a taste, or just after sniffing at them. He then heads to the next bunch of jar-caps in the line-up, one by one, until he finds some to his liking. How can a pet be spoiled more than that?

That's why I say, he lives like a king, and in fact, that's what he does, being served hand and foot, or better: paws and paws. But I like spoiling him this way, he is such a likeable pet who rewards me by curling up in my lap while I am resting or reading in my easy-chair, his "motor" purring in utter contentment while nudging his head on my hand, 'asking' to be petted again and again.

Wow, what a good life! I should have had the life of a cat! Instead I had a very hard life. My years as a prisoner of war in Russia have taken a toll on me. Without realizing it, after I eat my meal I continue to pick up each and every crumb off of my plate. My plate must be clean, that became a habit of mine. I do this for each and every thing I ever eat. I hate to see food wasted. Even though I barely survived with the little food I had as a prisoner, I still remember---- Kapusta----

That word is constantly repeated in my conscience. How I was longing for it, as a properly prepared, enriched and healthy vegetable soup, with more (fat) eyes looking up at you, than eyes looking in to it. No, there it was entirely the opposite, reversed.

Our prison Kapusta definitely had more eyes looking into the tin can than out from it. That was our saying as we described the green "tea" we were served and told that it was Kapusta soup. One was considered lucky, to find the resemblance of a leaf of cabbage on the bottom of one's tin can.

For the most part we only got the outer limp leaves that in the supermarkets here are removed and discarded before a head of cabbage reaches the shelf. In our case, we knew for a fact, that the good part of the heads of Kapusta, that were daily delivered for our consumption in the POW camp, wound up on the 'black market.' Snuck out of camp under the darkness of night by horse-drawn panje-wagons. Often we received a sparse amount of nearly rotten meat or fish, intended to be part of our "nourishment." I suffered once from severe fish poisoning and was near death in the POW hospital before I finally recovered and was returned to the Gulag once again as soon as I barely had some 'meat' on my ribs.

To this day I can't eat any fishmeal, except tuna, salmon, smoked fish or sardines, but only in moderation. Otherwise I suffer stomach cramps from undigested accumulation of other meals with fish as main ingredient.

Today, after so many years, as a result of being 'poisoned' by some of that food, I have a limited sense of taste as well as a modest impediment of being able to fully smell as a result of the frostbite of my nose I suffered in the bitter cold Russian winters. Now, when I try to eat and chew a piece of steak, it seems as if I am trying to eat rawhide or shoe-leather, no aroma taste at all, that others enjoy. Yet, I've learned to live life to the fullest, despite of it.

I believe it to be true when I say, that no one, in the civilized world or those in present-day times of war, knows what real hunger is like. Only POW's that were in the Gulags in Russia can be witness to the fact, that it was nothing less than pure deliberate and intended starvation!

Being in such hunger, I wrote recipes of various meals, of baked goods and desserts I heard described to me by a fellow POW, who was a professional cook and pastry baker.

Those were tediously written into my little booklets that I hid from the Russians and still have in my possession today. In doing so, I imagined eating those delicious meals and deserts. As the saliva built up in my mouth and was then swallowed, it seemed semi-satisfying to my craving for food. Of course, by doing that I was cheating my stomach and ultimately myself into believing in my imagination, that I was really eating. But at least, temporarily, it served its purpose.

So, what am I doing now? I'm sitting here in the dining room area of my house enjoying the Kapusta that I just made. I prepared it the way it is supposed to be, (and it's a damn good dish), with all the right ingredients in it. It's the kind I only dreamed about while in the Gulag.

With this one there are more eyes (of fat) looking out at me than into it. It has plenty of fresh cabbage head leaves in it, not those outer limp ones like we had in Russia. Along with carrots and some onions there's also some meat. But because I now have to watch my intake of salt, I can only have a few small pieces of ham, or corned beef. But nevertheless, I'm satisfied and content and it tastes great!

While I began eating this, it started to snow and the weather reports say that we can expect eight to ten inches of accumulation. Now reflecting back, I can clearly remember the morning when I had to shovel my VW bus out of the driveway and drive my wife to the Hospital, for the birth of our third daughter, little Lucie.

I guess today I will be home bound.

Petey is sitting at the window while alternately watching the birds at the feeders outside, and me. I put bird food out all winter long and throughout the Spring for my feathered friends, God's creatures. At the same time I'm listening to my favorite folk music, played by a Bavarian "Oompha" Band. I am thinking back and wonder, how I made it through all the agonizing hardships as a POW in Russia. Now I am able to think and write about those gruesome times of yesteryear without suffering nightmares.

Alois Rubenbauer just phoned and told me that the propeller blades for our ME 109 are now being repaired or replaced in Canada. Perhaps pretty soon we'll have our "Sweetheart" up and running. She'll just need some T.L.C. and fine-tuning.

We're also in the process of making the Hotel arrangements to attend the upcoming World War II air show/re-enactment weekend to be held in Reading, Pennsylvania, on June 4, 5 and 6. I'm certainly looking forward to that even though I will have to deal with the heat and humidity that is prevalent around at that time. At this event I will be one of the invited "Featured Guests."

I am expected to give speeches during specific times and one will be "telecast live" by a local radio station. A fine young man and good friend of mine, Bob Chubb, has become my sponsor as well as my helper and I am expected to be available for autographing and photos.

Just as I got off the phone my doorbell rang and it was Dianna, my dear friend and co-author bringing me a few final drafts of some chapters of our book. She drove despite the falling snow because she wanted to personally deliver the newly edited copies to me. Then I asked her: "Would you like to join me with a Bowl of Kapusta, and a piece of bread?" She replied: "Kapusta fine, forget the bread!" So together we enjoyed "Another Bowl of Kapusta".

> ***And This Is Not The Final Chapter of my life because I'm
> still surviving and there is still more to tell…   God and
> my Guardian Angel continue watching over me.***

My Nice and Easy Basic Recipe For Kapusta (Cabbage Soup)

First, shop for a nice looking head of crisp green cabbage, with outer leaves on it, because that's where the vitamins are. Many recipes tell you to remove them, but why? Cabbage heads are sold per pound at the super market and I have seen all kinds of different prices for it. Sometimes it costs twenty-nine, thirty-nine, forty-nine cents a pound. Even higher or lower in price, depending on the prevailing season it is offered for sale.

Wash the **Kapusta** head. Cut the cabbage in half leaving the green outer leaves attached. Put the other half aside for later, in case you want to add more into the pot. Sometimes, I make a side dish of fine-cut Coleslaw from it to have it on another day.

1 lb. of red potatoes, washed and cut into smaller pieces
Three whole medium onions, sliced
Six carrots, cut or sliced
A small bunch of celery, washed and sliced into small bits, with its leafy tops
1 ½ teaspoons of thyme
1 ½ teaspoons of oregano
3 bay leaves
some peppercorn s
Left over ham, corned beef or tenderloin cut into small pieces, they can still be on the bone.
1 large carton or can (32 oz) of Beef Broth (or two smaller cans)

Put all of the above ingredients into a large pot. Fill up with water to about two inches from the top of it. Add some more cabbage if needed.

A heaping tablespoon of butter or margarine to create the fat-eyes, if the meat you use is too lean. Add other spices according to preferred taste.

Set the temperature to medium, and bring it to a boil. Once it reaches boiling   point, lower the temperature to a simmer. Cover pot, leaving the cover at a slight tilt to allow for steam to escape. Check on it about every ten minutes, stirring it occasionally, adding more water to it if it evaporated too much.

Before it is done you may want to skim the surface to remove any froth.

After about one hour, taste one of the potatoes to see if it is soft. If it is, then you are ready to enjoy your Kapusta soup.

This recipe is quite flexible. There are many variations of it. You can always add salt and more pepper as well as a little garlic powder for additional seasoning. I use also Adobo spice, it gives it a distinct taste.

Some recipes allow a little sugar and / or some vinegar or lemon extract. Some people like to add a can of V8 juice, others prefer a can of diced or whole tomatoes, and yet others include some Ketchup. Other vegetables can be added to it as well.

You can be the "Chef," and it can be your Recipe!

"My Sweetheart" - ME 109

From Left: Ron, Gabby, Rudi, Al, Emil, Me,
At Front: Sal

Re-Enactment at Reading, PA.

Proudly We Stand, L.A.R.A.

Re-enactment, Frederick, MD.

Gottfried and Al having fun

Al Rubenbauer, Dawn Dupre,
Larry Mihlon

Grossdeutschland, At Various Events.

Chiccolini Mother
and Daughters

Dianna in Her Dirndl

Dianna - Co-Author
"Lady in Red"

Mary Ann Esposito
Al Rubenbauuer (owner
ME-109)

Presentation at Dowling College

Grand Finale - Front Left Bill Wheeler, Ruby Bostic, Vic
Torrelonge, and Me!!

Bob Chubb Proudly Holding
Enlarged Plane Illustration

2004 With my Presentation at the WWII
Weekend at Reading, PA.

Twelve

Afterthoughts In the 21ˢᵗ Century

It is now approaching close to sixty years since I first became a prisoner of war in Russia (1945-1948). First of all, I want to say is that chapter eleven was not the final chapter of my life! I have been blessed with fairly good health, despite a few set backs and impediments, and a few surgeries, aches and pains that usually come with the aging process. As the expression goes, I still have "a lust for life." I continue "marching on." With the Good Lord's help I've come this far and I'm not giving up yet! Now my goal is to reach the age of one hundred and beyond.

Somehow, I like the term "centenarian." When you finally reach that plateau, and join that "club," you receive a congratulatory letter from the President of the United States. It is true that each and every day of my life I still re-live my past experiences, especially now while re-writing my book, but so does everyone else as I presume, no matter whether they were good or bad experiences. So, we must move on as life continues.

I struggled and struggled and still struggle with my survival today. Only today the issues are quite different. They are the challenges of the so called "Golden Years," Health Plans, Medicare, Social Security and so on. I live in a society, where a lot of usable things get tossed away, or otherwise carelessly disposed of. The poor population could survive on what the American people discard. Poverty and starvation here in America is not on or part of the fine line between life and death.

I know what real starvation is, I lived through it, but with the help of our merciful God I survived. As a nineteen-year-old POW, at one time weighing only thirty-one kg, sixty-two German pounds, equal to sixty-seven American. Only real and genuine hunger can bring you down to that level of starvation, being on the brink of death, holding on to a shred of life. That is starvation, as I know it to be and barely survived from. So, I know, what I am talking about, R E A L H U N G E R !!!

Now isn't it ironic that from the very place where I was held as a starving POW at the Pensa-oblast region of Russia, and from the Delta of the Volga River, comes the most expensive, finest, most desired and exported Caviar in the World? The natural reproduction (spawning) of the sturgeon occurs mostly in the Volga Delta, flowing into the Caspian Sea. It accounts for at least sixty percent of the world's supply of that most wanted Caviar. Actually, the Beluga sturgeon is the largest fish found in the Volga.

To compare my present morning routines between life then, and my life now, well, all I can say is that "it's a whole new world." All these gadgets and gismos that I'm living with must all be kept in working condition; otherwise I start a somewhat "bitchy" morning. Not to say that I'm moody, but do I need that unnecessary frustration?

Do you realize that with each new item you purchase and bring into your home you are on your own once you make the purchase? A rather crude and often misunderstood instruction sheet comes with the newly acquired item, telling you how to connect or assemble it. They call the people who write these instructions technical writers and with that job title they have a wonderful career, usually with steady work. Only when I read the instructions after I bring whatever I bought home, do I end up taking it back. Many times I just don't get to understand those "How-To-Do-Its!" Often parts or screws that are listed in the description are missing; sometimes the instructions are for another type of those items and don't jibe with that what you have before you.

Then, as I continue throughout the day, I have to check if my TV works, the microwave, radio, CD player, alarm system, also if my car will start up, etc., etc., etc. Not to mention the initial frustrating task to correctly connect all the wires and diverse cable systems necessary for my TV and also the computer to work. Also not to mention the tricky task to connect all the wires, plug-ins, the power-lines and electronic gadgets and all that must be done in a certain way, so that the components will function properly. Many times after you've finally assembled the whole thing, you find out that it does not work and you have to disconnect everything and start all over with those un-intelligible sets of instructions. That task along with all that technical jargon is the protocol for today's survival. Now I've learned to adapt to it and cope with.

In my opinion, the computer and the Internet are the most important and greatest inventions of them all. Of all the new inventions I have seen and used in my lifetime, they are it! The radio and the airplane and cars were already in existence during my early years. I remember in our family, we used to sit together in the living room at home and listen to the radio. My father had to fine-tune it for the long, short-or middle-wave and it made those terrible hums, screeches whistles and other funny noises.

I remember that radios and TVs were built with vacuum tubes and that each tube had its part to play in the overall functions. Many German companies like Grundig, Telefunken, Saba and others exported fine, high quality radios and later in more recent times other electronics to the United States.

Yes, the computer is truly an amazing piece of equipment and it's here to stay. I guess they did all they could with the advanced technology for TV and radio therefore we now have all the added components to create various audio/ visual systems. The whole world comes to me with the computer. Technology in all fields is steadily progressing.

I believe that the concept of the Internet started to come into reality in 1995. Imagine, that in just a little over nine years all these advances have been made to develop everything further and still is going on? Every source of information and question I ever had could be answered with a few clicks on the keyboard or mouse.

My dilemma is, that I am only capable of using two fingers to type. I never formally learned how to type using both my hands. So this handicap makes writing this, my story as well as sending emails, extremely time consuming. Yet, in my life span I overcame the many obstacles, so here I am, now attempting to do this task. The computer contains it's own operating system of data, sounds, visual effects, a scanner, printer and high speed modem. One is a companion to the other. But if one gets zapped out, then it can trigger a general breakdown of all of them. Not to mention a new vocabulary and 'viruses' that goes along with the whole system and one has to cope with.

Now I have to worry about things called worms, viruses and even something called Trojans? Wait a minute; what on earth are we talking here about? The word Trojan refers to the ancient town of Troy that their enemy attacked unsuccessfully for a long time. So, a strategy was devised to bring troops into the town undetected. A huge hollow wooden house was built by the enemy, which was capable of concealing a certain number of selected soldiers. This horse was presented as a gift to the town in admiration of their valiant defense. The town of Troy accepted the "gift" and the horse on wheels did get rolled through the gate for everyone in town to admire.

At night, when the towns-people were asleep, the hidden soldiers emerged from the horse undetected. They opened the town gate and let the enemy army enter. They took the town over without a fight. Hence, the name Trojan, was a sneaky way and device to invade the computer un-detected.

Where are we going with all this stuff? To me it appears like a type of intricately complicated sneaky and spy- like World War III behavior taking over! Take me back to the old and peaceful time and way my life used to be. To an established era and quiet environment when people spent more time with each other than with machines and fancy complicated gadgets. There was much more appreciation for the simple things in life and how we spent our time. It used to be so nice to go for a walk in the park and go on outings to the forests and countryside having picnics and being in touch with nature.

I have to say, stop, look, listen! As the expression goes: "Take time to smell the roses." I strive to do that. I enjoy my garden and also manage to keep a small greenhouse that I created in the upstairs of my house. In 1958 I added a dining-/ living area to the downstairs of my house. The greenhouse is directly above that area on the second floor. When you walk through it, you come out to the open sundeck where I place my potted plants for the summer months. It is a joy and a pleasure to observe my many seasonal tropical blooms. I've been successful growing and maintaining orchids, geraniums, hibiscus, poinsettias, amaryllis and Christmas cactus. They all seem to thrive in their warm sunny space. Now that I own a digital camera (another recent and marvelous invention), I not only make photo shoots of my gorgeous flowers in bloom, but I also take the pictures to my computer and turn them into what I call "masterpieces." Imagine all the things I can do in the privacy of my own home.

Now in 2009 that little greenhouse does not exist anymore, it was taken down because it got too much for me to take care of all those growing and accumulating plants. The work was done in the later month's of 2008 by a contractor in conjunction with the new installation of roofing above the living / dining room, also a new ceiling and insulation and the painting of the entire downstairs area. Several leaks had developed at the flat roof ceiling, when a severe storm had punched holes into it by a projected broken heavy branch coming from the adjoining maple tree. Luckily, we had good insurance that covered the entire cost of the repairs.

While doing research for this book, I found out that Gulags and labor camps for political prisoners also existed in other parts of the world. The Russian Gulag prison camps existed until approximately 1953, at the same time that Hedi and I came to America. But yet, unlike the battlegrounds, and memorial sites that are recognized as being historical, other less known are often completely forgotten. Little remains as evidence to what previously once existed.

There are no real and official memorial sites in recognition of the pain, suffering and loss of lives; there is little or nothing written about the prison camps, the Gulags of Russia, and whatever was made known earlier was rather vague in description. The fact is, there will always be some type of war going on at some place in the world, and prisoners will be held against their will., mostly under dreadful circumstances.

Making comparisons of the ongoing fate of thousands upon thousands of poor souls, both as victims and sufferers, I am of the opinion that not only for myself, but also all former POWs that were in Russia as well as all others that are surviving from the horrors of

World War II, should receive equal compensation and publicity for their suffering.

I did not receive as much as one red penny for having been such a victim, having withstood all that pain and suffering in the Gulags of Russia without any compensation. Just because I was not residing in Germany on that target date in 1955 or 56, when I was already here in U.S.A. as an immigrant but was still a German citizen. Did the German government think that I deserted my country?

The government office responsible for that so called "law", rejected my numerous applications, even with my seeking legal assistance, trying to claim my entitled back pay for the time I was a POW and technically still a member of the German armed forces.

It's the law, I was told! Only those former POWs, that were residing in Germany and were citizens there on that target date, got compensation in the form of back pay with interest in sizable lump sums. That was for their time spent as POWs anywhere, not only Russia.

Documented proof had to be submitted to get what you were entitled to. I had submitted all the proof I had, including a copy of my official Russian discharge document, but again and again, I was denied my certainly "earned" payment of compensation.

Now, isn't that nice? Here I was, a former POW, having fought for my fatherland and suffered the same brutal and inhuman treatment, just like any other former German soldier in Russia, who was "present" on that target date in Germany. I got nothing---zilch --- they got their deserved back pay plus interest.

I am left here empty handed, wondering what the logic might be? Who persuaded the German lawmakers to come up with that unfair and ultimately ridiculous law of denying reparations to those former POW's who had left the destroyed, mostly bombed-out and over-crowded post-war Germany to seek a better life? <u>One thing is 100% certain: None of them were ever POW's in Russia!!!</u>

Besides that loss, and the fact that because I was taken as a prisoner of war, after my 5th Air-Victory, I never actually received that Iron Cross medal for which the paper work had been submitted to the Luftwaffe Headquarters in Berlin. Now I can only admire it by seeing it in some museum or private collection. But I was allowed to wear it as re-enactor.

During the Nazi Regime, Hitler commissioned Artisans designing about four hundred and eighty-five different medals and award pins that were given to mothers, civil service workers and of course, the Military. In comparison, the United States only made eight or nine medals that were only awarded to the Military.

Now I wonder, what actually is the difference between my state of circumstance and those fortunate comrades of mine who received their compensations?: It is the circumstance of being an aspiring citizen of our good old USA!!! Thus, I paid a very high price for becoming a proud naturalized American in 1958, when I was sworn in on August 19th, a day I will never forget! I still have that original certificate of naturalization that quotes in the last part:

"In testimony whereof the seal of the court is hereunto affixed this 19th day of August in the year of the Lord nineteen hundred and fifty eight, and of our Independence the one hundred and eighty third."

Sidney R. Feuer
Clerk of the US District Court
By Richard J. Gelardi – Deputy Clerk.

The signature of the Deputy Clerk, I could not decipher accurately, I am not sure, if I got it right, but that is not too important. On this certificate by the Department Of Justice, the description of me states, that I am 6 feet 1 inches tall, weight 195 pounds. Today, in 2009

I am 5 feet 11-1/2 inches and 170 pounds, the result of 50 years of hard work and toiling to make a living here in the land of the free.

I am still proud of my heritage as a former German, but it is hard if not impossible to forgive the present German Government and it's unjust, unfair law, for having denied me compensation that I surely had earned by sweat, extreme hunger and the cost of impaired health in particular.

In the United States of America, any war veteran leaving the service, particularly all those from WWII have received and are still receiving special honors, medals, recognition, medical help and assistance and even now National Monuments. The younger ones also receive schooling for jobs after discharge when needed. After passing away, the retirees get honored burials in a veteran cemetery.

All that does not exist in Germany as a home-comer as POW or having been discharged from the service you were on your own; at least that was the case when I still resided in Germany and I am not aware of any changes since then.

We Are Now Living In The Twenty-First Century,

"We Are Still Not Here Yet!"

Upon returning to Kennedy International Airport, in New York, after my most recent trip to Germany in the Summer of 2003, I took my Passport and filled the usual customs form out, ready to hand in. Because I am a naturalized United States citizen, my form is quite different than the one for visitors (and possible future citizens) entering the U.S.A.

Non-immigrants (meaning visitors) entering the USA by land or sea must complete a long narrow green form known as I-94W. Most people, whether foreign or American, as well as English or- non -English speaking, have no idea what this form is all about and also the content and significance of the questions being asked may be misunderstood.

The U.S. Department of Justice, Immigration and Naturalization Service prepared this form. That means: The United States (Federal) Government, INS. The form says at the top of it: "Welcome to the United States." I-94 Nonimmigrant Visa Waiver Arrival/Departure Form. Then there are instructions to read and you are to fill out two sections on the front, followed by a series of seven questions (labeled A-G) on the back, followed by more questions, waiver or rights, certification and your signature, and so on.

First of all, it strikes me as being very "odd" that when I entered Germany now as a visitor, in 2003, I did not have to fill out anything that even slightly resembled a confusing form like this. In other words, I did not have to fill out a detailed form, and no questions were asked.

So, as I further examined this US form I-94W I also noticed that it is completely outdated. It seems, that the last time it was updated was indicated in the parenthesis (05-29-91).

To continue, when you start reading the questions on the back of the form: Starting withA. Asks: Do you have a communicable disease; physical or mental disorder; or are you a drug user or addict?

B. Asks: Have you ever been arrested or convicted of an offense… and so on,

C. Asks: Have you ever been or are you now involved in espionage, sabotage; or in terrorist activities; or genocide; <u>or between 1933 and 1945 were you involved in any way, in persecutions associated with Nazi Germany and it's allies?</u>

This multi question is very misleading to an older German person who is visiting the U.S.A. for the first time. Anyone who lived through World War II in Germany was alive during the period of time specified in the question. If you know very little English but you can distinguish the years of 1933 and 1945 and the word Germany you may check off "yes" as your answer to this confusing question.

That is exactly what happened to my dear friend Sieglinde, who came from Germany with her grandson to visit me for the first time about four years ago. She was not prepared as to how to answer that question. She did speak some English but because she was confused and checked off "yes" for the question related to Germany she was detained at the airport for more than two hours, at my expense, (as I wanted to surprise them with a limousine ride from the airport to my house) and had to pay waiting time by the hour.

That delay created for her unnecessary stress and aggravation while I waited and presumed that she had missed her flight to New York. All arriving passengers had long since passed by and left. I inquired several times as to her arrival and got only vague answers. When she finally exited from the Arrivals section, more than two hours later, she told me why she was detained.

This un-necessary 'inconvenience' (Better said: Harassment) should never have taken place; it leaves a bitter taste for the innocent visitor. So, I am asking this question in all seriousness: Have we really advanced forward into the twenty first century or are we still stuck back in time?

Just think about it, here comes an elderly Lady as a visitor to the USA and gets practically arrested and interrogated for over two hours just because of those (Stupidly arranged) 'ill-conceived' lines of confusing multi-questions, that only an idiot could have written!

Is that the way visitors get "welcomed" to the USA???

I still continue returning to Germany about every other year to attend the Dulias family reunions as well as visiting family and friends. At last count, there were worldwide only fifty-two male name carrier descendents in existence. Because I have three daughters and two Granddaughters, unfortunately, my line will not be carried on for that branch of the "Family Tree" to grow any further.

My dear friend Sieglinde has been a widow for quite a while, but she is the mother of three grown sons. That is a very interesting fact because I had three daughters. What would have happened if we had made a life together? Sieglinde's only brother, a Doctor, who was my best friend, Helmut Link, was killed in a car accident many years ago. Yet, I enjoy visiting her whenever I return to Germany, she would be very disappointed if I failed to stop by for a few days.

More recently, we vacationed together and went to Ziericksee, Holland for a visit. I had invited her for a return visit to see me here in Patchogue but because of the unnecessary 'stress' that she had to endure at her last visit she politely declined. In other familiar words: "She had her nose full", that harassment on her last visit was enough for her; never again she said.

Now you can understand what damage can be and is still done to innocent visitors just because of those tricky multi questions on those stupid entry forms.

This year 2001 Sieglinde will be celebrating her seventy-fifth birthday. When we recently spoke on the phone, she reminded me that she still has a fountain pen that I had given her as a gift before I joined the Luftwaffe. Maybe when I return to Germany next time, we can go together to see if the initials I had carved way back in 1949 into a beech tree up at Angels Mountain in Fürstenfeldbruck is still there,

Irmi, my other close lifetime friend, is married to her third husband and lives in the same house that she grew up in. It is tragic that she lost her only child, a son. When I last visited her in her backyard house she had a young man as a tenant at her old front house. He was like a son to her and had a pet raven called Felix. The bird performed several funny antics and tricks.

Unfortunately, my younger married sister Gisela and recently also her husband Werner are now residing in a brand new nursing home near Fürstenfeldbruck, in Germany. During my last trip I was able to visit her there. She is alert yet not functioning to her former full capacity. I almost did not recognize her due to her poor health she is rapidly aging. I was so sad to see her end up that way.

2009 update note:
In 2006 she passed away and I attended her funeral representing our family. She got interred in our family grave where both our parents Lucie and Paul Dulias rest in peace at the North cemetery in Fürstenfeldbruck.

My youngest sister Gerda and her family are still residing in Goldsboro, North Carolina. My oldest sister Ursula, a recent widow, is the mother of two married daughters as well as a grandmother to five grand-children, she lives near Patchogue in St. James, Long Island, New York.

My oldest daughter Angela is married and lives on Long Island. She is Vice President of Human Resources at a big defense plant. Now she owns a quarter horse, as her love for horses and owning one has been her life long dream since her early childhood.

My middle daughter Elisabeth has two daughters, my only grandchildren, Lauren and Danielle. The younger of them, Danielle is in High School and Lauren is in a College in Boston, studying Electrical Engineering. Elisabeth is lives in Denver, Colorado and works in a Studio as an artist and sculptor specializing in metal works and welding as well as a Lease Administrator of Railroad Real Estate for a private firm.

2009 *Update:*

My grand daughter Lauren is now an Electrical Engineer working on Long Island. My grand daughter Danielle is a certified nurses assistant, massage therapist and is studying to become a Licensed Practical Nurse in Denver Colorado. In addition I am now a Great Grandfather to my handsome, four year old Great grandson Nicholas Lucian.

My youngest daughter Lucie is also married and living in Chicago, Illinois and is a successful Office/Network Manager .

My former business partner, Clyde and his wife are still living on Long Island, New York. It has been their tradition every year to have an "Open House" party on New Years Day, and that is when we are celebrate and to get together. Both of us still carry in our wallets a keepsake of half a twenty-dollar bill. When we first worked together we argued over who would pay for our lunch. We finally 'settled it' when Clyde split the $ 20.00 bill with the intention that we both are putting the two halves together at a future date, for another lunch. So far it hasn't happened.

2009 update notes:

Gerda, my youngest sister and also her husband William Moneypenny are both in nursing homes near Raleigh, NC. Bill, my brother in Law is afflicted with Alzheimer's and Gerda had a severe car-accident and later in several falls broke both her hips her shoulder and some of her ribs. At present she is unable to walk due to extreme weakness, is wheelchair bound, can hardly talk and despite hearing aids has trouble hearing. For her upcoming 80th birthday on the 5th of April most of us family members were planning to visit her to celebrate and cheer her up. But my present health situation and also that of my older sister Ursula will not permit us to attend.

Angela visits me daily and takes good care of me. I was confined to the hospital for eight days, suffering from COPD but am at home now recuperating and getting stronger from day to day. I am hooked up for twenty-four hours to an oxygen machine by a fifty feet long "leash" that allows me to go everywhere about the house. My two kitty cats are playing with that constantly moving clear plastic hose and have fun with it trying to catch and hold on to it.

Lucie and her husband Mike have moved to New Jersey not far from the beach at Colts Neck. Mike has been promoted to a large territory as district manager for NJ and MD in his job. They recently bought a very neat house there and after getting settled Lucie took a good job as office manager only 25 minutes from her home.

Clyde Fader, my former partner, sadly passed away in 2006 suffering from severe emphysema. He ruined his lungs by smoking too much and stopping too late. Joan, his wife still keeps up that tradition of open house on New Years day. Those two halves of that $ 20.00 bill we finally put together again and Clyde took it along with him in the left breast pocket of his funeral suit. When we meet again in the new system of things we can reminisce about it.

Bill and Marianne Burns, my longtime friends have since also passed away, but more recently I was able to attend the second wedding of their daughter Linda who married her former childhood classmate. We all are hoping to get together real soon, along with my daughters this summer, when they come for a visit. I can then show them the home movies that I made some forty something years ago, when they were little girls, at Tupper Lake and from earlier times, here in Patchogue.

My dear friend Irmi too has passed away since my last visit to Germany and so as time goes on, more of my friends of long ago will depart from this life; it is up to Jehovah God to appoint the time and place in His divine will.

I am hoping and praying, that He will grant me the privilege to live to be 100 and beyond.

In Washington D.C., on Memorial weekend of this year, 2004, there was the "Dedication" of a new World War II Memorial Monument. I have not yet visited it, but I have received comments about it, in my fan letters. Americans are not too pleased.

One lady expressed to me the fact that what she found when she went there was an "unexpected history lesson." She is of the younger generation of the post-war "baby boomers." She claims that on the Pacific side of the new Memorial there are words engraved from the speech given by President Franklin Delano Roosevelt announcing the attack on Pearl Harbor.

"Yesterday, December 7, 1941, --- a date which will live in infamy ---the United States of America was suddenly and deliberately attacked." "With confidence in our Armed Forces, with the unbounding determination of our people, we will gain the inevitable triumph."

The quotation from the speech continues, and then abruptly ends. But wait a minute, according to the monument, the speech stops before it really had ended. What happened to the end of the quote directly from Roosevelt?" "So help us God!" Those who made a special trip to go to see it, shook their heads and walked away.

They could have fooled us, but we are aware of the prevailing history and of the speeches that were given by our Presidents. "Truth and authenticity, not a distortion of 'history'," is all that we look for. Are we living behind a "shadow?" You can't fool the people who were there! Roosevelt's words are engraved in their hearts

THE FINAL AFTERTHOUGHT

Now, that my life's story has been told, I sincerely hope that this, my writing will result in a better understanding of how war has spiritually and physically maimed so many families throughout the world. It is the sad sense of loss of their loved ones who have disappeared into oblivion.

If I figure out in mathematical terms the gruesome fact of human lives that were wasted while I was serving my time in the war, and as a prisoner of war in particular, I come to the conclusion, that ninety eight to ninety nine percent of all prisoners died there deep in Russia and never made it home. They ended up in mass graves, nameless.

This reality of the truth puts the name: "The Un-Known Soldier" in the light of understanding, namely, it's real meaning.

Today's population hardly gives a thought as to what the "Tomb of the Un-Known Soldier" in Washington, D.C. really stands for.

Therefore, I feel compelled to remind and to enlighten those people visiting the tomb, and all Americans in general, that the names of the unknown soldiers disappeared and no one knows, what really has happened to them. The fact is, that most of those comrades-in-arms died for their country on far away battlefields and prison camps, but no one knows their names any more.

That is the real reason, that in most countries that were involved in WW II and in all other wars, these memorials, "The Tombs of the Un-known Soldiers," were created as a sad reminder. But also with recognition and in the memory of them: Those who never returned home; were often forgotten forever, and many others remained missing in action. (MIA)

So, I want to urge all of us, to never forget those brave men and women who gave their lives, so we can freely enjoy our lives in peace and prosperity. Let us give thanks to them for their supreme sacrifice.

Let us also be reminded of, what the philosopher Immanuel Kant stated so convincingly:

Peace Is The Masterpiece Of Reason!

In God's Peace,
Gottfried Paul Johannes Dulias

I Never Found Out What Ever Really Happened To Them.
These Were Some Of The Inmates With Me At The Gulags
Up To *Now It Was Too Painful For Me reflecting Back To That Horrible Time,*
But I Had Their Names Tucked Away In My Little Notebooks For All These Years.

(There Could Be Misspellings Because The Old Writings Were No Longer That Legible)

I hope, that the relatives of these former fellow POWs will recognize familiar names here and may want to know more about them, I will be glad to tell all I may remember about them. My E-mail address is: sailud@aol.com my telephone: (631) – 475-9467.

1. Basin, Harry From Berlin NW
2. Birkhahn, Fritz at Karl Fischer From: Potsdam/Berlin *(He personally wrote something in my Promptuarium booklet)*
3. Bongratz, Martin From: Munich 8

4. Buchberger, Hubert From: Linz/Austria
5. Burmann, Rainer From: Polsdorf/Vienna, Austria
6. Chicbizziura, Werner From: Munich/Pasing
7. Ditzel, Heinrich From: Hagen/Westfalia
8. Düthorn, Georg From: Kempten/Bavaria
9. Fischer, Franz From: Munich 8
10. Girschick, Erich From: Leipzig/Lindenau
11. Gruber, Hans From: Perach/Bavaria
12. Gruber, Ludwig From: Jettingen
13. Guthseel, Karl From: Geroldsgrün/Saale
14. Hoffman, Karl From: Günzen, Waldshut/Baden
15. Ilina, Max From: Munich
16. Keplinger, Rudolf From: Reichenau/Friedberg
17. Knippe, Max From: Bautzen/Saale
18. Köglmeier, Max From: Munich
19. Kreitschmann, Gerhard From: Berlin O
20. Laugsch, Otto   From: Berlin/Johtal *(**Died while in Prison 1946)***
21. Lüdicke, Paul From: Breslau
22. Mack, Hugo From: Munich 23
23. Maschinski, (Maschner) From: Osterode, East Prussia
24. Müller, Willie From: Berlin-Treptow
25. Naumann, Karl From: Chemnitz/Saxony
26. Osterloh, Fritz From: Hude/Oldenburg
27. Perchan, Paul From: Berlin SO
28. Renninger, Xaver From: Sontheim, Schwaben
29. Schmid, Xaver From: Kempten/Bavaria
30. Schmidt, Otto From: 23 Bremen
31. Schreyer, Fritz From: Vlotho/Weser
32. Seitz, Anton From: Oberegg/Krumbach, Schwaben
33. Thierbach, Walther From: Chemmitz/Saxony
34. Timm, Otto From: Garstead, Hamburg
35. Töllner, Karl From: 23 Bremen
36. Treus Larr, Ewald From: Münster/Steinfurt
37. Vogt From: Puch/Fürstenfeldbruck
38. Weber, Hans From: Fürstenfeldbruck
39. Weigel, Johann From: Neudrossenfeld/Bayreuth

40. Weigele, Willi From: Oberderdingen/Veihingen/Würtenberg
41. Welther, Wilfried *(He personally wrote something in my Promptuarium booklet)*
42. Wiehr, Paul From: Rostok
43. Wuchener, Dr. Gustav From: Munich/Solln
44. Zander, Walter From: Steinach/Thüringen
45. Zart, Alfred From: Darwitz/Gr. Kreuz

SPECIAL THANKS TO:

George Andree
My Computer Technician,
Without him I'd still be lost in cyberspace.

Michael J. Chorney, Ph.D.
Guest Relations, Coordinator
At The Mid-Atlantic Air Museum
Reading, Pennsylvania
Who gave me the opportunity
To be featured as one of the
Guest Speakers for the WW II Weekend

Bob Chubb, and his Wife
A Fine Friend and Sponsor,
who found it in his heart to find a way for me to tell my story
*at the 13*th *Annual World War II Weekend*
in Reading, Pennsylvania June 4-6, 2004.
He found two artists who were able to accurately render
illustrations of
"My Sweetheart," the Me-109,
according to only written specifications as to how the
Aircraft actually looked like

They did a "Magnificent" job!

EXTRA SPECIAL THANKS TO:

Alex Methenitis, now residing in Greece,
(Profile, wheels up rendering)
Virgil O'Neil, residing in the United States,
(Wheels down rendering)
for drawing my ME 109 G 14 A S

Emil Cassanello,

A Fine Friend, Former Pilot of a Cessna 172
Team Member of S.O.A.R

Mary and Peter Durniak
Russian-American
Consultant / Correspondents

Mary Ann Esposito,
Team Member of S.O.A.R.
And always a "Wonderful" Hostess

Larry Mihlon
A Fine Friend and Re-Enactor,
Founder of L.A.R.A.
(Luftwaffe Aircrew Re-Enactment Association)

"Ace," William Prechtl
A Fine Friend, Pilot and owner of an N3N
And
All Members Of The Early Flyers Club
All Members Of The Bayport Aerodrome Society
All Members Of The Antique Airplane Club in Bayport.

Al (Alois) Rubenbauer, "Hauptmann"
A Fine Friend and Re-Enactor
Founder of S.O.A.R.
(Society of Aircraft Restoration)

Arthur Ruhl
Librarian and Consultant,
Acting as Editor-In-Chief.

Steve Robbins
Teacher and Editorial Consultant.

Dr. Ron Sinagra

A Fine Friend, My Chiropractor
He sure knows how to relieve my "Aching Back".

Ronald Spencer
A Fine Friend and ole' WW II Veteran,
Was the Navigator for the B24's, 8th *Air Force Division.*

William Tucci
A Fine Friend, Artist and Film-maker,
Crusade Fine Arts.

Bill Wheeler
A Fine Friend and ole' WW II Veteran,
Tuskegee Airmen.

Elisabeth McGuire
My second daughter. She served as proofreader/editor for this
revised edition.

I did not want to forget mentioning my sincere thanks to my neighbors, other friends and acquaintances, and last but not least to my dear family. My three daughters who are very concerned about my health and helping me wherever they can, and often call me. Especially my oldest daughter Angela who is the only one still living here on Long Island, she visits me often and has been taking care of a lot of tasks for me and is always helping me. She still is faithfully fulfilling the promise she made to her Mother, my dear Hedi on her deathbed, to take care and look after me. My heartfelt thanks to you, Angela.

And here is my sincere thanks to all of you, my friends and relatives from the bottom of my heart. You each have effected and still continue to play a very important role in my life, in my existence and my being.

Vielen Dank
Many Thanks

Gottfried Paul Johannes Dulias

ADDENDUM

Now it is 2009 and five years have gone by since the original version of this book was finished and printed. Many things have happened since then; some of which I added in chapter 12 of this new revised and expanded version as 'updates 2009' at the end of some sub-chapters.

To distinguish them from the regular text, I printed the updates in Italic lettering.

Some of my friends and relatives have passed away; Emil Cassanello, Ron Spencer, Bill and Marianne Burns, my brother in Law Alphonse Rinaldi, and my younger sister Gisela, her husband Werner and also their daughter Elvira in Germany. I flew to Germany to attend my sister's funeral, representing our family. May they all rest in Peace, awaiting their resurrection to the new system of things.

So, life is going on for me and I pray for and hope to live to be 100 and beyond. I still have many things to do and accomplish and with Jehovah God's Loving Kindness and Blessings I will achieve all of them.

In 2005 I welcomed my first Great Grandson, Nicholas Lucian. My daughter Elisabeth, his grandmother, tells me that ever since he was tiny he has always looked up at the skies. He is fascinated by planes (which he refers to as jets) and says he wants to be a jet pilot. Just like I did when I was his age; though there weren't any jets at that time, but I wanted to fly and be a pilot whenever I heard and saw that big five engine Junkers Hindenburg on its way to Berlin every day. Maybe Nicky will become a fighter pilot too, as I did?

Many other things had happened in my life since 2004. Dianna's pair of Siamese cats had six kittens and after weaning from their mother Blinky, she gave them away. I chose one of them to take home to be a companion to Petey, my black longhaired American kitty and they get along very well together. Moulin is her name and she is now fully grown and as I sit here writing on my computer, she is resting on my lap and likes to be petted, showing her contentedness by purring and licking my hand in appreciation. Moulin and Petey play together often, running up and down the stairway to my upper floor. They both sleep in my king-size bed at night on my dear Hedi's side. They both give me a lot of pleasure and companionship. When I am out shopping, they greet me at the door and want to be petted. When I am away for a few days to the events with LARA, or on my almost yearly trips to Germany, my good neighbor and my daughter Angela take care of them.

In the past five years I got around quite a bit attending most or all of the events that Lara was attending and also others I personally was invited to as a VIP guest speaker, such as the yearly Expo 2005, 2006, 2007 and 2008. I am invited again this year with my friend and aide, John Kunze in Minneapolis, Minnesota. Twice I was invited to the Flying Air Museum in Palm Springs California as a guest speaker and also twice to the Show of Shows exhibition in Kentucky.

I was also invited to speak at a history club in Ohio, a library in Pennsylvania, a church group in New Jersey, in three schools here on Long Island and in three hospitals here on Long Island as well as four Army Reserve Posts and twice in the L.I. Westhampton Military

Reserve Airport, named after my good friend Gabby Gabreskey. I also made many presentations at the diverse organizations and clubs I am a member of. So I am not kidding when I say I got around extensively. I am looking forward to continue that regimen.

The next upcoming event I will attend will be on May 15th- 17th 2009 in Virginia Beach, VA at the fighter factory Air Show and Military Aviation Museum.

June 5th-7th 2009 I will be at the WWII weekend in Reading, PA. That event is one the biggest annual Air Shows in the country.

If time allows I would like to fly to Wisconsin with John Kunze to attend the Oshkosh Air Venture 2009 starting on July 2nd, 2009.

I definitely will be attending the Air Show in Minneapolis, Minnesota where I am invited to attend as VIP and speaker with my aide John Kunze July 17th to the 19th, 2009.

After that, I will be at the Geneseo Air Show in upstate New York. The Air Show in Lancaster PA, August 22nd and 23rd, 2009.

So as you can see, we have a very tight schedule that keeps me busy. I really enjoy these events and at all of them I have the opportunity to sell my book and autographs. I can be seen at all these events barring any unforeseen circumstances.

The most outstanding event I ever attended is the five glorious day event I spend at the Maxwell United States Air Force base in Montgomery Alabama.

Each year since 1980 the Air Force Academy created a program whereby sixteen veterans of WWII and later wars are selected to become honored Eagles of the USAF Veterans who distinguished themselves in combat fighting for their homelands. Not only American veterans but soldiers from all nations that were involved in the WWII and later wars like Vietnam, Korea, Iraq.

Since I am considered to be an Ace with my five air victories here in the Untied States according to the established count, I was selected to be one of the sixteen candidates for the year 2007. I was asked to send them some documents and pictures pertaining to my service in the Luftwaffe and a brief synopsis about my life.

After two weeks or so, I received a letter from the Command Staff at Maxwell Air Academy explaining the whole procedure for the five days of activities and celebrations of the graduation of the 2007 school of cadets. I was also informed of what to take along and that I had to select a companion as my aide for the duration of all festivities. I chose my good friend and fellow LARA member, Woody Barnes, who also received a letter about the procedures of our five day stay.

At the appointed day two Majors of the USAF came to my house with two extra large suitcases containing 800 copies of the two side-panels of a large three-piece poster, each with eight lithograph images of the candidates as they appeared as young men serving in the Armed Forces. An artist, who for many years worked for the USAF, drew those images from provided pictures. He did an excellent job!

Each of the candidates had to sign 800 panels under the pertaining lithograph! What a task that was! At my dining room table we set up an assembly line; one Major handed me the panel, I signed it and handed it to the other Major, who put it back into the suitcase.

At lunchtime I served them each a bowl of Kapusta soup that I had prepared the night before in my slow cooker. Of course it was not like the kind we POWs received in the Russian Gulags; this one had plenty of corned beef and some potatoes and baby carrots and it had plenty of "fat-eyes" swimming at the top. The officers enjoyed it very much and asked for seconds as they ate the soup along with slices of buttered German Farmers rye bread.

We continued the signing process and made good headway, so we had time for them to take the short trip to Brookhaven Calabro Airport to see and photograph Alois Rubenbauer's ME 109. Both Majors were very impressed and each sat in the cockpit for pictures. After driving back to my house I continued to sign the rest of the 800 panels and then the Majors went back to their hotel.

Both of them stayed overnight at the Holiday Inn and had to go to another assignment the next day to interview and assist with the signing of the panels by the well known Tuskeegee Airman, Lee Archer, a friend of mine who lives in a Village just North of New York City. He was also one of the selected candidates for the 2007 Eagles.

Now here is the report I wrote about the…………..
….Five glorious days at Maxwell AFB June 5th to the 10th 2007

THE GATHERING OF EAGLES

The 16 selected outstanding persons to be honored as this years Eagles of the USAF arrived with their aides on the 5th of June. Among them four retired Generals and ten American war heroes, one British Captain of high fame and also fortunate me as former WW II German fighter pilot.

We all were treated like Royalty and including our aides, each were billeted in well prepared special private suites in an elaborate Officers guest building. Welcome-goody-baskets and -letters from the commanders of the various departments, AF-unit-coins, AF T-shirts, gift-bags with sweets, festivity schedules, maps of the base, etc. were waiting for the soon to be inducted Eagles. An assigned car for each candidate was parked just outside the feudal building. A great welcome reception with a scrumptious buffet dinner and cocktails was held at the Officers club just across the street.

All the hallways in that club were decorated with the 3-panel posters of all previous groups of 16 Eagles since 1980 and our group poster will be added there too for posterity in the hall of fame along with pictures of notable individual heroes of earlier times. The three panel posters had on each side the lithograph images of eight new Eagles of the USAF and the larger center panel pictured all the types of planes they flew in combat at the wars they were fighting for their fatherlands. My ME 109 G yellow six appeared next to the lithograph of me, as were all the other planes next to their former pilots.

On the four following days, after delicious breakfasts at the officers club, four of us honored guests each were interviewed on stage for 45 minutes in front of an audience of about 800 spectators including the entire class of this years graduating cadets of the AF College. Followed by elaborate lunches alternately held at the officers club, the cadet mess-hall, the Montgomery Zoo, sponsored by the Alabama Power Company, where each of us 16 were presented with specially minted one silver dollar double Eagle Coins in velvet gift boxes and congratulating letters. After the luncheons we had free time to roam around the base or rested in our feudal suites for a nap followed by scrumptious dinners at the Officers Cub.

Each day brought more surprises and honors, including two evening barbeques in one of the large hangars attended alternately by each one half of the graduating class of the cadets including their families to mingle with us and of course we were busy signing autographs for the visitors.

An A T- 6 trainer and a P-51 were displayed in the hangar and I got to sit in the P- 51's cockpit for picture taking. I found the cockpit much roomier than the one in our ME 109 and felt, or better yet, assumed, that the pilot in combat by the sharp turns would have been shoved sideways if he wasn't tied down enough. I liked the 109s narrow cockpit better with my shoulders touching the sides of the fuselage so you felt like you are part of the plane. Outside the hanger a Hue' Helicopter and an A-4 jet, as well as a C-130 transport plane were displayed for all to see.

In between the various festivities Woody and I drove around the base and took pictures of the numerous war planes on static display, Even a B 52 was displayed in front of one of the buildings. Also on display was a full size metal replica of the Wright Brothers flyer with both of them sitting in it. This monument was erected in memory of them in a special plaza. At those elaborate luncheons and dinners the newly inducted Eagles and our aids socialized and had a nice time together talking about our war experiences.

We all received one of those three panel posters rolled up in a shipping cardboard tube including a brochure featuring one-page synapses of all new 16 Eagles with their lithograph images and also pertinent information about the Eagle program. A list of all previous Eagles since 1980 sorted by the diverse countries those Eagles came from. I was listed as the sixteenth German Eagle among such high scoring Aces of the Luftwaffe, like Erich Hartmann, Günter Rall, Adolf Galland and eleven others. I really felt out of place with my five air-victories, because in Germany with such a low score you were only an "also ran". Those posters were also sent to each of the sons and daughters of the new Eagles as a memento of that high honor that was bestowed upon their fathers.

On Saturday the 9th of June a festive luncheon was held at a nearby country club. Each of us 16 was presented with a large golden medallion with a blue-white-red neckband designating us officially to be the newest Eagles in the program. We also received a trophy, an artfully made model of the Wright Bros.1903 flyer. The size of them was about of 10 " all around dimension, made of lacquered mahogany and delicate brass wiring, at the fuselage and frame-struts and at the wings. It was held up by a hand carved stand with a base featuring an honoring brass label showing individually engraved the names of each of the new Eagles. Because of the delicate nature of this art piece, it was mailed by the Air Force staff in proper packed and crushproof boxes to each of us. Mine arrived un-damaged a couple of days after I arrived home.

In the evening the Graduation Ball of the new cadets was held at the historic Union RR station in huge connected tents accommodating the about 1000 festively dressed participants with all graduating cadets and their families and we Eagles and our aides as honored guests. An elaborate rich assortment of many different meats and vegetables that was also featuring many other delicacies at that buffet dinner with diverse beverages that started with a champagne toast to the new Eagles and the graduating cadets. The dinner was followed by music and dancing. The televised welcome speeches on several big screens throughout the huge combo-tent preceded the dinner. All attendants had a marvelous time and we took pleasant memories with us when we left for the airport on Sunday morning to fly home to our various home-locations. As a special thank you gesture to us new Eagles a donation of $ 200.00 individually in the name of each of us 16 celebrities was made to a charity and we also received in the mail a check for $ 300.00 as honorarium for our speeches and interviews and additional re-imbursements for the various expenses we Incurred in traveling to and from this great event. I will never forget this once in a lifetime great honor-event and glorious experience.

My heartfelt thanks to the staff Command committee of the Eagle program of the Maxwell US Air Force base for having selected me for this greatest of honors, to be an Eagle, I am so proud to be one of them.

Gottfried P. Dulias

"Ace of Spade Squadron"
("Pik As Geschwader")

Gottfried P. Dulias as a Cadet,
Berlin-Gatow, June 1944

Me 109G-14/AS of Lt. Gottfried Paul Johannes Dulias 3./JG 53, Budapest, March 1945

"Pik-As"
Fighter Wing 53, "Ace of Spades"

The Me 109G-14AS flown by
Leutnant Gottfried Paul Johannes Dulias
3./JG53, Budapest, March 1945

ABOUT THE AUTHORS

The authors orginally met via the Internet. His screen name was ME-109 and she didn't have a clue as to what that meant. As his life story was revealed to her, she found that he was a former Luftwaffe Fight Pilot and Prisoner of War in Russia, during World War II.

Hearing his story was for her like taking a trip back through time. Working as a team, they tried to find the best way possible to present this never before told true story , to you.

They both hope that by your reading "Another Bowl of Kapusta" you will come to a real understanding about the true happenings of what life was like before, during and after World War II.

FOR IMMEDIATE RELEASE
EDITORS: For review copies or interview requests contact:
Promotions Department
Tel: 800-839-8640 ext. 5244
Fax: 812-961-3133
Email: pressreleases@authorhouse.com

A True Time Capsule

Authors Explore History through a True Life Story

PATCHOGUE, N.Y. – The Hitler regime; a life-altering time for anyone in the world to survive, but especially horrifying for Gottfried P. Dulias, a citizen of Königsberg, Germany, who would endure three years as a Russian prisoner of war. Dulias and co-author Dianna M. Popp offer firsthand accounts of World War II through his flashbacks to recreate the challenging life of a Luftwaffe fighter pilot in the eye-opening new book, *Another Bowl Of Kapusta,* (now available through AuthorHouse).

After 60 years of hellish nightmares and repressed memories, Dulias reveals his deepest secrets about the events that forever shaped his life. Born in 1925 to an upscale family in Königsberg (present-day Kaliningrad), Dulias came of age in a country struggling to rebuild after the destruction of the first World War. He abandoned the dream of becoming a pastry chef to join the Luftwaffe, where he scored five air combat victories before his Messerschmitt Me-109, "Gustav 14," was shot down by ground fire in the spring of 1945. He was captured and held as a POW in the Gulags of Russia.

Another Bowl Of Kapusta ("kapusta" means cabbage, the staple for Russian POWs) is not only the story of Dulias' miraculous survival against insurmountable odds, but also his journey both to that point and after the struggle. Outfitted with the strength and determination to live, a positive outlook on life and an unfailing trust in God, Dulias survived the horrendous conditions and was released in January 1948, eager to begin a new life.

Dulias is now an advisor and Luftwaffe re-enactor with the newly established Luftwaffe Aircrew Re-Enactors Association (LARA). A widower since 1997, he lives in the same house he and his wife bought 50 years ago. Popp met Dulias on the Iinternet, was fascinated by his story and felt compelled to document it. Popp is an artist who has previously written articles for several newsletters and newspapers.

AuthorHouse is the world leader in publishing and print-on-demand services. Founded in 1997, AuthorHouse has helped more than 20,000 people worldwide become published authors. For more Information, visit www.authorhouse.com.

Another Bowl Of Kapusta is now also available for purchase at a variety of Bookstores including: www.Amazon.com, Borders, Barnes & Noble, Walden, www.Booksamillion.com, just to name a few.

9 781418 488369